World War III

PHIL
SALERA

WORLD WAR III
The Hour of Our Death

2006

World War III

To My Friend Dave And My Sister.

PREFACE

No matter what one chooses to believe terrorism gripped the first decade of the 21st Century. Though the span of terrorism was truly worldwide its origins and causes could be narrowed considerably. The list of terrorist groups was long and noteworthy: Al Qaeda, Salafist Group for Call and Combat (in Algeria), Moroccan Islamic Combatant Group (in Morocco), Kurdistan Workers' Party (Turkey), Lashkar-E-Taiba (Pakistan), Lashkar-E-Jhangvi (Pakistan), Jaish-E-Mohammed (Pakistan), in the Philippines Moro Islamic Liberation Front and Jemaah Islamiyah. This list also included the Palestine Islamich Jihad, Al Aqsa Martyrs' Brigades, Kach and Kahane Chai, Hezbollah, Asbat Al Ansar, and the Islamich Movement of Uzbekistan. All of these groups were in some way tied to Islamic Fundamentalism, and it was these groups that caused the world to spend so much time, money, and lives hunting them down. However, when the leaders of these groups were dead there was shortage of men willing to take their place.

The leaders who assumed power in Islamic nations realized they had to adapt, or they too would be short-lived. So this they did by the devious means of conspiring with others in dark corners of the world. The new Islamic fundamentalists appeared disguised as peacemakers, as friends, as true politicians. By the year 2010 their metamorphosis was complete. This completion marked the end of the old way, and the destruction that became the new.

CHAPTER 1
THE NEW IMPERIALISTS

The clouds of war hung ominously over the Earth, and grew like shadows in the late afternoon sun. Alliances were about to be formed between unlikely nations, and the great curtain of carelessness was about to be raised, which will lead to an unimaginable destruction. The year is currently 2017, and many people in the world are enjoying what are to be the final moments of their lives.

Global terrorism has finally been eradicated, or at least the more notorious factions that were known to the planets civilized governments. Ironically, with the end of terrorism the Arab League was dissolved—in 2010—by a single man who showed the league as weak and impotent, and on that basis must be discarded. It has been said, however, that the Arab League and the New Imperialists who destroyed it conceived a child in the end. That child soon became a formidable opponent in government, military, and economics. The new ideas, personified by the Arab Union soon brought the Middle East to the forefront of world politics, and began to stand in direct competition with the west.

And then there was the west. The cost to eliminate terrorism was massive for the soon to be allies in dollars, lives, and time, while severing all their ties to the Middle East. More importantly, the "War On Terror" used up irreplaceable resources, and gave the rest of the world time to catch up to United States development. Later known as "Pyongyang Syndrome"—becoming more powerful because your enemies are engaged elsewhere—began happening around the world.

Before the Arab Union, the Middle East consisted of nation states divided, competing with each other through weapons, and ideologies, and always through the economy. When the United States left Iraq, it left behind an economy capable of grinding out goods, and officers capable of training soldiers. In any case the Americans left in 2009 feeling secure that another September 11th would never happen again, and the Europeans felt that another May 2nd (on this day in 2007 a low-grade germ bomb was exploded in Paris, eventually killing 6,000 citizens) was a distant memory. Both continents were all too happy to "let them do whatever, as long as we're not involved."

When these events were over, an event, which seemed to be of little consequence when it was going on would have a massive effect on the Middle East as well as the course of human history. A peasant boy had come to power.

Ali Annan was born in 1970. His parents were primarily peasant farmers/traders, and since his birth in Iraq, he continually saw his homeland harassed by more powerful nations from the 1980's-to 2010. Prior to that he had witnessed atrocities firsthand in a war with his neighboring country Iran as well as numerous wars within his own. He greatly admired George Orwell, and Winston Churchill. He was most influenced by United States history, and wanted to discover their blueprints of civilization, law, and lifestyle. But he could never think of any good reason why his country was constantly retarded from progress, after all who was the U.S. to decide whether or not Iraq could have certain weapons under any leadership. He argued that government should be a search for responsibility, and if any regime was responsible the regime should not be controlled by external forces. Annan did not think of journeying for responsibility, or becoming a politician until an uncanny opportunity presented itself.

In 2003 Annan had seen his dictator deposed by U.S. forces. Although, Annan never liked Hussein, he believed his country needed a strong leader to give its people an international voice. He much preferred a homeland government to the assembled subservient puppet government. After watching the new administration dawdle for a number of years Annan believed they had little credibility. So tirelessly he decided to help one of his idols take power, Sadam Abin. Somehow Annan found himself giving a speech to his citizens on the streets of Baghdad, and immediately his people responded with intrigue to him. The following is an excerpt of his speech:

> "And I say we are Muslims, let us unite, there is no reason we should not stand for each other. I see in my dreams a powerful Middle East making decisions ruling the world; Mohammed tried to spread Islam, we will rule with it! We will evaporate everything that stands in our way, and introduce a new set of morals to the nations who have felt superior, and give each Muslim the right to persecute himself! Persia unite; again! In the name of Abin!"

Annan was a captivating speaker, he had a dark complexion with a powerful hawk face, and he resembled a Napoleonic Middle Easterner. Annan was a man of rare talent, one of those people who could rally thousands just by saying comforting words. In this day in age he would be compared to Hitler, but a more civilized more informed group would compare him to Queen Elizabeth because he lacked violent intentions originally. More importantly though, Annan was well liked by his country for his family attachments, and his undying loyalty to his sick wife, whom eventually died May 17, 2013. He had resisted taking public office in order to be with her, as a result he wrote many influential books in his leave the most important being, "The Power of Persia"—a lengthy treatise on the world's first empire. Abin eventually stepped out of the leadership role after only two years because he lacked health and saw no chance for government longevity.

Annan took power in December of 2013 and turned Iraq into the strongest Middle Eastern power within three years of his arrival into office. He bought grain to feed his people with oil revenue, put many to work, and even had set Iraq on the path to becoming a manufacturing nation. Although, industry was still weak, Annan had jump started the most powerful economy in the Middle East. Placed there by the direct intervention of the United States. Neither Abin nor Annan's wife would live to see the great Dictator finally unite the entire territory of the Middle East. By the end of 2014 the unthinkable had happened; Iraq, Iran, Kuwait, Bahrain, Yemen, Oman, UAE, Syria, and Jordan had joined Annan's new Arab Union. By 2015 Cyprus, Lebanon, Palestine, Saudi Arabia, Qatar, Afghanistan, Turkmenistan, Tajikistan, and Pakistan forgetting their differences had all joined the ever-expanding Arab Union. They had joined in an effort to pool their resources, but mainly because these nations felt Annan had the Muslim interest in mind and a vision for the future.

Each time nations joined the Arab Union they would be given a stake, and all money made between the nations was divided up equally to improve the overall standard of life. The idea of unification was Annan's creation, and it developed very impressively from the colonial American model he so wished to emulate. What he did not realize is that his system was most comparable to conjoined communism, but instead of people there were nations, and instead of the State—the Arab Union was supreme.

All was not bright for Annan though. Many Arab strongmen felt loyalty only to a higher power/cause, and because of Annan's actions they felt Islam would lose its religious essence to evil capitalism. Annan became the number one target of nearly the entire Middle Eastern underworld. However, when they saw the returns they received on their preliminary investments they willingly accepted Annan with open arms, called off the hit men who Annan had already killed. Annan was extremely bright for the peasant boy he once was, but needed to find a way to hold on to the Muslim religion—it being the most powerful unifier- but bring the AU out of primitiveness (read theocracy.) In order to do this he sentenced a Muslim, who was accused of planning an attack on him to death. Minutes before the man was to die the great Saladin appeared, pardoned the man, and said, "I will never murder a Muslim, from any Muslim nation, in any Muslim nation- never!" Although he had already violated this on numerous occasions this single act gave Annan complete support among the people who constantly sang his praise, and a very dangerous attribute, undying loyalty from his people. Slowly, Annan's dreams for expansion past the Middle East began to get the best of him, he looked towards another approaching technological power to the east- China.

In 2015 a romantic high-ranking Arab official, Abu Saddhis wished to set in motion plans for an alliance with the Chinese. Undertaking this effort he wrote a letter to his counterpart in the Chinese government Mao Ze-Tse. Saddhis's letter inquired as to what the protocol would be if the Chinese would export weapons, goods, and influence to an accepting AU. Also, Saddhis wanted Arab soldiers trained by Chinese officers to strengthen the ties between the two nations. Saddhis's dreams were to create a modern day incubator in China in order to have an army, and air force prepared to eliminate foes. Lastly, Saddhis remained open to any possible way the AU could accommodate China.

Tse was completely dumbfounded when he read the letter, but he was half appalled, and half intrigued. He thought if the Chinese were caught training the AU for war with Israel, Beijing would be penalized, and serious consequences levied—maybe even war! However, when he presented it to Zhen Zui, the Chinese Prime Minister, he gladly accepted the invitation, and even questioned Tse on his friendship with Saddhis, and Annan. It seemed the Chinese leader was very intrigued with Annan, and very bored with the rest of the world. Zui had grown weary with Europe, and especially with North America, he felt the Old Power Nations (a Chinese term for the U.S., Europe, and Japan) were solely responsible for trying to keep his nation in the Dark Age through unfair trade policies. But often dumped surplus goods into his market—the largest in the world. Determined to prove Chinese superiority he happily accepted a meeting with the AU, and began sending his officers to train the Arab Union officers and units.

The Chinese knew they were 1/6 of the world's population and had outlined contingency plans to conquer the world. They dreamed of domination through an all-Chinese society complete with living space, capital, respect, and they were resolved to acquire it with tacit help from someone. Eventually Zui hand wrote a secret letter to be given to Annan in Baghdad. On a rainy overcast day the letter found itself in possession of Hoang Chin who would personally bestow it to Annan. It stated: *"My fellow strugglers, I feel we have been put into an impossible situation. Certain forces have driven us into each other's arms, and it is time for the China with the AU to accomplish dominance. It is very possible that a Chinese army would fight alongside your army against Russia, Europe, and the U.S., but not as a Chinese Muslim Army."* *Zui*

Annan set the letter down, glanced around his palace and said to Chin, "I wish to meet your leader as soon as can be arranged." At last the stage had been set for the great leader to finally meet the population king, deciding decisively a significant turn of events in the course of history.

Annan had been invited to Chung King, China by Zui. The meeting was to be completely private no media allowed, and the Chinese took all the necessary precautions to deny any knowledge of the event to leave the airfield. Even Annan's personal plane had been painted with a Chinese design to make it un-noticeable. Annan stepped out of the plane, and was quickly escorted by guards to a private compound somewhere in Chung King.

Zui led off, "I am terribly sorry about all the inconveniences you have had to deal with on your way here."

"It's quite all right, but tell me something was this show of force meant to impress me, or to intimidate me?" Annan questioned.

"I assure you neither Mr. Annan, I'm just sorry we could not do more. Especially stop the rain, but, who controls the weather, and this is a secret meeting. So may I begin?"

"Of course, I am very interested to hear what you have to say."

"Mr. Annan, what do you picture the world to look like in your head? I was very pleased to read your expressed wishes for a contingency plan for an assault on the United States and Europe."

"I said nothing of the sort, I'm grateful for the expertise your army will lend us. Besides your forgetting many important specifics, with all do respect, our countries do not have the Air Forces, Navy's, supply lines, experience to compete in any type of warfare. In any prolonged attacks our supply lines would be so immensely tenuous that it's doubtful we could carry out an offensive past the immediate terrain. I have gone over this many times in my head. I would love power, and dominance, but first we need hope!" Zui discovered in a few moments why Annan was so loved, he had a passion about him that was unmatched by contemporaries.

"Then we shall give it to you. I realize Mr. Annan that your conglomerates will experience numerous difficulties, please allow the Chinese to look into ways to solve them for you. First let me put some ideas on your mind. I have decided to offer you our latest fighter, the JH-27F (the JH-27F Fighter was one of the most advanced fighters of the time. The Chinese had been looking to find a jet comparable to the approaching Joint Strike Fighter Series II designated F-37. The JH-27F had rocket, and jet propulsion, thrust-vectoring, and vertical boost-thrust which allowed it to climb at a rate just as fast as the F-37. The tactical designation JH- 27B Bomber was equipped with 16 hardpoints, the capacity for 30,000 lbs. of bombs, 20mm. cannon, and 4 dummy jettison packs to detract surface-to-air missiles). Your country will soon possess the craftsmanship to manufacture it. Take this as a sign of good faith. Second, you are aware of the fact that around 75% of the oil in this hemisphere comes from your nations."

Annan interrupted, "We estimate 55% comes from our Union, if not more." Annan began to see where his counterpart was going with this point.

"Keep in mind that with both our countries resources we would fit together perfectly production wise. Also as a rule of thumb the allies will not be able to move without gas, tires, petrol, at least think about that," Zui said waning. Zui's face looked to be happily distorted; his glasses shined his eyes to Annan. "One more question. How committed is the Arab Union to fighting a war against Europe, and the United States?"

Annan felt a fire light inside of him, he shot back, "Our men are ready to die for Allah, can you say the same for Tao!"

"Then I am correct when I say that Europe, Russia, the U.S., and I imagine Israel will all be dealt with in May 2017?"

"May 2017? What do you mean? That is only two years away! We can't possibly make attack plans that soon, it would take at least five years to acquire what we need to be competitive."

"So sure are you, Mr. Annan. Precisely at this moment our countries technology is more even to the west than ever before in our history. We must strike immediately while we have a chance, or end up like Russia did after the Cold War, before they became the Republic, and gave away too much military power. My general staff has already drawn up preliminary plans of conquest; at our next meeting I suggest we share them with you."

Annan delayed, "I would be most curious to see them."

"Good, then I will draft a directive." Zui turned to his guard, "Call in my secretary would you." A few moments later a short stocky man came in with a small notebook. Zui continued, "Directive Number 1, a general order for the invasion and subjugation of Israel, India, South Korea, Taiwan, and Japan. Combined with further efforts to undermine the allied cause in all military institutions located in proximity to our respective homelands. That is all."

There was quietness in the bunker that Annan had never felt in his life except for the lonely nights he spent looking up at the stars as a boy. Annan did not show the pleasure that was in his heart; he had now looked at himself as a modern day Mohammed. He was determined to eclipse the Prophet with his greatness.

"Just one more thing Mr. Annan it is imperative that no belligerent move be made that allows any nation to know of our intentions. We must keep up a great poker face. Therefore no stupid aggressive moves are to be made, and under any circumstances do not initiate terrorist attacks anywhere," Zui said with impatience. "Continue exporting all you were before, in fact ask the allies if you can do more, that is the best way to deceive the allies."

"I can easily arrange all you wish, however do not expect us to enjoy it. If we follow this course I will rather go the entire way to war than shame my people with acts of weakness." The Arab Union had become a world power from the brain of Annan, and under no circumstances would he play a weak mistress to the west. That was enough to shame his people to the core.

"I understand Mr. Annan, it is all part of a great plan, a man of your talents is exactly what we need to conquer the west. I will contact you for our next meeting to discuss both our interests. But let me be honest Mr. Annan the man with the notebook was a fraud, we have planned these attacks for over 4 years already. We will just redraft them with your cooperation."

Annan braved the wind outside. It had begun raining, and he ran to the car waiting for him. It was not until Annan had gotten back to his palace in Baghdad that he gave his aides the next day off, and retired immediately to an early slumber. He complained he had a headache, but in his mind he felt his life had been altered for the worst, and any attempt to recapture it would be futile.

A thin man was sitting over a table examining several files. Anyone could see that he had worked tirelessly for an endless amount of time reaching peak physical exhaustion. He was about 35 years old (but looked older at the moment), had light brown hair, and was a prodigy concerning international affairs. Benjamin Wolfshiem received the job as the Israeli Head of Secret Services because he was highly skilled, but most of all he was trusted by all members of the Israeli government who listened to his suggestions concerning affairs abroad. Evidence was that Benjamin could ultimately schedule an appointment at any time to see top officials for any reason. He was what every college grad wished they could be, and despite being young Benjamin was well suited to handle any meticulous situation. However, at this moment Ben's concentrations were completely exhausted concerning information about Ali Annan.

"Why did Annan visit the Chinese?" This question came from Ariel Wessler who was currently the Israeli President. Wessler was also exceptionally capable of occupying his countries post. He was well loved, and highly respected, undoubtedly Israel's best leader since Netenyahou.

"That is not what worries me sir. Why was he visiting with no one knowing he was there? The Chinese media even though controlled by Zui could not have just become invisible. Ordinarily a meeting like that would have been all over the papers. Annan going to China was strictly confidential, and I imagine it must have concerned vital issues that other governments are not to be made aware of." Benjamin said this in the most serious tone he could manage; he needed to make Wessler feel danger so that he could get cooperation on his ideas.

"Benjamin what do you think was the purpose of their meeting? Could it be trade? Weapons dealing? But more importantly what would you recommend we do about it?"

"Sir, my first thought of their meeting is that the Chinese Republic, and the Arab Union are consulting each other on a possible alliance. I know it sounds crazy, but do you remember the Chinese war draft we intercepted about 3 years ago concerning Zui's feelings about a war with Russia. (Zui had unilaterally attempted to convince Russia to prepare for war against the West by flooding false rumors, but the Russian President at the time ignored his overtures completely). Whatever the results of this meeting were, I would like to get the opportunity to explore additional possibilities. I want to meet the CIA, KGB, and all remaining friendly services in the United States. I believe that since the first day the Arab Union was formed it had been created for the sole purpose of power, and Israel stands in their gateway. The Arabs will not be settled until we are destroyed."

"Then," said Wessler regretfully, "Benjamin, you shall have that chance."

It was a sunny day when Benjamin arrived in Washington, D.C. exactly one week later. He walked through the airport terminal, and saw a number of improved safety features designed to detect items that could be dangerous to the flight of the airplane. The new FAA "satellites" in the airport terminals would show a picture of the baggage inside in infrared, and would also use that infrared scan to locate anything from keys to knives. The truly amazing part of the machines was they could tell the difference between something sharp, or something harmless from the scans. Expert Systems had finally caught up to detection devices. All in all terrorism through the use of an airplane had become antiquated.

The sun was bright outside, and the weather was warm, nicer than usual for a late September afternoon, even in Washington, D.C. All of a sudden a calendar caught Benjamin's eye, he had nearly forgotten what day it was because the flight was so agonizingly long. The date was September 23, 2016; he quickly realized a connection, 15 years earlier the World Trade Center had been destroyed. How fast had the Americans bounced back, he thought, nothing seems to faze them. What a remarkable race! How he admired them.

A car was waiting for Benjamin outside; hurriedly he rushed to the car where in turn he was taken to the pentagon. At the Pentagon he noticed many memorials Pearl Harbor, WWI, WWII, the Civil War, and Patriot Day, which were placed there because the Pentagon also was a target during the fateful attack.

"We will be ready in a matter of moments for you to speak, Mr. Wolfshiem. Is there anything you require?"

"No, thank you, I'm fine, but could you show me where a washroom is? I would like to wash my hands before I meet anyone."

"Of course, right down the hall, second door to your left." The steward replied.

"Thank you," said Benjamin; he noticed how nice the halls were. Almost as if they were an ostentatious advertisement for American military might. Upon coming back, Benjamin was taken inside an office room. He noticed there were seats for intelligence representatives for the countries: England, Italy, France, Germany, Russia, Ukraine, Canada, Mexico, most of South America, Poland, Finland, Sweden, Norway, Belgium, Ireland, Spain, and Greece, and of course the U.S. When Benjamin asked for friendly nations he did not think it would be this many. Compulsively, Benjamin began alphabetizing the nations at the conference until he shook back to reality.

"Mr. Wolfshiem? Please present the findings you insisted were so important to call this meeting." A man repeated.

Benjamin took a deep breath, he was undoubtedly the youngest one in the room, how he hoped they wouldn't give him the brush off. "I have come here today to spearhead an investigation, one which I hope you, my contemporaries will support. Ali Annan made a secret visit to Chung King, China around three weeks ago. Our intelligence managed to discover this fact while working in a Chinese airport. He met with Chinese Communist leader Zhen Zui, the meeting could best be described as lengthy. The Israeli nation believes they are planning to launch a small-scale attack within the next 6-18 months. I have flown here as soon as possible to help stop this from happening."

"I have a question Mr. Wolfshiem." Antonio Gallezeo a recognized Italian statesman stood up. "What proof do you have of this attack? Neither China nor the AU has made any demands upon us. Furthermore, are you sure that your country is not suffering from paranoia concerning the AU's close proximity and obvious hate towards you?"

Benjamin decided it was time to fight back, "I looked for a rational reason that Annan would be in Chung King *secretly*, I couldn't find one. I looked for an irrational explanation for a *secret* meeting. The most logical one I came up with was war, *or some aggressive act*! They need to keep their actions secret so we do not suspect any of their intentions—I believe this. I would like a cooperative intelligence approach between our nations to discover what exactly is happening."

The overseer of the meeting looked to be from America, he asked Benjamin, "Would you please excuse us a minute Mr. Wolfshiem?"

"Certainly."

"I know that the opinion of my country would be that this is a request born out of paranoia."

"The people of France would disagree perhaps we should allow it—but limited," said Pierre Aqui, the French consul representative to Nikolai Chernigov his Russian counterpart.

The American stood up, "Go retrieve Mr. Wolfshiem."

The American looked directly at Wolfshiem as he walked in the room. For a moment it became awkward to Benjamin; almost as if the mediator was checking Benjamin for a madman. "Mr. Wolfshiem some of your contemporaries feel your story has been misunderstood by your country. However, we have decided to advise you that Israel should in no way make any moves towards the AU that may be interpreted as a sign of belligerency, but the world's intelligence agencies have agreed to help—in a very limited state."

Benjamin was relieved, at least some form of study would occur over the next few months. "Thank you gentleman, it is a great relief to know that we can stand together in order to get to the bottom of this peculiar event. Good-bye gentleman."

Benjamin trudged out it was time to go back to the airport and inform his countries leaders of the vast undertaking they now had to shoulder. Knowing his mission was half a success, he stood outside smoking a cigarette noticing the sky had turned overcast, and it began drizzling. Benjamin's feeling were barely paid lip-service for the next few critical months.

"I wonder why the young Jew is so worked up." He heard in his mind over and over.

CHAPTER 2
THE YEAR OF THE DRAGON

It was the New Year 2017, and in America the celebrations were normal if not a bit old- fashioned in the eyes of posterity. It was a great time to be an American, optimism reigned supreme, and living in the greatest country the world had ever known was a blessing in many ways. For now though, a New Years Party here, or a get together with some old friends there was protocol until the ball would magically drop, and begin another course of human history. Another course greatly anticipated.

As the international dateline passed through Europe the nations and citizens felt content, happy, and very much secure with their station in the world. Unemployment was a problem, but one they had pulled through before. There were two very different ends to this spectrum that bear further study. A new philosophy was beginning to emerge in the Eastern European nations as opposed to their western neighbors. Western Europe struggled under economic setbacks carried on by social programs, clogging government budgets. But countries like Rumania, Hungary, and Yugoslavia were developing rapidly economically, and reached a point where many took notice of their progress. They were becoming the first of the little powers that would inherit Europe after the war.

Russia had become a Representative Republic—propped up by millions of international dollars—taking more than just a page from the United States. Altogether, a new feeling of pride was unEarthing from the depths of Russian government. Russian citizens looked forward curiously and anxiously to a new hereto inexperienced future. It seemed something was just too right with the world at the time.

At the beginning of 2017 there was Ali Annan who looked upon the world as an independent animal, about to be reconditioned. Annan felt he had already done an impossible job uniting Muslims from the Azeris, Gilaki, Mazandarani, Kurds, Arabs, Lur, Galachi, Turkmen, and Persian backgrounds, not to mention there various religious schisms. He looked upon any job lying ahead as possible as long as he was the catalyst. After all when one accomplishes a miracle (as he did) they soon think about the next one to accomplish, not reflect on what had been already done. In any case, by the end of 2017 he was to become an Emperor.

Chinese leader Zhen Zui had announced a major trip to Baghdad, although he outwardly announced them under fallacious pretenses. Zui had "gone" to the Middle East as a campaigner to help with the current Chinese oil shortage crisis. The Arab Union had stated they would no longer continue to pump the same amount of oil from their wells, and openly directed this statement towards China. They felt they were exhausting what was left of their oil stores, and wished to have oil for future generations. In reality there was no such shortage, a campaign was just five months away, which needed supplied, and since the AU made money from industrial export production the oil funds were no longer a major priority. The time to stockpile these resources had already begun. Annan and Zui had successfully tricked the rest of the world. Zui announcing his trip under these false pretenses was a way of creating a clever form of cover, allowing him to jump back and forth from the Middle East with no one suspecting his intentions. So why then did Zui go to see Annan? Zui felt he had to accompany his generals to Baghdad, and because he was the focus of attention no one would pay any to the plane landing 75 miles away, which contained the opening plans to World War III. All the nations grumbled; what will he do? Few paid attention, few cared, and it was only Israel that watched with a tedious eye.

The rest of the world would have done well if they had followed the Israeli's suspicion. It was five a.m. when Zui arrived at the new Baghdad International Airport. Unknown to the second string media who had burden of covering this "meaningless" event, Zui's generals had arrived two hours earlier in Iraq, including four additional officers—2 Air Operations Commanders, and 2 Naval Admirals.

Zui greeted Annan indoors, as soon as Zui went to say a word Annan urged a weak, "ush."

Annan then led Zui into his private chambers through three separate hallways, and sitting back on his favorite chair he opened the statements, "Greetings, Mr. Zui, I took an opportunity earlier to tell your generals 'welcome to our country.' The reason I had to bring you in here is, in Persia, ears often appear on walls, and close to the ears is the mouth. The Americans say loose lips sink ships." In reality Annan had begun receiving reports that the Israeli spy ring had constructed artificial termites bearing microphones for the sole purposes of spying. Annan would always take guests to the basement because elaborate jamming devices were built into the walls which could not penetrate his favorite retreat.

"I understand Mr. Annan, a very wise precaution indeed." Zui was even more impressed with Annan this time because of his ability to speak with such articulation. Especially with the way he looked one in the eye, Annan could have easily made it in any field he chose based on that look. The funniest thing to Zui was had Iraq never been transformed by the United States, Annan never could have risen to power, but despair had always held the country, whereas Annan offered salvation. Salvation in a country bereaved.

"My generals will inform me of the plans, then I shall decide if we will go to war on your side." Annan wanted to make this statement sound uncompromising. He did.

"*Your* generals will be quite impressed with our plans." Confidence oozed from Zui's voice.

"Let us assume that is the case, there is one thing bothering me, the Americans. They remain our greatest threat, and I feel they cannot be allowed to bring their full military capabilities to bear, especially in a war of length."

"Mr. Annan, What does the Vietnam War mean to you?"

"A war between the North and the South. The Northern forces wanted to unite the entire country under communism, whilst the South said they wanted independence. However, the Viet Cong made life miserable for the combined Southern forces of the U.S., and their Vietnamese partners."

"I am very impressed Mr. Annan, but what do you know about the American home front during the war? What do think happened to your nation 15 years ago?"

"The majority did not want to fight, but may I remind you Mr. Zui Vietnam was in the middle of the 60's revolution, many extenuating circumstances that we can't count on now. In my country the war was unpopular because no provocation took place. I have studied America very well, who do you think the AU is based on." Annan started laughing at his last comment.

"Let me say this Mr. Annan, the U.S. today is very liberal and weak, they are going to destroy that great nation, liberalists have no place in America. The Americans don't even understand Jefferson. You must have seen it during your war for liberation, how nearly the great nation was split in two." Zui's voice growing desperate.

Ali Annan took a deep breath, he looked at Zui, and said, "Remember, Mr. Zui, this is speculation, I believe the Americans will fight, *I feel I must remind you*. Intellectual error is innocent, physical error is another story. Don't count on too many maybes, or there will not be too many tomorrows."

Zui thundered back, "the Americans have never had bombers bomb their mainland, fighters over their skies, or troops set to invade their coasts. There heads are in the clouds, they suspect nothing." Zui calmed down, took a seat, and delivered his last line, "besides, the Americans should stay out of it all together, unless they care more about Taipei, than New York. Foolish people!" Zui urged a happily frightening smile at this last, sardonic comment.

Meanwhile, in a dark room in Iraq, Hung Nguyen, China's most senior general was shaking hands with his Arab opposites. Nguyen had studied in America and France thereupon returning to China to conduct their military operations. The half-Chinese/half-

Vietnamese general's career was unparalleled in Chinese peacetime history. At the moment he was in an AU building greeting his newfound Middle Eastern friends. Papers in a folder were covered up with the emblem of a Chinese flag; later the AU generals found out they were the plans for the upcoming assault.

"Has everyone arrived?" Nguyen asked.

"Who else were you expecting, Genghis Khan?" A young AU general had blurted out that statement, which was followed by a round of laughing between the generals.

Nguyen, still half smiling from the poke of military humor, began delivering the lecture that would make the Chinese and AU brothers-in-arms. "Indeed, gentleman, this is a map of the entire world, one which, according to our plans will be conquered in 18 months. The tactics we bring you are designed to utmost thoroughness, flawlessness, and specifications that your leader has given us. In short, in front of you, lays perfection."

"Isn't 18 months a bit ambitious, we all know the first phase must be short and decisive, but 18 months for an entire campaign?" The same young Arab voice as before spoke up, this time he was recognized as Abu Rahim, it was no coincidence he was the AU's youngest general.

"The Arab Union will not be anything above dirt until they realize, command, and receive the best of their troops." Nguyen's temper had begun to flare up; he would make the Arab Union great if no one else could supply the discipline. "As I was saying the opening phase will play out like this, we propose to attack the following nations on the opening day at the same time: India, Israel, Taiwan, South Korea, with a minor strike at Japan."

The resounding sound of, "whaaaaaaat?" had filled the room. "An attack that large, we'll never be able to coordinate it. We can't use nuclear weapons the U.N. would respond with everything they have. It can't work." This was the voice of one Arab general, but the opinion of many.

The nine Chinese leaders stood firm while the Arab's bickered at them. The Arabs could not help but be impressed with Chinese discipline. "Gentleman, gentleman, please, you haven't even learned how you can criticize our plan yet. When we attack at these five points the allies will be so confused they will never know where or how to react. There will be no use of nuclear weapons; at least not at the beginning so we must use our advantages in numbers and training to crush the allies. We have our own ready allies: North Korea, Vietnam, Cambodia, Bangladesh, Thailand, Laos, Mongolia, and Malaysia have already pledged their forces and land in support. Keep in mind we hold equal with the allies in planes, lack their naval resources, but outnumber them greatly in troops. We will turn these advantages into victories. The Chinese have waited many years for the chance to strike, our armies have increased since the 1980's, we will now show the world the military machine we have created."

"You hunger for profitable lands, we know you want Taiwan, and the entire collection of Pacific Islands, you feel threatened by a navy, which could pounce anywhere along *your* Asia and attack." Auda Bakr stepped in for the first time, he was the AU's top general, he was pure genius, and maybe the only man Annan trusted with military matters. "Fortunately for you, my leader has given me orders to evaluate your plans so we may coordinate the attack, you see we are finally powerful enough to determine our own fate. But we also thank you for assisting in the training of our troops, and for the officers you will loan us." Bakr's last statement left a bitter taste in his mouth.

"Powerful enough to determine your fate." Nguyen said. "But not your officers, quite a contradiction. However, you are very welcome. First, our plan for the invasion of India. General Tran present the invasion."

Chinese generals had worked for months to assure that these were the best-case scenarios to give to the Arab Union. After all, the AU would study the plans themselves for weeks after the meeting.

Tran was another in a line of formidable military minds who had been nicknamed the "razor brains" by Zui. Tran led off with Asian twang in his voice, "Thank you, sir, as we all can see India is surrounded, dangerously may I add, by enemies and oceans! I have studied the terrain carefully, I want no armored units only foot soldiers, armored units will hold back our speed in the conditions of India. A two pronged attack—from Pakistan to the southeast, and China traveling southwest -aimed to encircle Rewari , which is just south of New Delhi the objective. Also on the first day, another attack—composed of Chinese forces—from Nepal to Baleshwar a 500-mile trip, will isolate West Bengal from the rest of India. Two weeks after the opening day this"—Tran pushed a division marker on the map—"a fourth force of Arab Union troops will strike due east 500 more miles from Pakistan to Agra this will cut the northern Indian forces from the southern. India will have no choice but to surrender. Once our forces meet at Rewari they will cut of Delhi—the center for communications—from every other important position. Without Delhi the Indians lose all their means of communication, and after that they will have to fight individual survival battles rather than a coordinated defense. It is important the AU troops hurry into Agra. Once they arrive the Indian forces gathering to win back Rewari will be hopelessly surrounded by Arab soldiers. We calculate it will take 4-5 weeks for us to force unconditional surrender."

Bakr thought about the plan, "What if the Indian forces in the south do not surrender? The whole reason for taking India is to eliminate a nuclear threat, and not give the allies a place to put weapons that could force a time consuming war, or a starting point for an attack on our homelands."

Nguyen fielded this question, "If they do not surrender when we have taken the north we will simply threaten them with nuclear weapons, they would have to surrender, seeing how they already lost control of most of their nuclear weapons and forces. Furthermore, I do not believe they would use them on their own soil. Next"

The third Chinese general Chiang Zu stepped forward with the utmost confidence; his job was to present the AU plans for the attack on Israel. "As you all know the Israelis are highly mechanized.

On the same day we strike India, the AU is to arrange for 2 army groups enormously strong in armor positioned north and south of the Dead Sea. You are hereby ordered to proceed to Hebron, cutting off whatever part of the Israeli army you can. As soon as you get to Hebron you will divide into 3 groups. This will confuse the Israelis, while they figure out how to defend it; the Northern group will go to Haifa, Middle group to Tel-Aviv, and Southern group to Gaza. This entire plan should be finished within 3 weeks. You are also ordered to flank, surround, and bypass the Israelis wherever you can, since you will have great superiority surround them whenever possible or justified in your eyes and move on! You must do this as quickly as possible so that the forces you use can be redeployed in case we run into any problems in any other theater. I have also been permitted to tell you that we will be giving you the brand new Chinese Type 3000 tank for use in Israel. However, that is all I'm allowed to say presently. It is a very simple plan, but with a technological advantage and brilliant execution Israel will be subjugated in a matter of weeks."

Bakr felt inclined to interject again, "China does not understand that Israel will strike us with mass bombings and possibly nuclear weapons, smashing our cities, families, and forces. We could be defeated in one day."

"No, no you're wrong." Nguyen seemed to have an answer for everything. Just how long had China planned this attack? "Israel will not use them without the approval of other nations. Europe won't risk nuclear annihilation because of a breakthrough on the Israeli frontier. They're smarter than that. We also have reports that the Americans have a missile defense system capable of stopping 55 missiles, and may have provided the specs to Israel. You see, neither one of us would use nuclear weapons. It would be an absolute waste to launch them knowing a full retaliation could eliminate life from Earth, but the Americans won't strike us because they don't believe in using nuclear weapons to settle wars, they will want to win the conventional way. If America uses nuclear weapons first they will damage relations with the entire world, and possibly bring the world into a holocaust, something they will never risk! And now gentleman the attack on South Korea. General Hu"

Chou Hu the last general from China to present an attack strode up to the map with a slight limp, he was an older man, and it seemed that his day for large operations had come and passed. He spoke with a belabored hum. "The assault on South Korea will be completely undertaken by North Korea. The North Koreans hold a massive advantage in numbers on their Southern counterparts. Unfortunately most of their weapons are outdated. As a result, they must ask our navy for assistance in order to carry out numerous landings. There will be 3 North Korean landings: 1. Inchon, as long as it is timed correctly. 2. Kunsan, and 3. Pusan. We will land here to give them too much to fight, they will not know where to commit the bulk of their forces, this way our numbers become more of an advantage. A lightning thrust straight to Seoul then southeast to Yondok will not give the Americans a chance to reinforce them from Japan until it is too late. We will then be masters of everything from the South China Sea to the Nile."

Nguyen stepped forward again, "I will now show you the plans for us to take Taiwan and Japan. Taiwan is very simple; we will land at six points on the Taiwanese coasts, with the main goal of finishing the job that Chiang Kai-shek started with Mao Zedong. I will command the entire operation from land and sea. Once we land—the toughest part of the entire campaign—we will drive east eliminating every possible part of the Taiwanese army across the island. As far as Japan goes we will start bombing them on this day, but will not invade until all other operations are complete, we do not wish to take on too much of a load at once, although we certainly are ambitious. However, AU soldiers may be called upon for the Japanese invasion if and when that becomes necessary. It is better to weaken Japan now, and avoid costly losses than overextend ourselves to the point where an invasion could falter. There you have it. Keep in mind it is not at all complicated to carry these steps out, but it is difficult to execute it. We could master the world in 2 years."

Deep down China was hoping to starve Japan into surrender, or even better, turn them to neutrality.

"One more question General Nguyen," Bakr had one more skeptical thought. "Where are the Russians to be during all this?"

"General Bakr, as is always the case certain specifics to the plans cannot be spoken of here, but please let us worry about prewar plans, and let us especially take care of our Russian friends. Tell me, what are your first thoughts of our plans?"

Bakr looked at all the Chinese officers in the room. "I feel your plans are nothing short of magnificent. But when are the operations expected to begin?"

Nguyen looked confidently at Bakr, and responded, "They are slated to begin with luck on May 17, 2017. A short few months away," Nguyen said flatly in passing. It looked as though the Chinese had covered everything. For hours after the meeting the generals pursued discussions on a wide variety of topics before retiring into the warm night to take the rest deprived of them for so long, especially the Chinese.

Benjamin Wolfshiem had been studying surveillance photos for what seemed like years now, however in actuality it had only been 3 months. He thought that the new satellite photos of underground equipment were nearly amazing, and it was up to the United States, Israel, and Japan to continue to pioneer this technology.

He was working with one of his associates when he turned to them and said, "Why are all the training camps filled with soldiers? They are raising quite a military over and above what the AU originally said. Does that seem friendly to you, or more of an act of war?" By now thousands of "spy termites" were overrunning Baghdad. The latest series burrowed into the dirt or sand to avoid detection.

"Maybe you should try to get the attention of other countries now. At least you have more than your own conjectures to back you up this time." One of the smart asses chimed in.

"That is probably the best thing to do, but I'm so damn sure I'd get brushed off again. All the other nations want is to turn a blind eye, pay no attention, they'd happily sacrifice us to avoid conflict. Don't think they wouldn't." Eventually Benjamin got the initiative to pick up the phone and get in contact with the United States Middle East Intelligence Bureau. This branch had been created prior to the U.S. leaving a friendly government in power in the Middle East. It was created after the second Desert Storm for the implicit purpose of monitoring military strength. After a long waiting period the bureau finally decided that it was worth taking a look at Benjamin's material—if just to shut him up. Also they had been noticing peculiar events happening in the Middle East. Masses of troops being moved from place to place, Chinese commanders giving instructions, and new types of tanks and planes that they had never seen.

Finally, on April 15, Benjamin got the response he had so agonizingly been waiting for. He watched excitedly as a wire message came over his desk, but it was not the one he wanted:

Mr. Wolfshiem: after studying your material for a number of weeks we have the following observations and recommendations for you: We have confirmed movement of mass AU and Chinese forces. At the present time we have no concrete information on what this means or a reaction. Warning: you are not to provoke these nations in anyway or become belligerent. Since we have no stated objective it would be unwise to show any signs of aggression to your believed peace loving neighbors excluding preparation of military forces. Repeat do not make any moves which would be considered warlike until we have confirmation of a materialized assault. Below is the information you requested. Will continue to monitor.

Total
Army groups in China: 27
Army groups in AU: 19
Armored Divisions China: 47
Armored Divisions AU: 25

Aircraft China: 12,000
Aircraft AU: 8,000

Benjamin ripped the paper out of the machine, and jumped to the telephone, "I need to speak to Wessler right away, Prime Minister Wessler!"

The connection went through, "Hello. Benjamin. What good news do you have for me?" Wessler's voice was to the utmost of sarcasm.

"Their massing on the borders, all the signs lead to attack. They cut down the sale of oil to dry other nations up, and there is little to no contact between the AU, China, and the rest of the world. We are going to be invaded, and damned soon." Benjamin said exasperated. "The intelligence report is nothing but double-speak. There will no one helping us."

"I believe you Benjamin, but no other nation has told us anything."

"Nothing." Benjamin agreed. "But we must be prepared."

Wessler hung up the phone on Benjamin and called his military leaders. "I would like all of you to draw up contingency plans for a war with the Arab Union. As soon as this order is completed immediately mobilize our forces. Time is of the essence."

Benjamin had talked with Wessler shortly after he gave the order, Wessler told him to appeal to all nations willing to listen to ask them for help. Do not be afraid to show every piece of information to other nations even if you must scare them. Anything that may help us gain allies against this new most dangerous threat is entirely encouraged.

Deep inside Benjamin greatly admired Wessler. Benjamin was the first to realize what his country needed was someone who would fight no matter what the odds. Whatever their chances were by themselves, Benjamin was supremely confident in his nations leadership. April had turned swiftly to May.

"Do you believe it is possible?" The room was completely dark, it must have been hours past midnight. Ali Annan was having an audience with Auda Bakr the man who would lead his unseasoned Arab Union Army.

"Yes, sir. The Chinese have seemingly thought of everything. I believe we are strong enough to conquer the west with Chinese assistance. Perhaps we will even become more powerful than they are."

"Auda. Would there be any advantage in waiting. Say we wait 5 or 10 years would that harm anything? I'm trying to say what would be the difference. I have all the time in the world."

"The difference sir, would be the fact that the world, for better or worse would be twenty years more advanced." Bakr said profoundly. "The major difference is that we could be robbed of our ultimate destinies. Five years would not make much difference, ten would rely greatly on us being in power, and twenty—who can say for sure we would still be alive, sir?" Bakr's reference had been taken as a point made about Annan's wife.

Annan leaned back in the quiet of the night. Looking up he asked Bakr a blunt question, "Do you think our destinies intertwine Auda?"

"I do not think I stand here by coincidence, sir. Neither should you."

"A leader's destiny intertwined with a general's, I never like it, even when I read it."

"Our forces have now completely mobilized sir."

North Korean General Khang Tro looked at his deputy officer with a smile, he would be leading the North Korean forces against the South. The invasion was completely up to North Korea, except for a few ships, aircraft, and pilots they required from China. "What an absolutely brilliant sight, these men will one day be victors over the entire world, and I will begin by leading them to victory here."

"Morale is extremely high sir. Our preparations call for us to strike straight to Seoul, then rush to Yondok so no forces can be landed to counterattack our positions. Coupled with the landings from China we will be able to trap entirely all their defensive forces."

"I know petty officer Duang, I have reviewed these plans day and night. Over and over again in my head, I cannot see us losing. We have superiority, comparable technology, a fine fighting force, surprise, and an iron will." Tro looked back at his understudy, "The commanders in chief believe we can conquer South Korea in ten days despite our obvious handicaps."

The North Korean troops had marched up to organize their lines, singing songs, and playing games. They showed so much happiness for what they thought was the right thing to do. The whole scene must have been very profound; men looking forward to fighting because of their feelings of virtue. It was unimaginable for any other countries to have treated war this way at this time, but the North Koreans, and soon enough the Chinese, and Arabs would be remembered for it. They did not know the terror they would soon cause, it was probably better they didn't.

A strange occurrence happened on May 14, 2017. Something, which was quickly thrown aside because of the upcoming war news breaking in three short days. For a period of two hours the sky over the Atlantic Ocean turned blood red, and all communications were rendered impossible. No phone calls, faxes, or any type of electronic transmission could be sent out or received. Panic stricken people took it as a sign of danger, and as strange as it may seem some claimed UFO's were involved. They were only half right. Some cited sources of a similar event that did occur one time shortly before the beginning of World War II, was this premonition a precursor of things to come happening just days before the outbreak of war?

Benjamin Wolfshiem was working rapidly, he knew he did not have much time, and other nations were beginning to take a vested interest in the happenings of the Middle East. If Benjamin could work quickly enough perhaps he could rally them.

"Look at this assembly of soldiers on the borders of India, soldiers and tanks on North Korea, ships loaded with men and supplies in eastern China, and an armored formation—the largest I have ever seen—on our border. We're going to be attacked in the next couple of days." Benjamin was exasperated and his words were piggybacking on to each other making him difficult to understand.

One of Ben's associates took a copy to fly to the U.S., "I'll arrive there tomorrow morning, maybe we can finally convince them. They have to be seeing the same thing we are."

"For our sake, I hope so." A quick glance at the calendar confirmed it was the night of May 15. The panic in the room continued for the next 72 hours.

The time to unleash this massive offensive had finally come. General Nguyen sat in his office praying, and hoping that the first phase of the offensive would be greeted with optimal success. It would be impossible to continue the war on the scale they planned unless major victories were achieved in each theatre at the commencement of the war. Nguyen could hear the hours approaching, and it occurred to him that the nations he planned to attack had made no responses, perhaps they knew, in which case it would mean devastation to his land, and perhaps they had mistaken the troop movements for exercises. Either way it was too late to cancel it. He picked up a microphone and announced, "This is General Nguyen to all units, I have utmost confidence in your abilities." Then an announcement came over, "the stand down is over. The planes and units are in position, we attack in 5, 4, 3, 2, 1."

The time for careful planning was over. In moments the world was engulfed in destructive war.

CHAPTER 3
LIGHTING WAR

Today our countrymen, brothers, fathers, sons, and soldiers went to destroy and rid the world of oppression, despair, and evil. This morning our comrades attacked and together with our allies carried out assaults in India, South Korea, Taiwan, and Japan. Our brothers to the west also launched an assault on the nation of Israel with our complete support. All of our allies who are close to us in both thought and proximity were deeply overjoyed to join in a combined effort, which has taken us to war with the aforementioned nations government's and the United States. However, no nation or coalition will remain as united as our states! Our men are of the highest morale, and know that right is on our side because of this war now grievously forced upon us. In the coming months of our campaign we will be as hard as nails, and as unflinching as steel. We will never be deterred, but always determined, never showing weakness, and always appearing with fresh strength and a firm will. No number of men or level of technology can stop us from this crusade we now undertake to restore justice to an unjust world. On shores, lands, islands, oceans, and in the sky victory awaits."

For now that was all. This was a make or break speech for the career of Zhen Zui—sending his nation to war—but on the morning of May 17, 2017 these words came spewing forth in a great tribute to all those who ever rallied men. Zui chose his words carefully, and in some instances, flatly lied altogether. Words like "forced", "oppression", "evil", conveyed a message that the Chinese had been severely wronged, and were now the beacon of hope to the "struggling" world. A concept the newspapers of the outside world would soon run with as being an absolute lie and completely unjustified. Whatever could be said of Zui's speech it had one characteristic that all should. It was a stirring masterpiece in the grand scene and context of time; it gave vigor to an already lively country, and turned supporters into fanatics. In short it was a gem.

By 2017 the Chinese wanted war, they had made too much progress and spent too much money in pulling their technology closer to that of Japan and the U.S. than ever before in their history. The Chinese did not want to end up in an un-winnable arms race; so they chose where, when, and how the "race" would ultimately stop and the war begin.

The Chinese needed the Arab Union as much as the AU needed them. The Chinese did not trust the AU, but it was necessary to act as though they did for obvious purposes and mutual benefit. Most importantly, with the AU holding down the entire European continent the Chinese were then free to focus on their immediate problems also known as the Pacific and the United States. The Chinese gave the AU supplies, vehicles, equipment, and added expertise. In return the AU gave the Chinese a blank check on their resources of which fuel was the most foremost. The Chinese never needed to develop a hydrogen fuel cell, or any other technological advancement in fuel as did the allies. They could turn those efforts elsewhere with the vast AU resources, while the allies scrambled for alternative energies. The alliance was solid but what it lacked in trust it made up for in convenience many times over.

Many guessed at the reason why China went to and wanted war. There were many eclectic reasons for their newfound aggression. First, they had spent massive amounts of money to upgrade/create military equipment. Another large part of their defense budget went to further their technology; where they came up with ingenious inventions like the JH-27F, which would soon terrorize the skies both east and west of China. Another wonder weapon they created was the Type 3000 tank. It featured twin 118-millimeter cannons, a great invention that could deal with two targets at a time, perfect to offset the numerically superior numbers of the allies.

In fact, the reason it was designated Type 3000 was because of the running joke between Chinese generals that the tank would not be obsolete until the year 3000. These new weapons forged a new attitude in China and brought confidence that the Chinese nation was destined for greatness. The Chinese had procured much of their national budget to military means, and they became determined not to waste materials. They had seen the wholesale despair in Russia after the cold war, which was caused by overspending on arms, and promised themselves a similar event would never happen to the world's strongest communist state without using them first.

The Chinese also had a timely habit of exploiting opportunities that did not occur all to frequently. The United States had begun to drastically cut down the number of military bases overseas; everyone felt war "in this day in age" on a grand scale was over. Twenty-first century wars would be fought with technology the experts said, but the Chinese never bought into this philosophy, and by not doing so created an advantage. If soldiers had guns, they will fight, until other soldiers with guns stop them. Therefore the only unfriendly nation that would offer formidable resistance in the immediate area of China was Japan.

Second the Chinese had always felt that Taiwan was a jewel of their empire, which had remained untapped for decades. Ever since Chiang Kai-Shek had established independent Taiwan the Chinese Communists had been waiting to knock it out. Taiwan came to symbolize in some strange way the motif of World War III. The forces of totalitarianism and dictatorship trying to eradicate the democratic views of anyone would get in their way for one last time. In this theory, Zui had become a logician. Able to play roles so as to convince his country Taiwan was extremely profitable, and extremely American. The former could be taken by the Chinese for their benefit, while the latter must be smashed for their national satisfaction.

However, Zui's most profound thoughts and attitudes centered on America and the probable reaction of the Americans. He felt the American race had no stomach left for war and could barely survive anything that tested their patience. "A fashioned crazed debauchery laden republic has no stomach to fight," he once said. A country with a short attention span could never endure a war of long tenure or remain united he uttered frequently—the feelings of China as a whole. The Chinese were resourceful, efficient, and pragmatic, but they would soon find out never is a long time, and the Americans would fight them. The cost China eventually paid in lives; this quantifies what Zui could not.

Pieces of land have been fought over thousands of times, conquered, defeated, overthrown in a cycle all to familiar to some, and not familiar to others. To the Armies of the East, as the combined AU and Chinese armies came to be known in the early days of the war there were only three types of land: conquered, defeated, and what is to be defeated. In any case the chance to stop the AU and People's Army of China was lost in the beginning moments of World War III.

Early on Wednesday May 17, 2017 crack Chinese troops poured across the unstable border of India, and began using the most valuable asset of any army—speed. Two army groups enormously strong in infantry raced to their objectives. The Chinese—attacking from mainland China—numbered around 550,000 men being supported by 105mm Light guns, 155mm FH70's, and 159mm Type 3 guns making up the largest percentage of the artillery support. The reason the Type 3 was made at 159mm was so the Chinese could fire the NATO standard 155mm shells, but the NATO guns could not use Chinese shells. This was another advantage of always making weapons after another country produces their line. The Chinese tried to take advantage of any allied attribute, and more often than not capitalized.

Chinese troops moved so quickly that Indian air and artillery could never stop them in a certain area long enough to use these weapons to inflict any severe damage on the enemy. Without any stopping power India was helpless to defend itself. Meanwhile, the Arab Union infantry (attacking from Pakistan on the same day) numbering around 2 million men was almost exclusively supported by 159mm guns. The truly amazing fact of the invasion was save for Type 4 light infantry vehicles—another Chinese creation based on Russian designs—there were almost no armored vehicles used by the here named Axis. Meanwhile, the AU relied on dinosaur equipment like Russian BMP-2's having had them around for countless years.

Although these numbers and weapons did not seem very impressive, they were offset by a major tactical advantage in the air. JH-27F's supported two types of bombers the JH-27B's and the Xian T-92's. Furthermore, the Chinese sent demolition crews to live in India months before the war quickly helped sabotage Indian airfields while the time was right and the Indians were off balance. Combined with the first Chinese air strikes, which focused on knocking out Indian airfields, much of India's air force was destroyed before it could get off the ground.

As a result, this made the only impediments to the invaders the terrain and Indian artillery. India was prepared for war, but in any case they were not given the chance to completely mobilize and in one week the Chinese found themselves 100 miles away from there objective of Rawari. At the same time another smaller force of Chinese troops was dispatched to cut off West Bengal from the rest of India. Its ultimate objective was Baleshwar 500 miles away. Here is where Indian generals thought they could stop the Chinese, however Chinese soldiers continued to show amazing fortitude. They continually beat the Indian soldiers on their own terrain, and the Chinese Air Force devastated Indian troops wherever they appeared. Coupled with the fact that India needed to fall back to protect New Delhi, Baleshwar was left wide open. Tran beat the Indians all the way back to Baleshwar.

The AU troops were moving at a slightly slower rate across the terrain of India when an opportunity presented itself to Kotah Gawla. At Dadri, some 100 miles away from the AU objective of Rawari, Indian General Kotah Gawla drew in reserves from all around and boldly counterattacked the main Arab assault on Rawari. The Battle of Dadri raged on for five days, but while it looked indecisive, General Tran stepped up the Chinese offensive, and eventually forced Gawla to retreat in order to protect his supply lines.

Another invasion from the west, launched on May 31 consisted of 700,000 more AU troops set out on a straight line to capture Agra, thereby cutting India into two parts—north and south. This attack by the AU was not only unnecessary it clogged up Axis resources. After Gawla retreated from Dadri the war for India was a foregone conclusion. No support was given to India, and probably none would have helped. On June 8, the Chinese forces crushed the Indians at Baleshwar, and two days later the pincers snapped shut at Rawari. Delhi was now completely isolated from the rest of India, and the leaders of the Indian nation fled to Australia.

Tran called on his Arab counterparts to speed up their invasion, which was easy since India was crumbling fast. Their government having already left and army in disorder. A few days later Agra was reached and the Indians—reluctant to use nuclear weapons on their soil—were vanquished. In one month of fighting the Chinese and AU had eliminated their only serious mainland threat at little cost. The Chinese and AU suffered 100,000 casualties, while India—now defeated—suffered 310,000 casualties. Soon to become a note in history the campaign in India was far from perfect. However, when one considers it was fought by nations who participated in almost no war for a great period of years it becomes much more impressive. Though the Axis made mistakes, they were learning.

"Did you hear, we're being attacked, and rumor has it they've already broken through our frontier defenses!" The voice belonged to one of Benjamin Wolfshiem's understudies. Ben looked at the digital calendar it was May 17.

"Thank Yahweh I sent Ilan to Washington a couple days ago. I think we can still hold them, but it depends what they have in the field. Where did they strike us from?"

Ben's understudy walked over to a map to pinpoint the location from where the attack had originated. "They hit us from north and south of the Dead Sea, but all they have done is disrupt our sentries, and I've also learned they seem to be moving forward on both fronts with a very small number of their troops."

"They're planning to surround and destroy us then, probably trying to lure us into some kind of a trap. I hope our generals sense that." Just then the phone rang, Ben picked it up—"yes, yes, yes, ok, we will leave as quickly as possible." Putting the phone down Ben jumped to his feet, "Get everyone we have and get out of here, the AU has put heavy bombers in the air, and this base is vulnerable, no doubt a target. Hurry!"

As Ben ran out, he was in such a panic that he forgot to destroy the encrypting machines, a few minutes later this communication came out:

From the U.S. Dept. of the Middle East
To the Israel Head of Secret Services:
Be on watch we have reason to believe you may be invaded within the next 24-48 hours. We will send more information as it becomes available. Good luck.

The assault on Israel was very well conceived even though it did not mark great success to begin. It was not supposed too. There was good reason for that; the AU armies used infantry to push a short way into Israel. While the bulk of their forces, especially the armored divisions waited to pivot then encircle Israeli divisions. The Israelis sent some of their best divisions to force the AU back, and establish a defensible perimeter, which they did quite successfully. This was the reaction Generals Bakr, and Zu were hoping would come to fruition. Once the Israelis tried to mount an offensive—on May 22—they found themselves encircled by tanks they had never seen, and subsequently lost a substantial amount of manpower.

The Chinese Type 3000 tanks chewed up Israeli built Merkavas, and then turned their attention to the British made Centurions. The Arab's proved they were capable soldiers when given modern technology, even though they struggled where they were still using, by now, long outdated T-90's that were harpooned by the Israeli Air Force like a dead beached whale.

Nevertheless, by May 31 the AU had reached its main objective of Hebron almost directly in the heart of Israel. Although a little behind schedule they had already eliminated the best Israeli defenses. From there the second phase of the Chinese plan was carried out. The armies met at Hebron, separated into three parts, one to the north at Haifa, one to the middle at Tel-Aviv, and one to south at Gaza. The Israelis tried to patch a defensive line to meet this new threat, but on June 2 the AU troops hit this line like a pile driver.

Israeli soldiers—some of the best trained in the world—were falling back all along their land. They were brave, but were outnumbered at least three to one, and even more in some cases. The air was the only place they were capable of winning victories, but the sheer numbers of the AUAF made up for all axis losses. Israeli C2's, and French Mirage 2010's were capable of carrying the fight to the invaders, but there simply were not enough of them. And as soon as the JH-27F made its appearance with Chinese pilots the AU could strike anywhere with virtual impunity. The AU eventually won command of the sky, while the Israelis lost all of their airpower in forward positions.

By June 10th all of the AU army groups were within days of forcing unconditional surrender. At this time the Israelis appealed to other nations to begin using nuclear weapons against the Arab Union. The United States had its hands tied, and now found itself hard pressed at war with China in the Pacific. Japan was in a precarious position, and had no way of helping. They were too far away, and under constant bombardment from Chinese aircraft and missliles. The only answer could have come from slow moving Europe, but at this point they were more impressed with the AU. In the end the Israelis did not use nuclear weapons, but had to be content to fight again another day. Europe was not prepared to risk war—save for England who was already at war with China, having declared it on May 18.

A solemn day occurred on June 14th, 2017, the AU generals accompanied by Ali Annan arrived in a small schoolhouse near Haifa in Israel. There was an odd fog in the air as the AU generals, with

Chinese General Zu arrived. Papers were signed and in minutes the Israelis had put themselves at the mercy of the AU. The AU suffered 30,000 killed in the entire campaign. A number so small they felt they could push their way into Europe in a few months time of course. The Israelis suffered 40,000 casualties, but 75,000 soldiers escaped—they would, some of them, walk their country again one day victorious, but currently they left on ships from land with heavy hearts and soiled spirits.

The United States watched as their newly acquired enemies began to gather up land, and crush allied armies. No doubt the situation was desperate, but with too many fronts opening up America had no idea where to commit their forces. Chou Hu would get the first opportunity to fight against the Americans in the one place the Armies of the East it was thought could be stopped—South Korea. On May 17, while India, Israel, and Taiwan were under siege South Korea was called to war.

The North Koreans charged frontier defense lines—and even with American and South Korean troops—could not be stopped. The initial landings at Kunsan and Pusan (southern most point) were so successful they hampered all further allied military operations. Originally the Chinese had planned to land at Inchon, but this was deemed unnecessary by the North Korean General Staff. There was no reason to land there because Inchon was not an area of importance to an army looking for an offensive miles south. Inchon was surrounded and bypassed which worked out just as well.

The main North Korean drive headed straight for Seoul, and nearly reached it in 4 days. United States General Matthew Brighton made a remarkable stand just north of Seoul on May 23, but without receiving fresh supplies and soldiers it was next to useless. Brighton retreated south, and declared Seoul an open city allowing North Koreans to waltz through at their own leisure.

A greater danger from behind opened up on May 24th! From Pusan, a Chinese southern force was trying to enclose the entire defensive position of the allies in South Korea. The Chinese force came close to trapping nearly all of Brighton and his men south of Seoul. Adding not only another dangerous front at this perilous time, but one capable of encircling Brighton literally.

Pusan had already been captured and the pure numbers of soldiers for the "Armies of the East" was beginning to tell. After Seoul was taken a great pincer began to close around the allied armies. The only recourse for Brighton was breaking out to Yondok and trying to evacuate as many soldiers to Japan as possible.

On May 25, Brighton boarded a ship, along with his staff, and remarked, overlooking Korea, "What a tremendous waste!" The allies did eventually evacuate 33,000 soldiers, but the ones who were left had to fend for themselves and deal with punishments handed out by North Korean's gleefully returning to power.

Initially, Nathan Moore, U.S. commander of the Pacific, felt that South Korea was just a minor defeat, but losing it put Japan directly in the line of fire, and sealed off Japan from Russian aid. Moore turned his attention south to the best position to stop the Chinese momentum, the small hereto-undisturbed little island of Taiwan. The best place to make a stand, and possibly force the Chinese to retire, or at worst prevent them from gobbling up other Pacific friendlies. Either way Taiwan alone could dramatically influence the course and duration of the war. In what culminated in another Chinese victory disasters occurred on both sides.

The first movements and landings on May 17 were at Taiwan, although they were not well planned by the infallible General Nguyen. Naval landings were choppy, and by the time Taiwan picked up radar on the Chinese Navy, it met stiff resistance. Nguyen called on his best troops for the second landing knowing China would still have a tough time offsetting Taiwan's naval and air power. However, by May 19 the Chinese had established 5 of 6 beachheads with one being completely destroyed by accurate missile fire and Taiwan's stellar Air Force. It was hailed as a major victory, but was of little consequence because the Chinese had exercised the campaign with only 3 jump off points. They had already persevered two more than what they really needed. Because of the brutality the allies now needed a long period of recuperation. At this point though China had a much better chance to win without delay.

The President of the United States Thomas Powwer, mentioned for the first time here, was a Republican fighter. And his reputation took over here; he fanatically supported anyone who would fight against China or the AU. Taiwan was no different in his eyes. U.S. troops began landing on Taiwan on May 25, the world now said, "China would run into real soldiers for the first time." However, they were only a token force of around five thousand, the rest of the allied fronts were in full retreat, but a relations nightmare would occur had the U.S. stood idly by.

Nguyen on the other hand was not stopping, his main objective was Taipei, but only two of the forces went to encircle it. His prestige was beginning to wane, especially with the disaster of losing one force, and around 2,000 men. Undaunted, Nguyen proved to be an extraordinary commander, at least wherever his naval difficulties were not hurting him. On June 2, at about the same time the Arab Union drove to Agra, Nguyen had completely surrounded the American and Taiwan forces at Taipei. He later wrote:

> *Our soldiers proved themselves superior to Taiwan's and America's. Although, they (the allies) had a small amount in numbers when compared to ours. Since they needed to protect cities it was easier to plan the campaign, and it was most easy to predict where they could be encircled. This was the underlying strategy of the entire campaign. I often wonder if they were on the offensive, and we then tied down to protect our cities could have fought the mobile war, which was so important to our victory.*

Nguyen would eventually get his chance to fight the defensive war, but it was still many months away.

As his troops began to put Taipei under siege, Nguyen watched with delight as Chinese soldiers—outnumbering America's and Taiwan's 3 to 1—were closing in and cutting off allied forces left and right. Skillfully transferring troops from one place to another, The Battle for Taipei was a complete Chinese victory. It is important to remember that the Chinese forces vying for Taipei were not the same that originally landed, they were fresh, and despite Taiwan having a very modern air force there was not enough aircraft to stem the Chinese tide. Especially, since all other air forces were heavily engaged elsewhere. Nguyen did not care about the number of casualties on the beaches; his concern was keeping his best troops far from the fight until a beachhead had been established. As a result fresh, well-trained, well-equipped soldiers could battle tired soldiers at the point of exhaustion. By June 9th it looked as though all of Taiwan would fall into the hands of China in a few days.

Nathan Moore, decided to attempt a daring invasion of Taiwan. His plan was to land on the east coast of Taiwan and drive to Taipei hoping to free it. Moore knew he could basically go where he pleased for superiority at sea was overwhelmingly in favor of the allies. The importance of this island could most easily be noted because it was the only place the allies attempted an immediate counterstrike during the early days of the war.

On June 14, the same day Israel surrendered, the first invasion armada raised by the U.S. in World War III appeared off the coast of Taiwan with 2 carriers, 5 cruisers, 10 destroyers, and 8,000 marines. It was crushed. Nguyen proved himself superior to the American generals on land tactically fighting The Battle of the China Sea. He waited as long as possible before sending aircraft to attack in order to inflict one massive debacle on the American invaders. Once on the beaches the Chinese used murderous artillery fire, breaking up the Americans. Over 4,000 marines lost their lives while another 2,000 were taken prisoner. The rest retired back to Hawaii, waiting to strike again.

The United States now realized Taiwan was gone. All they had to show for it were 7,000 casualties, and around 41,000 troops they successfully evacuated. Thomas Powwer locked himself away for one day in the White House contemplating what to do after one of the worst defeats in American history.

While the Chinese and Nguyen had grown in confidence and skill, remember his superior numbers opened the doorway to the Chinese victory.

For the moderately trained, technological, Armies of the East everything went according to their best-laid plans, they had lost less than 30,000 dead and wounded—a number easily made for with their manpower. While inflicting 3 to 4 times that number on the allies, and eliminating the two most prestigious tigers of the Far East. The first four phases were complete and opened up the idea that the war would be long or short—long if the allies were to recover—short if the Armies of the East would simply annihilate what was left of them.

The Chinese had also started bombing Japan on May 17, but as yet had no real plans to attack them. It was not that they did not want to; Zui's generals felt they would risk being overextended. As soon as Taiwan was taken, Japan prepared for an immediate invasion, but it did not come. China was unsure of Japanese intentions and was in no mood to "waste soldiers in an area we already dominate." Tokyo, Hiroshima, Nagasaki, and Kobe, were all bombed daily even though the Japanese were able to shoot down around 8% of China's bombers the Chinese kept coming. The Japanese imported most of their supplies, mostly oil, tires, iron, and had a way of molding these things into remarkable technology. The invasion of Japan was postponed until such time as Japan was isolated from receiving supplies from the west.

Zui had decided not to attempt an invasion of Japan. He realized his border was still unstable; an unfriendly Russia to the north could possibly cause problems. However, the Russians were in no shape to go to war. Radical rebels in provinces were being financed by China to initiate chaos, thus creating a fifth column, which would not allow the Russians to break free. As a result most of the Russian army congregated around the border looking to fight a defensive war. Zui knowing this preferred to stay out of Russia completely, better to extend east and west than to get bogged down in Russia like so many other armies vis-à-vis Napoleon's and Hitler's.

The only encouraging sign of the entire first part of the war was the reaction from Eastern Europe. Rumania, Yugoslavia,

Greece, Poland, etc. all the nations that had lived under Communist oppression put themselves squarely on the side of the allies. They had come to know the "American" or "Western" way of life, and were resolute not to lose it. They resented increasing Muslim citizens who had tried to take hold of their country for so many years. Thus a large air force, navy, and military had now become strictly allied. The eastern Europeans had joined Britain, and the United States as the only nations not directly attacked to take part in the war. This would have a tremendous impact on the war later, but for now the U.S. and Britain cheered excitedly, Western Europe grumbled, Russia held hope for a successful alliance, and the Chinese and AU won.

The first phase of the war was now concluded, and the axis powers could claim complete and total victory. They had yet to be put on the defensive, and had grown in skill and confidence and were at that point the most effective troops on the planet. Zui laughed, Annan cheered, and their armies enjoyed the best of all possible worlds. They looked forward to their next offensive with supreme confidence, and as Zui had once stated the Chinese were unflinching towards their enemies.

My would Abu Saddhis be proud to see his dream come true, his dream that had begun in a letter was solidified in the orient. There was little left to do in the immediacy for the Chinese who would recharge their strength for the next round while the AU would wait to see what China recommended. The Chinese were the leaders, but the AU would eventually put themselves in their own plans, and that is where the war would turn, giving the allies their only chance.

CHAPTER 4
LONG LIVE ANNAN

On May 18, one day after the outbreak of hostilities the United States declared war on China. Just minutes later before *President Thomas Powwer* had dried on the declaration of war, 22 U.S. Air Force B-52H bombers—taking off from Kansas—smothered Beijing under a cloud of smoke and rubble. The air war had begun. Beijing was the first Chinese city to feel the brunt of the allied bombs that struck so suddenly with an ultra devastating affect. Fire hydrants and fire alarms were exhausted, and while many key economic and military areas were destroyed with precision-guided bombs there was a greater overriding factor. Zui could not guarantee security for his people. Despite the fact that the attack was inconsequential to the outcome of the war China was ever threatened from above.

This was the major obstacle that hurt Chinese morale after their successful subjugation of India, South Korea, and Taiwan. The Chinese military leaders also had other problems to deal with from other locations. First, the isolated island of Diego Garcia, about a thousand miles away in the Indian Ocean was a developing nuisance as the allies tried to slow the Chinese war machine production with stealth aircraft. Diego Garcia was a British Protectorate being used as an air force base by the R.A.F and the U.S.A.F. It was from little Diego Garcia that British attack jets along with U.S. stealth fighters and bombers—primarily the B-2—were hitting "Industrial China." Combined with full-scale bombing raids from the U.S. mainland they inflicted a solid one-two nearly around the clock blow. These punches dealt deadly setbacks to Chinese confidence, but production was barely affected, if at all.

Together these air attacks only stiffened Chinese resolve to eliminate Diego Garcia, thus halting one piece of the daily civilian terror. Taking Diego Garcia would also crush the remaining allied forces in Chinese territory. However, a much more pressing issue was the fact that China did not have the naval capabilities to strike the U.S. in the Pacific with any efficacy. In every theater of study they found themselves compromised where they could not provide land based air cover to their tiny naval flotilla. Nguyen hoped to remedy this problem by taking strategic islands for the purpose of creating airfields. As a result, Pacific nations that relied on American supplies from the east could be cut off indefinitely. Nguyen wanted to use Douglas Macarthur's philosophy of "island hopping," but inversely in regards to the great general. His plan was to take only islands critical in gaining island bases in the fastest amount of time, while inflicting the highest number of casualties. It was a good plan. He carried it out masterfully. But there was a problem.

Nguyen wanted the AU forces to remain in the Middle East, specifically there to offset a sinking Russia, far from fighting a long-term war. Russia was still capable in proving to be a difficult enemy especially with the support they were receiving from the UK and U.S. This was an unrealistic point of view from General Nguyen because the AU had no desire to fight Russia. They were not willing to play a secondary role to their Chinese counterparts, or act as China's home defense force. Thus, Annan and the AU looked toward a still non-combative Europe for expansion.

Without giving any concern to Russia because of their weakness, Annan considered attacking Turkey. For years, he had aims to punish Turkey; it was Turkey—more specifically the Ottoman Empire—who had once subjected Arabs to tremendous torture in the early 1900's; Annan knew his history. It was Turkey who had semi-supported the U.S. during the Persian Gulf wars vastly undermining the entire Middle East he now ruled. In the mind of Annan, Turkey must be dealt with in a harsh way for their impudence towards the Arab nations. But where to go after that?

Many of Annan's generals told him after the Israeli operation they should stop, and take the necessary time to train their soldiers to the level of China's in case the allies tried to invade. But the main idea behind this suggestion was to strengthen the Arab Union if and when they were to invade Europe. However, Annan favored staying with the attack, and desired a year-end campaign. In the end he took advice from the only general that truly mattered, Auda Bakr. After Turkey was taken it was Bakr's plan that Annan eventually agreed on; it was on Bakr's plan that Annan would eventually lose his empire.

Conversely, by the fall of 2017 the American people were reminded of the Sir Thomas Moore quote, "You never have war unless you choose it." This was but a sick joke. Ironically, Moore wrote those words almost exactly 500 years prior. The Americans with many others never chose war; they were forced to choose between subjugation and war. The U.S. chose to fight, with Britain, Europe, and Russia. In a time of crises these nations still came together to defend themselves from oppression, and more surprisingly for each other.

The United Kingdom had long been a supporter of the United States, and had profited greatly during the last half of the 20th century. Although the sun had set on the British Empire long ago, Britain had become the elder statesman of the world; dangerously lingering towards becoming the sick elder man. Watching a young and thriving AU, along with an aggressive upstart China the elder statesman responded the only way they knew how on May 18. The British parliament resounding declared war, and began working immediately with the U.S. and Russia. In the hearts of the British people there remained a firm belief that they were needed once again to save the world from catastrophe so a better way of life could emerge.

The Russians were another story all together. Russia chose to fight because they were extremely threatened, attacked, and all at a time when they were just getting back on their feet after the formation of their shaky democracy. They were the only real military power in close vicinity to China, but years of cooperative training with the Chinese left Russia with few secrets. Russia was particularly desirable to China because the Chinese were the highest minority group living in Russia and had been for a long time. When President Salaval found out that China had financed and sponsored a ring of rebels months before the start of the war (much like in India during the outbreak) to purposely stir up trouble in the Motherland, he and his nation became resolute to march victoriously through Beijing. Salaval had to deal with many Chinese sympathizers still in their government, and consequently some hardliners still leftover, who wanted Russia to delve dangerously back to communism. Salaval was in a precarious position between the citizens who supported him and those in government who wanted him removed in favor of friendship with China. But Salaval was unrelenting. He recognized who the enemy really was outside his country and inside. He saw that his nation's only hope was to fight and win because Chinese soldiers would not be coming to liberate Russia.

Living in Russia at this time was a very tough life to endure, and it is a great tribute to Russian resiliency that they overcame it. Not only were the streets dangerous, the constant threat of invasion from China or the Middle East was alarming! There were food shortages, crime, and pollution had hit an all time high. For once Russia had trouble finding enough soldiers to defend itself. Terrorism was common everyday in Moscow, St. Petersberg, Ulan, and Krasnoyarsk. Daily attacks could be found openly on the streets of these cities in front of eager news cameras. Workers rioted local industries to find food, people left shot in the streets, left for dead with empty pocketbooks. After the war started Russia went from a powerful republic into a state of complete turmoil and chaos. Thanks completely to Chinese.

A state of civil war now existed between Chinese minorities and money passed from Zui under various guises, pitted firmly against the native Russians. One United States newspaper headline described it as "Bleeding Russia", which now reared its ugly head in austere reality. The American, British, and Europeans citizens wept and felt for the Russian people. However, the allied world did considerably more about it than weep, and these problems would be taken care of one by one. First with help from the Ukraine—and later America—the Russians stopped the Chinese rebels, and eventually achieved remarkable victories in their land. Russia saved itself before invasion allowing them absorb the vast Chinese blow that eventually came.

Had Zui ignored the American conflict for as little as four months, he could have won a major victory in sparsely defended Russia. But he had a choice. Either give the Americans time to strengthen and organize by attacking Russia totally, or finish the Americans, and hope then isolated Russia is silenced soon thereafter. Had China invaded Russia in late 2017 it is doubtful they could have been defeated, but whatever Zui thought of the Americans he thought even less of the Russians. Of all Zui's prophecies his strangest concerned the Russian Federation. He never thought they would overcome the uprisings, he never thought they could stop an attack, and most importantly he did not think they could win total victory. It is easy to see how Zui assumed Russia would fall apart, nearly everyone thought the same. But in the lessons of history a country not taken finished during a vulnerable time will always come back hauntingly to inflict sorrow. Under this premise how shocked Zui would be!

The Russian President, Darius Salaval, departed on August 10th 2017 to meet with Thomas Powwer, and the UK leader Henry Bollingworth in London. Security was tenacious for the three leaders gathered in one place for the first time. Even though Western Europe had not openly declared war yet, they watched tediously. The outcome of this meeting would affect the course of war, and determine what would become of the world. Former enemies would become friends and help would be accepted on terms never before seen among nations. Undoubtedly, this was the most important political event of the war. The outcome?

Russia, America, and the United Kingdom all pledged allegiance to each other steadfast to win total victory. If any of these nations were attacked the others would rally to their defense.

This arrangement became advantageous to Russia who benefited immediately from UK and U.S. capital and equipment. Even though their first victories were still months away their beginning cooperation in London made them possible. America gave the Russians equipment, supplies, and it was agreed to eventually land troops to help Russians defend Russia. The UK promised to be the go between for supplies, and to carry on the fight wherever possible on the plains of Russia. The lend-lease act was reinstated by the United States to give as much aid as immediate as possible to Russia, so short of war.

Amazingly by November 10th—three months after the conference—the Russian army began to collect its strength, and getting back on its feet. Towns and cities organized militias, Siberian troops arrived in key cities, and even though the country would not be completely cleansed of these Chinese funded rebels until early 2018 these victories allowed the Russians to accumulate men, equipment, and supplies. When they were eventually attacked, they were prepared to fight, and ridden of the enemy within.

After the Taiwan operation Nguyen was campaigning to Zui that the next logical operation should be to strike Japan or the Pacific islands—mainly those islands with U.S. interests. Zui held the power and felt that the aforementioned island of Diego Garcia must be taken as a compulsive matter of pride. Zui's pride interfered with his judgment; he had an undefeated army, but a country that was being bombed. There was no way he would let the allies continue to hit his nation's mainland if he could do likewise. As a result, preparations for an invasion, which would comprise almost all-Chinese naval strength, were aimed at Diego Garcia.

The British could marshal 4,000 men to defend the island, but they were woefully short of supplies and needed time to refit. On August 14—just four days after the London conference—Zui sent his most prized possession—his only large aircraft carrier: Peking, along with 10,000 troops and 2,000 paratroopers against the small British garrison. The Chinese soldiers captured the island in 5 days, but took severe losses. Chinese losses were 3 destroyers, 4,000 men, and the most irreplaceable piece of Zui's navy: the Peking. Allied forces on the island retreated to Australia, and found themselves greeted to wonderful applause. As a result, frustrated Australians were finally able to declare war on China the next day, now putting those nations in an unfriendly circumstance.

More importantly, however, was the fact that Diego Garcia was not a necessity to conquer, American bombers just moved elsewhere, or took off from U.S. bases to continue pounding China. Zui losing his only carrier—the world's newest—was inexcusable for an operation that achieved nothing of substantial value. Zui fettered away his only means to provide his Pacific naval operations with air cover. This provided a major morale boost for the allies, and showed the Chinese that their leader was capable of making grave mistakes despite their superiority. Had Zui not insisted on conquering Diego Garcia he may have conquered Hawaii.

The nation most ready to accept any type of support from the allies was Turkey. Turkish leaders nearly fell over themselves trying to gain support from anyone anywhere, but key allied nations could not at the moment spare any supplies. In the end Turkey received a handful of commanders who would help them set up their defenses. Turkey knew of the onslaught coming for them, and had deep fears that they would soon be conquered. Turkey had the double evil of being attacked before the allies were prepared, and before Europe was ready to do anything. The Turks needed weapons and experienced commanders; failing that victory was never possible over the invading Arab Union.

Ali Annan wanted to make the Turkish campaign the last operation before the winter of 2017-18. Because of this, Bakr rushed plans together, and they were in need of much patchwork during the operation. It is a great testament to the skill of Bakr that his plans were executed so successfully despite the lack of preparation. Bakr committed his newest tanks, about 1,000 Chinese Type-3000's, and the AU's version, the much inferior Majnun. He planned to drive a deep wedge into Turkey, allowing his forces to branch out at Zmir and Konya. Bakr himself would command the main drive aimed at Istanbul not Ankara. Bakr felt by driving straight to Istanbul he could cut off any allied forces inevitably arriving on shore. What he did not know is that these "forces" did not exist, and no one was coming to save Turkey. The Turkish Secret Service, receiving help from an Israeli colleague, Ben Wolfshiem, had fabricated them entirely. Turkey was hoping deception—the only attribute that could save them—was enough to prevent an attack.

Bakr unleashed his assault early on the morning August 25; he reasoned the conflict would last around one month. It took 19 days. Although Turkey did receive some allied help, they did not have the numbers of jets, tanks, and artillery to compete with the AU. Anywhere the Turkish lines were strong was where Bakr would aim to crush them. Bakr very much had the number of the allied generals at this time. He sent a wheeling pencil drive to ensconce Istanbul. As a result, he was threatened by a flanking counterattack, but his tanks could still chew up any equipment the Turks employed. Since he had a great advantage in armor the weak spots did not matter because the Turks could not exploit them.

The British Challenger 2 tanks were capable of dealing with Type-3000's and Majnun's; there simply were not enough in Turkey. Even if Turkey had the tank numbers AU pilots still ruled the skies above controlling the flow of the war below. Arab pilots, now fully trained, were shooting down Turk fighters at a frightening rate of 15 to 1. The Turks were handicapped by old jet fighters, which probably should have been retired or mothballed—one of them being the F-15.

The Battle of Zmir at the time was recorded as a minor skirmish, where the AU eventually won, but we know better today. Zmir was where the Americans would begin to find their victorious strategy, and it was at Zmir where a victorious leader would be found for the allies.

Thomas Edward at the time was considered a neurotic, arrogant, and reserved 37-year-old general. He excelled in everything he undertook before the war, including becoming an expert mapmaker, speaker, and leader. He loved technology, but felt he had a much better idea about what was happening around him simply through observation. When he combined these two beliefs doubly effective he became. He was a professional topographer, astrologer, and mathematician. He hand calculated nearly every figure because in his words, "the computer was not as accurate." He stood 6'1", had light brown, almost blond hair, and he saved the free world. Edward was a man whom continually doubted his own sanity, and believed he would do something great either success or failure. His gentle disposition and forced emotional stability made him a legend to his men. Luckily for the allies he perpetrated great success, Edward was described by many internationally as, "A walking human emotional contradiction."

At Zmir, Edward commanded Turkish forces attacking both sides of Bakr's pencil drive. Only Bakr's superior weaponry, and the advantage in the air won him the Turkish prize. However, Edward proved that if the circumstances were in his favor—meaning the air war—he could stop Bakr dead on. Then begin the long process of driving them back all along the front. However, he needed experienced troops and control of the sky which he did not have in Turkey. Unfortunately, Edward did fail in his first battle, but during the first week of September he evacuated to Greece, where he was promoted to Supreme Commander in Eastern Europe of all allied forces. Edward began planning immediately for another battle with Bakr—waiting patiently.

By September 13th, the AU was within miles of victory when they made demands on Turkey to surrender. By nightfall, Turkey signed an unconditional surrender, and the Turkish government became another one of those horrible governments—in—exile, which by now was all too familiar across the world. The Turkish surrender came as no surprise to the allies who realized the war had reached a critical point. Europe finally trembled with the realization that they could be the next to fall. In both directions—east and west—there remained no more buffer zones. Europe was open to the Arab Union and the west coast of the United States was open to China. Two gigantic armies could actually meet coming from opposite sides of the world in a huge victory celebration.

On October 1st Ali Annan with his advisors gathered outside the Emperor's Grand Palace in Baghdad. Annan greeted his citizens with lusty waves, and his supporters roared back wildly. Defense was overwhelming and thousands of AA guns and missile defense silos were online. When "all the kings'" men arrived inside, they had to deal with the first issue, which was primarily where to take their undefeated army next.

Annan led off the meeting by saying, "The first 6 months of this war have been better than we ever could of dreamed. In six months alone we have eliminated Turkey, Israel, and India. However, we must be cautious, but at the same time we cannot afford to wait and risk giving the allies a chance to recover! We are stuck in a difficult situation. Where do we go next year? What do you gentleman think?" Annan opened the floor for discussion.

Abu Rahim, the youngest AU general took the opportunity to speak with great passion. "I feel we should train the rest of our army to the level of the other great armies. It has only been in commanding and weaponry that we have been superior, and this trend will not continue if we fight Europe or the U.S. Now is the time to stop and train our soldiers, thoroughly! Our weapons will be matched in due time, and so will our tactics. We should consolidate then move forward."

"What do you think Auda?" Annan said, anticipating his answer still reflecting on Rahim's comments.

"We are in a very precarious position, we cannot afford to wait, but we cannot act carefree. The Americans, British, and Russians are worthy adversaries, and they rarely lose wars. Although, I have been thinking, why not strike where our advantage lies." Bakr stood up and walked over to a map. "Namely North Africa all great wars have always involved North Africa because it is the simplest gateway to Europe. Islam almost succeeded using the same strategy centuries ago. If our great leader can persuade Egypt, Libya, Tunisia, Algeria, and Morocco to allow our troops passage we could then try to invade Europe through Europe's weakness—the south."

"That is extremely audacious, and I like the idea very much," said Annan. "But where would you plan to invade?"

Bakr stood up straight, and seemingly glided over to the map once again. "This is North Africa, it runs almost below the entire coastline of Europe. If we, for instance, were granted the use of certain ports, we could then strike at the French port of Marseille and afterwards maybe a diversion in southern Italy. We could even attack Spain, and then go east. The only armies we have to fight are France, and Germany, and probably Spain, until we drive to Eastern Europe where the Americans have set up operations, but cannot reinforce these nations because they are busy fighting China. Who knows? The U.S. could be out of the war altogether by then." Bakr paused. "Keep in mind the allies expect us to strike from Turkey, and we could, but a landing in the south of France is, I feel our best hope. A landing from Turkey could be easily beaten back if the Americans decide to increase their forces in the area. The forces of Western Europe have been deteriorating for some time, and are ripe for a clean picking. I feel we could slaughter them in a summer's time."

Annan was very impressed with Bakr's tactical skill. "What would you require for an operation so large?"

"I would not attack France until I had in my command at least 3 million soldiers, 8,000 reliable aircraft, 7,000 tanks, 10,000 artillery guns, countless landing craft, and another smaller force to invade from Turkey causing a diversion. We have all the resources as far as men, and it is possible for us to get all the others. Comparable numbers of tanks and aircraft are required, but first we must get clearance to move our troops from North Africa, or the entire campaign will be compromised, and impossible to achieve."

Annan stood up sharply, "Then it is settled, I will personally invite the leaders of those nations you mentioned. While I am acquiring these political ties, all of our divisions will be trained for landing operations, and open country fighting. Read as much as possible concerning Rommel, Patton, and Montgomery's campaigns in these areas, and see how they fought in these amphibious situations. In a few months time we will all reconvene here, and decide which is the best course of action. I will tentatively schedule this operation to begin April 1st of next year—if at all—so there is no time to waste." Annan walked out, leaving his generals awed by his clear-cut thoroughness.

With that the meeting was ended, and Annan went to work on how he could use the neutral countries of North Africa to stage an assault. By Christmas, Annan had gotten Egypt, Libya, Tunisia, and Algeria to allow him use of their ports. However, none of these nations would directly join the fight against the allies yet. They wished to remain neutral—that is unneutral neutrals. In return, Annan told these nations he would not infringe on their governments, and at the end of hostilities they would not be punished in any way.

January 15, 2018 became one of the most memorable dates in the war. It left witness that still dawdling Europe was now on the frontline of the war. The AU's top divisions set out to Tunisia to reach their predetermined starting points before the invasion of Europe. Too late! France, and Germany finally realized Annan's true intentions, and desperately began to rearm for the coming fight. The French and Germans and even Spain did not want Annan to feel threatened so they never bothered getting prepared, but on January 16th they unanimously declared war in an act born out of survival.

Strangely, before the war, France had the best relations with the AU outside of China, but the goodwill France had endorsed on the AU was only a memory. Western Europe had better weapons compared to the AU, but at this point the AU military was a machine capable of grinding out victories in difficult places. The AU soldiers used to be laughed at and ridiculed by most news medias, and military experts as a dysfunctional force led by weak men with too much ambition. No one expected them to fight hard or win. By 2018 they had accomplished both. They were well organized, had excellent staff commanders, and their training had reached above average points. Their commanders made great demands upon them, and at this time—for a short time—they were considered the world's finest fighting force. They were no longer the easily defeated enemies that people had resoundingly believed they were. They approached every mission with confidence, purpose, and pride. The amount of respect they commanded was paramount; let that be your most enduring memory of them.

CHAPTER 5
CHINA MOVES EAST

It was October 1st 2017 and General Hung Nguyen stood outside the door of Zhen Zui's personal office; he was waiting for Zui to call him inside. Nguyen was expecting to receive massive amounts of praise showered upon him so gleefully by his commander, but there would no doubt be other news as well. For Zui never asked to meet him this way unless there was something he wanted. Nguyen was used to waiting for Zui to accept him. Zui had both the ability and the means to delay a meeting albeit in a manner of overestimating his importance, but in way of saying "I'm the boss." Zui excelled at this particular hobby of his, and it was something Nguyen could not stand to take even in small doses. Although, for all his leaders tendencies, for all his idiosyncrasies, Zui had led China to the most prosperous time they ever enjoyed. This factor was overridingly the most important, and it guaranteed Zui loyalty from everyone. The Chinese General Staff on down to the lowliest peasant.

The Chinese had a very real possibility to win the war in their planned 18 months, but in order to accomplish this they had to turn their attention, and more importantly the bulk of their forces to the Pacific Ocean. A very dangerous undertaking indeed! Only the most dauntless generals favored attacking the United States and traveling to the America's backyard at Hawaii. This topic ran through Nguyen's mind endlessly. The conference he was momentarily going to have with Zui concerned this issue.

Suddenly a door creaked open, a man peeked from the crack of the door that was created, and uttered forebodingly, "General Nguyen, you may come in now." The voice came from the unmistakable Zui who was already engaged in brushing his forehead because of a seemingly swollen brain. "Congratulations, General Nguyen, you are a man of endless genius, and now I will reward you. I am putting the entire Pacific operation in your hands, you have 1 month before I expect operational plans—November 1st. Is that understood?" It was simple. It was abrupt. It was Zui.

"Understood, I have been preparing since the end of the Taiwan campaign, I shall begin reworking final preparations today." Nguyen walked out of Zui's office appearing to be a man who was already beaten. He was noticeably disappointed to hear his leader had expressed wishes to attack the United States homelands. Nguyen knew enough military history to assume that this attack would end in failure. He knew it was logistically impossible to take an army 3,000 miles through hostile territory, reform, and then carry out an attack. With the Russian theatre left undecided, and the AU preparations underway to attack Europe, ambition was beginning to catch the "Armies of the East" placing them in dangerous situations. All the early coalition operations, which were so successful had now been thrown aside in an effort to end the war quickly. This was the first sign that a lasting alliance between China and the AU was in danger because both Zui and Annan wanted to pursue their own avarice-laden avenues. But all circumstances being subjective that did not change the fact that Nguyen would eventually have to order preparations for a Pacific assault in one month, and only he was capable of carrying them out.

Nathan Moore, the United States Commander of Pacific Forces (USCPF) was laying in wait for General Nguyen praying to avenge his prestige damaging failed landing at Taiwan. Moore knew Nguyen would invade because any other attack would have been useless against the U.S. Moore knew that China would not use nuclear weapons because of the U.S. insurance umbrella. The United States had a missile defense shield over North America now capable of stopping up to 1,500 Intercontinental Ballistic Missiles (ICBM's) at one time. The U.S. had secretly looped this together with a program in Japan, and the Japanese had further developed it to knock out over 3,000 ICBM's. Chinese systems were set to deliver tactical and strategic first strikes to the U.S. mainland. Unfortunately for the Chinese, while they had the number of ICBM's to launch, far less than 4,000 could be launched at a single time. Once those threats were processed and intercepted by U.S. defenses a devastating retaliation would usher in an eve of destruction reducing China to a primitive lifestyle, if any lifestyle was indeed left at all. While the U.S. and Japanese stood invulnerable to nuclear missile attacks many other nations had no defense at all. For instance, Russia and most of Europe were completely defenseless. Only the threat that the U.S would use them if their allies were attacked kept them from being pulverized by the Chinese. Conversely, being invulnerable never encouraged the use of these weapons to end the war. The unprotected nations would then be placed in ruinous danger because China could still attack them in a final wave with horrible success.

The Chinese who knew the U.S. could easily ravage their territory simply thought of a way to use their best competencies. These competencies were primarily the number of soldiers they could expend, which directly connected Moore to the idea the Chinese would attempt to invade the Pacific. Moore reasoned that Nguyen would have plenty of difficulty just getting across the Pacific Ocean. Moore thought it quite impossible to bring a large enough force over the ocean, organize it, and then carry out a full-scale invasion with coordinated, sufficient air cover and fresh soldiers. There was another factor that gave Moore an abundance of confidence as well. The Chinese Navy simply was not strong enough to compete with the American Navy. Chinese spending before the war had concentrated on aircraft, missile development, and tank design. At best they overlooked their navy. They had purchased some outdated aircraft carriers from Southeast Asian nations, but only recently produced one carrier, which was sunk at the siege of Diego Garcia.

Moore was in no doubt knowing he would get a chance to force a showdown with Nguyen's forces. Moore had an intact, well-advanced, well-equipped navy, and he had 6 first line carriers at his disposal against a single obsolete Chinese carrier that held about 12 aircraft. Moore also had around 10 times the number of screening vessels compared to the Chinese Navy. Moore's Aegis destroyers and cruisers were much more advanced than the Chinese Lulu and Zulu class destroyers. With a friendly Japan guarding the gates to the Pacific, and a technologically superior force Moore was sure of victory, despite the overwhelming quantitative numbers of the Chinese.

However, the Chinese were well aware of Moore's advantages—they knew their weaknesses—and decided to conduct feasibility study of their own. First, the Japanese presented a major issue, and could be a possible thorn in the side of the Chinese drive east—especially with American support. By 2017 the Japanese were the most advanced civilization man had ever known. China had been pounding Japan with air attacks coupled with cruise missiles since the opening day of the war. However, the Japanese Self- Defense Force had been prepared from the start. In fact, the Japanese were actually having the greatest success fighting the Chinese; stopping over 99% of the cruise missiles fired at them, while shooting down over 50 JH-27F's in a month and a half. The Japanese people were suffering, but they were nowhere near capitulating; food was short, and the Americans could not bring supplies over without facing fierce Chinese air attacks. However, Russia became a valuable go between to keep Japan stable, and help also came from Canada, Britain, and Eastern Europe. Nguyen stubbornly would not waste resources fighting Japan so he finally decided to bypass them completely and hope for a quick outcome in the Pacific. In any case Japan would be left at the mercy of China after an American surrender. He would get a quick outcome, although not the one he had wanted.

A common man at heart Nguyen did not enjoy the fighting he did it because it was his career. He hated war and he never deserved the barbarian iconoclast image the allies smeared against him. All over their newspapers Nguyen was an evil beast, but war is not a time for newspaper understandings. He much preferred diplomacy the way Annan did, but having no real government power vested in him, he was in a situation where he had no choice except to take orders or see his country led by a man less competent. Nguyen was the soldier who would take the hill, if it were impossible, he found a way, he was that soldier.

Nguyen pushed for a stepping stone seizure of the Pacific Islands where air support could be coordinated from one island to another. Nguyen's plan was half born out of realism, and half born out of shortcomings. When he eventually called in some of his generals his plan was as basic as it could be, for necessary reasons—mostly time.

Generals Nguyen, Tran, Hu, and Zu recalled from the Israeli victory, were the first to look over the Chinese strategy. "Gentleman let me give you first an idea why we will not fail." Nguyen led off with this statement, in an erect unflinching position. "The Japanese once tried to take Midway and force an American surrender. They failed. The major reason why is that they never determined what the main objective was. If it had been to capture Midway they should have sent all their resources straight to the island, ignoring the American carriers. If it was to destroy the carriers they should have sought them out before hand, and then struck Midway. Our operation will take us a bit deeper than that with clear objectives. We will drive to Hawaii, and if necessary Washington, D.C. We will call this opening operation—The Cluster Assaults. The ultimate goal—you ask—to land soldiers on the shores of California by February 2018." There was a brief pause while top-secret folders were distributed to Tran, Hu, and Zu. No one had sighed, no fear was shown, Nguyen's address was perfunctory for these confident men. They opened the folders calmly then Nguyen continued.

"The first step in subjugating the Americans is to stage an embarkation point on the eastern side of Taiwan, where we can base our communications for the entire campaign. We will start by taking the Bonin Islands, the Volcano Islands, and Iwo Jima. We will not have to face any attacks directly from American or Japanese concentrated forces. There will only be small garrison forces operating without heavy weapons and we will quickly eliminate them. From there, we regain our bearings and head 500 miles to

Marcos Island." He referred to a map of the Pacific and pointed out the location, "Defeat whatever small Japanese force is stationed there and build airfields, through the mountains if necesarry, and immediately move again. After we have taken care of that, another trip 400 miles more to Wake Island; the first American held island we will attack. We expect to encounter fierce resistance for the first time from U.S. forces, but nonetheless they will be shorthanded and we will prevail. We will consolidate our gains then go 750 miles to Midway Island because this gives us a base to threaten our ultimate objective Hawaii, which lays just 700 miles away. We will do it in this sequence, and the ground operations are yours to study, dissect, and memorize in the time being. Take them with you and prepare any questions or suggestions within two weeks. How does everyone feel about this?"

The question in that room went over with an uncanny silence that was meant. Almost all the Chinese generals were refrained from giving their true opinion ranging from confident to gung-ho about the job ahead. Finally, General Zu raised the first question, "How can we complete this with only one aircraft carrier carrying a maximum of fifteen planes?"

Nguyen shot back, "Because we have the ability with our Lulu class destroyers to intercept American planes with missiles and provide air cover from land bases. With this in mind we can achieve at least a stalemate in the air." Nguyen reset his shoulders, "Gentleman we are using our best, most experienced serviceman who do not doubt their leaders. Why do you doubt them?" Nguyen delivered his last question with a touch of animosity to his colleagues.

"I do not doubt our soldiers, General Nguyen, but asking this much, an operation estimated at 800,000 men, 22 destroyers, 5 cruisers, 1 carrier, and countless number of frigates and transport...I am dumbfounded as to why we want to do this so soon."

Nguyen responded, "I understand General Zu, but these are the orders I have received and it is up to us to carry them out to the best of our given abilities. We can accomplish this mission provided we do exactly what is prudent, there will be a chance of failure, obviously, but luck has smiled on us already, and my personal outlook for this operation is positive." Nguyen was a master of making men believe. In sense he was a hypocrite because the last line he uttered was something he doubted from the beginning of the war. Nguyen never truly believed the Chinese could win the war, even though it had gone well through 5 months. He was a positive person, but he knew much struggle still had to be endured. However, there was no other way to make his commanders believe unless he believed himself. So he had to lie or run the risk of having his entire staff receive a shattering loss of confidence. Nguyen had turned his colleagues doubt into disbelief in their troops. In truth this was not the issue. Nguyen had lied to his staff for the first time in his career. He walked out of the room alone with this thought: How can I begin a major campaign this way? For as unconfident as Nguyen was, Moore was juxtaposed at the opposite end of the confidence spectrum.

"General Moore, this is Captain Jeffrey Maddox, here to see you from Washington." Nathan Moore turned around to face the latest suit Washington had sent to consult him. These were becoming all too perfunctory for Moore who was tired of advisors recommending what he should do.

"I trust you had a refreshing trip, Captain. I suppose you would like to speak to me alone."

"Yes, sir." Maddox nodded his head out of trepidation. "First Commander Moore about a week ago plans were drawn up by Nguyen and his general staff in what we believe is an effort to invade the West Coast."

"I'm fully aware of the plans, I received that report as well. Does Washington know that the Chinese launched their largest cruise missile attack at Japan last night? All of them were shot down, but the Japanese did not retaliate. They have nothing to retaliate with. The Japanese intelligence service has noted that the start of a huge operation is at hand."

"Are you thinking the Chinese will invade Japan? Or aim for us?" Maddox asked this question with hope.

"No, the Chinese are going to try to get to Hawaii. I don't know how yet, but that is where they will dramatically attack us."

"How can you be so sure of this?"

"Captain Maddox, take a look at this map. If you were the Chinese, knowing you already hold Taiwan—and knowing that our latest intelligence reports show a stockpiling of supplies and men there—wouldn't you strike from your closest least threatened base and push outwards towards other Pacific Islands?"

"That idea does carry quite a bit of naval logic, I must say. Where do you think they plan to attack?"

"They will try to win the war in the fastest possible time, which involves conquering us not Japan. I think Nguyen will drive straight to Midway if he gets his way. The only islands that will matter are Wake, Midway, and Hawaii. That's Nguyen's ultimate objective I know it. I'll wait until he gets to Hawaii then release all of my naval strength, ensuring mind you, his largest invasion force is wiped out to the last ship. Then China will see what an American soldier can do when his back is not pinned against the wall."

"I think President Powwer would very happy to hear about your plan, he has sent me to convey his fullest support for you, your staff, and our forces. He wants you to know that his confidence in you is unflinching." Moore barely noticed Maddox's last remark. He knew he was the scapegoat for the United States after the disastrous opening of the war. Then Moore continued.

"His invasion force to Hawaii will definitely be his largest, it has to be. That gives us an opportunity to eliminate a large part of the Chinese Navy and Army. And when I speak of the army, I'm speaking of Nguyen's best troops. Second, I would not go directly looking for him because I have no idea what kind of traps he may plant throughout the Pacific. Nguyen's too smart of a man not to plan some sort of surprise for us. The Philippines are in the corner of the Chinese even if they are not fighting with them. Supposing another island out there decides to surprise us with fanatics who would trade their lives for our ships. I do not want to give the Chinese the opportunity to whittle away at our numbers and gain an advantage. I honestly feel better fighting right out here with our civilians sheltered. Nguyen's too smart of a man to haphazardly cross the Pacific. He will have defenses ready in case we try to attack him head on." Moore motioned his hand towards the Hawaiian waters which overlooked his office with such exquisite beauty. He figured that in a few months a great battle was destined to take place.

The Chinese had emptied their guns for the upcoming assault. They had Nguyen, Tran, Zu, and Hu, all of them commanding major forces for the so-called "Cluster Assaults." The Chinese had the best of their troops, and almost every ship from their navy save for 3 outdated destroyers ready to go. Sitting in front of them was 1,000 miles of ocean to the first round of invasions on Iwo Jima, Bonin, and Volcano Islands. These islands were not tactically important, but they were needed for logistics, once taken supplies, men, and ships could concentrate there until it was time for the next strike.

On the early morning of November 15th a 20,000 soldier armada was escorted by 27 destroyers, 7 cruisers, 1 carrier, and over 200 frigates silently headed for three Japanese held islands: Volcano, Iwo Jima, and Bonin. Chinese fighters and bombers made short work of the communications stations, and then turned their attention to Japanese airfields. Japanese built Mitsu F7's gave the Chinese fighters all they could handle—the Chinese lost 22 planes—but the caliber of the Chi Air Force training was too much for the Japanese to overcome. The Japanese never committed enough of their navy to offset China's striking power. Japan's navy was sequestered around the home island for defense purposes, and could not be used for any other reason on orders from their leaders.

As a result, the small Chinese Navy controlled the seas all around these formidable islands. Once the anti-ship missiles were silenced from the islands, 20,000 Chinese marines stormed the first collection of islands and the "Cluster Assaults" had begun. The Chinese had an easy time of it as soon as they got ashore. They were extremely well organized—thanks to Nguyen—and blunted every counterattack the under-equipped Japanese forces threw at them. The Chinese attacked these islands with radical emotions, and the Japanese simply were not prepared with most of their forces defending Japan proper. The fighting on Iwo Jima was ferocious, and many Japanese soldiers lost their lives forever entombed on the island caverns proving the war to be more than the sideshow the world claimed it was. The Chinese furiously motivated themselves by constant chants of Nanking (The Rape of Nanking was an offense the Japanese perpetrated when they attacked China. It is believed over 200,000 Chinese civilians lost their lives at the hands of Japanese soldiers). In one week the Chinese had possession of the islands they desired from the first part of their offensive, they could begin looking to the next step, specifically, Marcos Island.

Nathan Moore was sitting in his office when he first heard that the Chinese had attacked Bonin, Iwo, and Volcano. At first, he thought that this attack might have been the initial invasion of an attack that would hit Japan's homeland and culminate in Tokyo. He prayed this was not the case. Since May 17 any number of deceptions or theories could be possible from the Chinese. Their craftiness had already shocked the allies, and Moore had no idea where the next attack would occur.

Anxiously, Moore almost sent the balance of his fleet to meet Nguyen's head on in order to protect Japan. But you could almost hear Moore's own hand clapping against his head while he was saying, "I am so stupid." Moore logically referred to a map, and now fully understood exactly what Nguyen was trying to do, or at least he thought he did. He instantly noticed that Nguyen was trying to take an island and then leave it behind. If Nguyen planned to attack the United States this is obviously the only strategy he would employ. Moore now had the perfect idea, for he knew the next Chinese attack was aimed somewhere around Marcos Island because that was the next logical stepping-stone. Quickly he discerned a plan that would inform the Japanese of the Chinese plan, and let all American Pacific forces know that Chinese soldiers would be hitting Wake and Midway sometime soon after. Moore stuck his country's fate on the strength of these beliefs.

Meanwhile the Chinese had already completed the longest trip through their whole Pacific war. Every other invasion would be less than 1,000 miles, in many cases much less, and this propagated confidence from the top on down throughout the ranks of Chinese military. This gave Nguyen a tremendous amount of pleasure since Chinese aircraft had been refueled over the Pacific, and helped support naval forces allowing him to plan on the large scale invasion he intended. Nguyen also had set aside 300,000 of his best troops, and only invaded the first three islands with 20,000 men to keep all others fresh. As soon as Iwo, Bonin, and Volcano were taken he made preparations to bring the remaining 280,000 closer to the American coastline.

A short 4 days after the subjugation of the initial target—just 4 days! On November 26—Nguyen adroitly parried another 10,000 men, and all his ships 500 miles east towards Marcos Island. The quickness of orders, and the splendor to which they were carried out was an exceptionally remarkable sight. It was all thanks to Nguyen who had preached speed and detail from the beginning of the war. The "battle" for Marcos was one of the weirdest events of the war. Chinese soldiers fired not a single shot because there were no defenders on the island. When the Chinese came ashore all they found were remnants of a hurriedly rushed together military installation. A military installation where everything was destroyed while not a soul was left on the island. Chinese engineers were able to build an airfield in 2 days, and could start bombing the continental United States. Instead of being bothered by this no show victory, Nguyen was ecstatic. He did not have to waste supplies; he did not lose a single ship, and suffered no casualties. He should have been more concerned.

Little did Nguyen know that the Japanese—instructed by Moore—had completely abandoned the island to its fate. Moore wanted to see nothing of another pathetic defense the Chinese would rollover in hours. So Moore asked Japan to save men and equipment and not bother fighting in a hopeless battle. Or as Moore said, "The bloody battle that will accomplish damn."

Nguyen, on the other hand was not bothered, he simply figured that the Japanese had taken their forces back to Japan to help defend their island from what they thought could be his invasion force. Under this false pretense Nguyen continued his assault in the Pacific. Whether or not this invisible defense benefited the allies was a point of debate. The lost time compensated into a Chinese gain because it gave Nguyen two-extra weeks of time to prepare for the most critical point of his assault. Moore prevented Japan from losing more soldiers, and the Japanese had no desire to risk pointless losses from superior Chinese forces for no reason.

After waiting a few days Nguyen launched an attack on Wake Island where he knew resistance would be encountered. There was some irony in the fact that Wake was attacked on December 7th, and the last time attacks happened on that day it was 1941. China was an ally of the U.S. as World War II truly began. For the first time in the war a surprising technological event occurred as the Chinese were attacking. The Joint Strike Fighter Series II made its appearance under American pilots since the war began, and the training of the U.S. Air Force paid off noticeably.

There were only 10 fighters stationed on Wake, but those ten fighters accounted for 24 Chinese JH-27F losses. Furthermore, JSFII's sunk 2 Chinese destroyers. Unfortunately, for the small American force defending the island (600 soldiers) the Chinese had committed 4,000 men to subdue Wake. It was the same old story once the Chinese established a foothold, their superior numbers eventually led them to victory. They were well supplied with mortars and outfought American soldiers by simply swarming them. The fighting was terrifically close and often turned ugly. The Chinese were surprised that the American Navy was no where to be found during the slaughtering of U.S. service men. They won the prize of Wake Island in 6 days, while some 200 American troops evacuated to Hawaii. Around 300 were taken prisoner while the rest remain in memoriam.

Without a doubt the most crushing blow to the Chinese was the fact the JSFII or F-37's had outdone the JH-27F in combat. In preliminary testing the Chinese believed they possessed the key ingredient to defeating the United States Air Force. When their testing proper was carried out it looked very much like the JH-27F would be an improvement over the anticipated F-37. But once they fought rigorously trained pilots—like the Americans—the F-37 supplied a damaging blow to the Chinese morale. It was not the type of feeling they needed or wanted heading into their most dire battles at Midway and Hawaii.

After the Chinese had complete control of Wake, they began arrangements for the Midway operation. Nguyen, for the first time favored a brief two-week pause because it was imperative that he replaced his losses in the air. He also needed to bring more foodstuffs forward so the soldiers could rest and recover. The two-weeks would also give his troops another chance to familiarize themselves with the attack schedule and battle plan. Nguyen had a major job to undertake doing all of this, but where a lesser man would have failed, Nguyen achieved incredible results taking on as many roles as he could find. For this, his men loved him.

It was just past Christmastide when the Chinese formed for the last major attack of the year. This drive was aimed at the legendary Midway Island, and it was one possession the Americans had never lost before in warfare. Nguyen hoped to lull the defenders into a false sense of security, but the U.S. troops knew the attack was coming and were ready.

The Chinese launched 4,000 cruise missiles between December 24-27 in an attempt to knock out the U.S. Air Force, and weaken the island's defenses. It worked incredibly well! When Chinese ships and troop transports crept onto the beaches of Midway on December 28 they found only 13 fighters that opposed their entire navy. The Americans had not expected a full-scale missile strike, and were completely taken by surprise. There were only two Patriot 2 interceptor sites operational on the island. Chinese Special Forces had sabotaged the rest. It was impossible to stop the sheer amount of missiles from the Chinese Navy. A little over 3,000 crack Chinese troops poured over the island, and defeated an American force one-tenth their size. By the evening the Chinese rose the Communist flag over the communications station. The beautiful white sands of Midway were recklessly tossed everywhere in a careless array of destruction. There were only two identifiable substances on the island surface—metal fragments and blood.

The entire world was now thrust into shock and doubt. Doubt as to whether or not the United States could win the war, and shocked by what had happened. It seemed at every corner the Chinese had out thought, out fought, and out lasted the Americans. There was little comfort in the fact that the Americans still had a sizable army, navy, and air force. Other nations were more concerned the Americans would just dissolve or worse retire in a world ruled by oppression. From Russia to England to occupied Israel everyone human being was apprehensive—and nervous. Russian President Darius Salaval even radioed President Powwer encouraging him to "stay in the fight."

Every human being was worried that is except a handful. Nathan Moore was in danger of losing his career, but that was not on his mind. He was not concerned in the least about job security; he wanted a chance to face Nguyen in his home waters with all his forces at his disposal. He slept soundly, and was dreaming that his chance would arrive, he believed in himself and so did his men. When Moore first heard the news of his loss at Midway with water in his eyes he turned his back to stare out his window, waiting, hoping, and knowing he now deserved a chance to fight the battle that could change the course of this war.

CHAPTER 6
THE POLITICS OF WAR

The politics of World War III were as severe as a torture rack, and as electrifying as a pinball game. Government control in every nation was extended to unprecedented lengths in the history of organized society. Government intervention was commonplace from Beijing to Washington, D.C., and for a time all the home fronts resembled dictatorships under the constraints of the war. The nations who figured out how to win the war at home saw that success carried abroad. In the beginning it was China, but that turned along with the war. It was no coincidence that at the outset of the war the AU and China got the most help from its citizens and won, while the allies bumbled everywhere and fought against public opinion in doing so. The Chinese were thinkers, strategists, and realists who were very well prepared for whatever the political world would throw at them. Zui was a master politician and showed no fear when dealing with any world leaders when it came to trade, weapons, or Chinese aggression before and during the war. Zui made the allied nations tremble in large part due to the great Chinese dragon he controlled. By 2015 China controlled more money than any nation, more weapons than any nation, and a tremendous amount economical clout. They used it. And manipulated others through fear to get items like an aircraft carrier and submarines.

Every nation that took part in the war was organized on a political level making it extremely easy to topple these nations from a political point of view. Either by taking a country over or waiting for new leadership to emerge presented a double threat in determining a nation's fate. As Zui said, "The difficult part is conquering a nation with no leadership. What can you aim to dislodge or instill? It is much easier to simply conquer a nation with a firm political structure and introduce a new one. For in this you can easily identify who it is you are fighting."

The nations who Zui referred to were the United States, Russia, and all of Western Europe whose political structure was stagnant, stable, and in some cases (especially France and Spain) incapable of improvement. These nations were ripe and a hungry China wanted to set their appetite on gobbling them up after the United States was vanquished. Nevertheless, they were all too happy to cooperate with China before the war, and in the end were taken advantage of much worse than the Chinese labor class they thought they could exploit. But this was the same situation in the United States as well. Businessmen counted money hourly pouring in from China. The U.S. government sold military and civilian goods to China in large quantities. China purchased U.S. scrap steel and old warships at alarming rates and returned them to their former owners in the form of missiles, bombs, and bullets a few years later. But why should anyone worry now? Economic growth was occurring rapidly, and greed was a sacred attribute to many businessmen. There were enough distractions to occupy the "little guy" who would soon come to rescue the businessman who created the mess.

The Chinese were the economic dark horses of the world in the 21st Century. They controlled the largest market and the largest population and were not afraid to use that as leverage in a dispute to get what they wanted. They saw through foreign investment and saw many shades of green in between. China could demand foreign war machines or systems, and the political and economic leaders of other nations did the fighting to see it was delivered. This form of lobbying created the gigantic Chinese army that diced the allies in the beginning of the war.

The United States economy continued to grow throughout these years, but continued running high foreign debts. Economic hardship caused by the spending of previous administrations loomed on the horizon for the world's richest nation, and the American way of life appeared to be heading for disaster. But in 2012 a significant event reversed these eerie fortunes for good. Thomas Powwer won the election of 2012 and arrived in the White House in January 2013. Powwer was a Populous Republican who served no one else but the interests of the United States, "Whatever the best course for her is mine."

It was as if the common, intelligent, unafraid American had been placed in the White House. It took little time for Powwer's constituency to hate him unabashedly, but the other 300 million Americans loved him. When Powwer arrived in office he undertook the largest budget cuts in history, especially the Pork Projects he so despised. He saved everything worth funding, but his confrontations with congress were epic and unending. Powwer was not afraid of criticism, and one of his first acts was to push a bill that dramatically cut the salaries and benefits of congress. "Compensation in the government is too great to be justified. Hopefully by cutting it we will get people who really want to be here." The bill passed with only 18 total objections and the reason was very simple. Not a single house member who voted against it served another term in government ever.

Powwer was resoundingly winning victories everywhere the American could see. Grants to Hollywood activities were cancelled; overseas AIDS grants (amongst many other grants) were postponed indefinitely until countries receiving that money could be audited. Powwer also left his stamp on American political history by introducing the fair tax—in the form of a National Sales Tax. Payroll taxes were a thing of the past, and the IRS no longer existed. In one year America began yet another dramatic economic improvement, and to the common American things were never better. Powwer could have become emperor after one year in office.

Powwer did not stop there. He continued his fight to keep jobs in America by punishing companies who sought employment outside the U.S. Those companies who violated this doctrine were forced to sell their products at drastically reduced profit margins. Rather than lose the American market companies acquiesced, and

Powwer's new economic policies encouraged more insourcing from abroad. Powwer was not a slave to plutocracy in the least. He pushed for new technologies like the hydrogen fuel cell, which would greatly benefit the American military in the future. Powwer had a brand new restructured government policy on the first anniversary of his arrival in office. He cut his own salary by 25% in his first week.

Powwer had never lost touch with the common man despite reaching the nations highest office. He was born in 1965 into a small family with modest northern roots. His family scrimped and saved to carve a middle class lifestyle but Thomas always wanted more. Powwer spent 3 years in the U.S. army and after discharge graduated from Harvard with multiple degrees in law and business. Already a man after graduation he started working on political campaigns and became a formidable speechwriter. He won enough connections to run for governor of his home state—Pennsylvania. He was unanimously elected and went to work on keeping his campaign promises immediately. Huge numbers of jobs were created while taxes were reduced across the board when Pennsylvania experimented with the National Sales Tax. Powwer raised wages, lowered crime, and mastered the strategy he would use years later in the White House. It can honestly be said that the majority of people benefited from Powwer steering the ship. He was an honest man's politician who enjoyed alcohol, the occasional cigarette, and spending time with his family (wife & daughter). At the outbreak of the war there was never a doubt about how Powwer would react. Powwer had been tough on China and did not fear them in any way. In fact, part of Zui's rationale for starting the war dealt with his fears that Powwer would lead America back to greatness and impossible to defeat in less than 8 years. America was waning before Powwer. Of this Zui was correct, but the presidency of Powwer brought new strength to the American nation.

When Powwer was reelected in 2016 he immediately poured money into the military to match China's colossal buildup. As a result the U.S. went ahead for good in the arms race and developed weapons like the scramjet fighters, missile defense, and Rav attack helicopters that effectively won the war. Powwer introduced strict security regulations for defense employees who dealt with any technological developments keeping everything "in house." He even took security to a point that kept government out of technological developments altogether. The U.S. weapons and technology development flourished under this system against those of other competing nations. Due to the unprecedented monitoring of defense department workers' personal lives; when many U.S. weapons were introduced in the war they were completely unsuspected.

But Powwer also accomplished another great victory at the beginning of his second term. The U.S. Congress passed the Border Control Act (BCA) designed to combat the alarming number of illegal aliens passing into the U.S. The American public overwhelmingly supported Powwer and legal immigration was the only ticket into the United States. Powwer reduced illegal immigration and positive benefits soon appeared to everyone: the jails were less crowded, schools improved, tax burdens were reduced, and terrorist now had no easy avenue into the country. This also prevented the Chinese from sending their own fifth column to wreak havoc in the U.S. as they had done in Russia. The United States was on the way back!

However, Powwer's greatest achievement—and that is a mouthful—was undoubtedly the formation of the Missile Defense System (MDS) that kept North America secure from all forms of ballistic missiles. When Powwer came to office the U.S. was capable of shooting down 50 ballistic missiles, which was geared to stop rogue nations from launching suicide attacks through nuclear weapons. Powwer wanted security from all out nuclear attacks so he pushed it further even after most of congress was tired of paying for the program. "I do not wish to harbor the American people from one disaster. I wish to save the American people from all possible disasters. Anything less than that does not fulfill my sacred duty I volunteered for. I cannot feel good—and neither can the U.S. citizen—until I have placed the American citizens in immunity from the skies. To grow up in American the people deserve the opportunity to live without fear, and as we know this feeling has eroded recently. Missile defense is our greatest achievement to return back to this feeling."

On May 17, 2017 Powwer addressed congress bluntly: "Our way of life has been threatened to an unprecedented degree. The attack on India, Israel, Taiwan, Japan, and South Korea was a collective attack on the free world. If anyone here thinks that we can coexist in this world with the People's Republic of China or the Arab Union they are sadly mistaken. We can now fight to preserve our union—our sacred union—or we can begin subjecting ourselves to servitude immediately since that would and will be our ultimate consequence traveling this road. But the latter has never been an American quality, and that will never suit an American life! Everyone in America must stand up and say, 'Here I am, I'm your man, get to work on me!' WE WILL FIGHT KNOWING THERE IS A SPECIAL PLACE IN HELL RESERVED FOR OUR ENEMIES, AND THERE IS A SPECIAL PLACE IN HEAVEN RESERVED FOR US!"

For the first time in a long time America was inspired to do something led by the sheer fanaticism of their leader. But Powwer also pulled some devious strings as well. The laws of sedition and treason were reinstated allowing very little leeway to American journalists and newspapers. The right to print any negative opinion meant winding up in jail. Powwer constantly strove to tell journalists, "All we want are the facts. Please." Many members of the news media were jailed at the beginning of war, but Powwer refused to let any negative feelings creep its way into the American psyche. Anyone who spoke out against war directly was not only stopped, but could be put on trial for treason and face the death penalty. Powwer had no limit to his harshness, but he needed to keep American together in the difficult early months. The common citizen did not mind anyway because these laws did not affect them. The truth was Powwer's austere methods worked. The radical left and right wing were silenced for the entire war.

Also any company found doing business with the enemy—and there were a few—were shut down immediately and all their assets seized by the U.S. government. Powwer saw to it that the people responsible for hiding these transactions spent the rest of their life in jail or worse. There was only one more faction Powwer wanted to control.

Powwer foresaw that protests would be common to stop the war especially when the reinstitution of the draft (which was not one of Powwer's most popular doings) became necesarry. Any public protesters were rounded up, and placed in special jail camps, and if they were of foreign origin they were deported. Protesters quickly disappeared from the U.S. Powwer also extended them a special invitation: "Any protester who would like to go to China or the Arab Union to voice your feelings will receive free transportation to those nations. All you need to do is sign up for this expedition, and there will be no questions asked by your government." No one accepted his proposal and protests were broken for the duration of the war. This represented another reason people loved Powwer. He had a knack for doing things that no one should ever do in a position no one should ever do them. The realm of government had extended far beyond anything in history, but the postponement of these American rights was a necessity. The war could not have been won without discipline, and Powwer realized this automatically.

The United States also orchestrated many foreign events to frustrate Chinese interests. Powwer had witnessed some South American nations getting ever closer with China. The Chinese had built airports and given weapons to Venezuela. Venezuela being the South America's major oil producer might or might not have been a reason, but the fact that China and Venezuela were connected on many levels brought fear to Powwer. Powwer interdicted by sponsoring the overthrow of Venezuela's government in July 2017 allowing native Venezuelans to reverse its countries economic fortunes. Venezuela also became a major allied oil producer and was stopped from harboring Chinese forces and supplies. This event removed China from South America completely. Chinese influence was ended everywhere Powwer could find the resources, and he constantly looked for ways to evolve this ideology and frustrate the Chinese even further.

Powwer tirelessly worked with his allies, especially Russia, and never doubted he would win the war from the outset. Powwer was renowned as this century's Winston Churchill; a most valid comparison considering the circumstances. Powwer was the man who saved the allies during the early days of the war and promised the conquered nations the U.S. would strike the aggressors. He also sat through difficult times as well. He presided over the worst U.S. defeats in history, and looked like a responsible party in the so-called duped U.S. government. But Powwer implemented the allied strategy at the first conference in London and built the allied coalition. Eventually Powwer convinced Australia, Eastern Europe, and virtually all of Western Europe to join the allied cause or face extinction. Powwer's leadership through the war saved the United States, and he won a third term on the basis of a national emergency. He completed his third term in January 2025 after the wars end and stepped gracefully aside. In his last act as president he revoked all the national freedom and freedom of the press constitutional laws he had suspended during the war.

Politically the Chinese were the most united nation at the beginning of the war. Whether it was communist control or national will China already had the discipline Powwer wanted to instill in the American public. Zui had built nationalism throughout China and had avoided criticism from the world in doing so. A feeling of superiority emerged from China much like the Arab Union. The pride China felt was not in the form of development, however, China was already developed. China had accomplished satellite launchings, the world's most advanced airports, the highest number of knowledge workers, big business, and of course manufacturing. But because of their enormity they needed enormous amounts of resources to continue growing. They flexed their muscles and the world responded by making them the world's largest economy supplanting the United States. Zui was instrumental in the Chinese rise to power, but his own emotions often got the better of him. Zui despised America for many reasons. He saw no evidence of their strength. He saw no will in the average American, and went so far to describe them publicly as, "A pushover, and easy one at that." Zui also saw that everywhere freedom was desired—even in the Arab Union—the United States was the blueprint successful political leaders followed. Zui did not wish to defeat the U.S. he wanted to erase them from memory.

Zui had an image of China as the economic and political authority in the world, and from this idea he was unmoving. Nothing mattered to Zui except his vision and carrying out the steps it would take to accomplish it. Upon becoming the President of China in 2012 Zui had set out to overtake America. Zui campaigned wildly around the world reminding everyone that a new day was dawning where China would become the world authority. Zui had poured support anywhere he could to frustrate America including South America (until the U.S. helped overthrow the regime), the Arab Union, and numerous Pacific Island nations. Zui was merely continuing China's devious assistance that had started long before Zui came to office. For example, in the early days of Operation Iraqi Freedom Chinese engineers were killed in the bombing operations in Iraq. But these were all fringe matters in light of China's unmatched military buildup in history. Nevertheless, the secretive eggs of China's march to war were strewn everywhere from Iraq to Venezuela, and they should have been a clue.

These actions were known by the United States who planned on Chinese aggression thus preparing for confrontation years in advance. The Defense Department funded projects that would provide strategic advantages against the weaknesses of the Chinese military. However, China still chose to tempt fate and invade Taiwan squarely pushing the U.S. to war. When Israel and India were attacked U.S. interests were further threatened and total war had erupted between the two world powers. The dominos fell quite easily after that around the world. Following on the heels of U.S. belligerency the United Kingdom, Canada, Italy, and Japan immediately declared war. By May 17, 2018 Russia, Eastern Europe, and Western Europe along with Brazil had all declared war on China and the Arab Union. War brought with it many difficulties as well because the war reverberated throughout each nation fighting. The richest nations were forced to live like paupers as materials were increasingly difficult to acquire. Even U.S. citizens were forced to live without cars, clothes, shoes, food, and gas. But as one citizen voiced, "We still have houses and we're not in chains."

For the first time in modern warfare America had to live with the threat of invasion providing a great test to the American character. Judging the American character on the basis of their former leaders was the critical Chinese mistake. Thinking the America citizen was just as weak as these men and women was a fatal flaw because America had not lost the will to fight. Hundreds of thousands enlisted, while the draft was also brought back to fill out the various service branches. However, this was not akin to the United States alone. Every country that fought utilized some type of conscription to invigorate their armed services. Each nation was totally committed to winning the war, and showed the will to thrust soldiers into uniforms in few cases against their will. Since there was a shortage of manpower; technology and production became the two most sought after and protected advantages. The most protected political advantage was stability and to see that it was maintained. Over the course of the war not one single nation changed its major political leaders. Only one political change occurred before the end of the war.

There are many political questions that still haunt historians today concerning World War III. Some are shocking and some are overwhelmingly obvious. World War III was not caused by government as so many thought. Communism—or the spread of it—had no bearing as much as one word that can describe all the reasons—greed. Greed had many meanings from land to money to power. China and the AU wanted all of them, and the allied nations also wanted to keep what they had established in these areas. In terms of the world the fight was over goods and territory. As the dawn of the 21st Century approached it became apparent communism could not survive. China had become less and less of a communist nation because in their quest for growth the communist system could only hinder them. Economically in a competitive world communism was as close to a death mark as one nation could come. Most of Europe was paying the price for the socialized periods they elected to have recently, and as a result, their government leaders inherited an economic mess. These circumstances allowed China to become the economic powerhouse next to and above the United States. But China's plans went deeper. Zui felt that the entire world could be reduced to the workers, while the Chinese would step into the role of the international bourgeois. Communism then would cease to exist in China, but exist everywhere else.

Zhen Zui was a political character who had worked his way through the Chinese cabinet, and was the most logical choice to become the leader of the Chinese people. He exercised influence unmatched in Chinese politics and at first his arrival was a blessing to the Chinese people. However, Zui denied any legislation that called for Chinese social reform to keep discipline at a premium. He denied any liberal reform paying no attention to the cries of his struggling population not only because he was cruel, but because he had no desire for societal spending. All final authority in the Chinese government came from Zui and his cabinet. Zui did not allow Chinese courts to dictate anything, in fact, the Chinese courts worked together with the government to guard their mutual interests.

It can be said that communism pertaining to the 20th Century was formally dead, but a new kind of communism had taken shape— a strikingly familiar one—the oligarchy. The centralization of power within a few hands allowed World War III to begin and spiral out of control. The ability of elected leaders to ignore the clamoring of their people to pursue their own greed was 21st Century communism. Worldwide freedom had taken hold and in fifteen years the spread had been remarkable. In record numbers citizens turned out all over the globe to vote, but whether or not their vote meant anything was a vastly different story. The nations who had tried to resist freedom were dwindling in numbers so men like Zui had to rig elections to keep themselves in power. Zui had been a welcome addition to the

Chinese leadership when he arrived, but his intentions, which were welcomed by Chinese citizens, destroyed his country. World War III was the last nemesis that freedom and common sense had to face before it conquered all.

Being free and knowing what to do with freedom were two separate ideas that have always concerned intellectuals. Prior to World War III the focus was on achieving freedom, while after World War III the focus had shifted on knowing what to do with freedom and how to use it. It became the primary governmental mission of the allied victors to teach the destroyed citizens nations' how to use freedom, what to do with it, and how to keep it. This was the policy set in the second London Conference from July 3, 2021 to July 8th. But one caveat was added by Bollingworth: "The American way of life, the English way of life, the Russian way of life, and the French way of life. Insert any nation, and that is not the standard by which every nation aspires. There are many nations we remain peaceful with who believe in convictions dramatically different from ours. We must realize this, and build nations in the image they want with our assistance, not in our image with their tacit assistance."

Unknowingly President Powwer may have said it best in his 2016 State of the Union Address. "Freedom is a continuing battle that knows no specific battlefield. It must be fought in communities, courts, governments, and throughout the world. The freest nations must fight evermore to bring these opportunities to the less fortunate nations. It really is a never-ending battle that can only be measured in progress not measured by win or by loss. When every American and then every citizen who inhabits the world can rise together and open their door not to a fulfilled life, but to the ability to have one, we will know that our work is complete. It is my firm hope that one of our own state's mottos becomes the motto of every free citizen in the world, and that is: Our liberties we prize and our rights we will maintain."

The political shift that occurred from the beginning to the end of the war was the greatest in history. After nuclear explosions and the deaths of millions the political future of nearly every nation was placed squarely in the hands of citizens. There were still corrupt politicians, barbaric nations, and government problems, but a massive step had been taken to cure the world of the illness known as bad politicians.

CHAPTER 7
THE NEW ART OF WAR

The demons of mankind had finally caught up to the demons of technology. World War III brought with it the worst terrors man ever wished to bring upon himself. The weapons were paramount in the history of warfare and infinitely more deadly than any predecessor. War had drastically changed in the 21st Century. Large-scale troop movements were easily completed, but were not necessary to ensure victory. The way troops were handled was much more important than the sheer number. The later battles in Iraq showed this theory true as Thomas Edward was always outmanned, but because of superior weapons, and superior deployment the allies still pulverized the Arab Union Army. Unmanned Aerial Vehicles (UAV's) were common for reconnaissance and kamikaze jobs, but a human presence was still needed to react to unforeseen events. Unmanned Ground Vehicles (UGV's) were highly unreliable at the outbreak of war, but were established wonder weapons at its completion. For example, numerous projects to build robotic vehicles for battlefield use failed miserably, but UGV's were used successfully in short range situations near the end of the war. Much attention was put into the overall design of the weapon as in the case with later allied tanks like the Fortitude that struck with impunity. Soldiers were also more protected than ever with graphite armor suits against weapons designed to kill them faster than ever. World War III saw the creation of new weapons on almost a daily basis between the combatants, and new ideas were as valuable as battlefield victories. The war was staged with the most dominating weapons, in less time, causing more death and destruction than any war in history.

On the whole three issues came to the forefront in the minds of the world's military experts: technology, speed, and efficiency.

The technology used in World War III progressed at the fastest rate in history directly attributable to the advancement of the war. For nearly every innovative weapon another one was established almost as quickly to combat the new threat. Technology was constantly focused on vastly surpassing the latest invention, and there was no stopping point on who could top whom. For instance, the United States developed a brilliant missile security system, which China attempted to thwart with stealth nuclear missiles. To defeat them the United States created satellites to monitor in flight nuclear material, not missiles, and destroy them when necessary. It did not end there. The Chinese started with excellent superiority in the air and on land with the JH-27F and the Type-3000 tank. However, the Chinese grossly over calculated their ability to design weapons often clinging to the same weaponry for too long. The United States and their allies' on the other hand consistently caught up to and surpassed the Chinese latest brainchildren. China's fatal error was thinking they could develop one set of weapons in 2015 that would last until the end of the war. China reasoned the war would last until 2020 at the most. However, human ingenuity is only improved and measured by deadlines. Like the college student who produces a great paper at the last minute so to did the allies produce great weapons in barely the nick of time.

As a result the Chinese built up massive numbers, but they ignored the future, and were left with weapons easily destroyed by new battlefield arrivals. By 2018 the Chinese had handicapped themselves with a lot of old weaponry. They operated the way of a business only interested in short term gains and by the end of 2020 their days of profit maximization were over.

In stark contrast to the Chinese military spending the United States had been fettering money away for decades funding social programs, and infinite amounts of money spent on defeating terrorism. The war in Iraq was a tremendous drag on capital that could have been spent elsewhere or poured into future defense weapons. As it turned out the United States once again opened their wallets to fight World War III, but only because President Powwer dramatically reduced waste to become wartime spendthrifts. It could be said that the weapons that won the war deprived a nation of parks, swimming pools, and social programs. Given the two survival was more satisfying.

The Chinese military between the years 2003-2015 did not grow by large numbers. Instead China peaked training across all units, bought technologies from Russia and Europe while manufacturing the most advanced weapons they ever had by themselves. China did not waste these precious years and capitalized on an opportunity to challenge the United States for world supremacy. Their collective muscles became strong and soon they were sticking out their chest all over the world. In a scant 12-year period China gathered all the means to become the world power, and it started with an attractive economic market that enticed foreign investment, defense spending, and uncaring treatment to its citizens. China spent less money on social programs than Hungary in 2014!

Weapons like the Type-3000 tank and JH-27F jet were on the drawing board for years, but took a long time to perfect in the Chinese manufacturing yards. However, China could afford to consume years perfecting these weapons while attempting to instill in them staying power throughout the war. The United States was bogged down in the battle against terrorism, and conversely China with their fierce policies toward immigrants (not that there were many) never suffered at the hands of any in house disturbances.

When the United States spent money on defense they spent it on three major weapons: defense systems, attack choppers, and aircraft. The United States poured money into missile defense systems, and the new series of Firescout and Raven attack choppers, and the devastating jets that appeared later in the war. There were millions of opponents who took jabs at the missile defense system including high-ranking military officials. As the 21st Century progressed the technologies for this system became easier to develop, and much of that was thanks to the testing in the late 90's also highly ridiculed.

President Powwer reminded the American people on his election in 2012 that wars as we knew them are not over. Powwer's foresight kick started a program that had nearly been cancelled, but now enlisted help from Japan and Israel that finally completed a working system. The only reason the continental United States never suffered a devastating missile attack was because of these policies. Powwer kept America from sustaining a disaster equal to the proportions Russia would face at the end of the war.

The missile defense shield kept World War III from becoming a nuclear holocaust. China established an embarrassing amount of war materials that left them akin to going to war—soon. And no one was prepared to fight them conventionally. The defense departments in many countries focused on "the war of the future," but there was one more war in the past the world had to fight—and few were prepared. Many nations were flatly dumbstruck. After the war a few painstaking researchers discovered that France, Germany, Israel, Canada, Spain, Mexico, and Italy had no top-secret plans on fighting a war with China. Looking back this was inexplicable. How China was able to elude the radar of many nations while building a colossal army is a question that has still not been addressed.

China's awareness of this situation allowed them to reap vicious triumphs in the opening year of the war. But with the combined of events of China's Pacific frolicking ended, Russia entering the war, and the AU finally checked in Europe the writing was on the wall for China and their friends. As the war continued China was less vigorous, and when the news turned bleak after Hawaii the Chinese nation began backing into a collective shell. Sacking Nguyen after his failure was a mistake, but the overall capabilities of the Chinese soldier began to wane after Hawaii proving much more costly to the war effort. The average Chinese soldier before the war had a rigorous field-training period of 18 months. However, as replacements were rushed into combat after the devastating losses in the Pacific that same time period dipped to 3 months, and declined even further later in the war. Conversely, the United States took the time to nearly double the amount of field-training the typical soldier would receive. A human resources approach was adapted to the United States military during the war by a professional human resource individual. Corporal Earl Chadwick arranged intense training programs during the war to combat the amazing personnel advantage the Chinese possessed. Chadwick reasoned China could trade lives at a rate of 6 to 1. U.S. Army training programs focused on this inferiority of numbers, specifically weapons and tactics dealing with situations where soldiers were outnumbered. Soldiers were routinely drilled as surrounded units, and these programs addressed defense, stealth, and movement. Chadwick's philosophies worked, especially in Russia where nearly all of the soldiers had been trained in this manner. Finally, Chadwick never hesitated to switch topics, as China began losing this advantage and the AU regressed, the training was once again switched back to classic combat skills of advancement and consolidation. These drills also lead to the perfection of a new type of soldier—the Land Warrior. The Land Warrior Infantry program reached its full-scale in 2011, but many kinks were still in need of resolution. Land Warrior's were first deployed to Russia with dramatic affect. They brought with them that could fire multiple rounds simultaneously (as well as different sized rounds), HUBD (Head Up Battlefield Displays), and interlocking communications all generated through their helmets. Their visuals were similar to the looks of video games set in a real life display. These new soldiers checked the Armies' of the East expansion, regained the initiative, and kept the enemy on the defensive until the end.

As for the Arab Union they benefited from receiving the best of all possible worlds. After Operation Iraqi Freedom many civilian Iraqis were trained by some of the best U.S. officers. These men became the veteran officer corps of what one-day became the Arab Union Army created by Annan. These men also brought with them the best weapons they bought from U.S. arms manufacturers. In addition AU units purchased modern communication devices from Europe, and gained the ability to fight a war based on speed and movement. The antiquated techniques, which Iraq had fought with, were now forgotten; they soon gravitated to becoming a modern army in every sense of the term much to the credit of the American officers who gave them the knowledge. Fast-forward 10 years and Chinese officers became the teachers of the potent Arab Union, and the two sides shared information and intelligence. By this time the infantile Arab Union possessed innumerable amounts of information about western armies their Chinese counterparts gobbled up gluttonously. Couple all this with the fact that Russia and China were constantly staging war games, and over a twenty-year period the four greatest military powers had all interacted in one disastrous way for the United States and Russia. The exchange of tactics was unparalleled in history and the amount of information available was virtually unlimited to the Chinese and AU.

Nevertheless, the course had been set for the four greatest military powers of the day to square off in the most devastating war of all time. There were very few tactical tricks any side could employ against the other meaning any advantage reaped had to be done through superior planning. The Chinese were the first to realize this factor and they exploited it professionally. By the time China began allying with the AU they could not ally themselves with a now threatened Russia. Russia immediately lurched back to stop involving themselves between China and the Middle East. China had already decided the Arab Union was the future of the world, or at least China's future, and Russia with their birth rate barely above zero was dying. Chinese planners were determined to undermine Russia by indirectly striking them, and keeping them at bay until they surrendered or China marched through them with ease. At one time Zui had desperately tried to hint at war with his Russian ambassadors, but each time he received a deaf ear. Had Russia fought alongside China and the AU there was precious little that could have been to stop them from conquering the Earth.

The even split between China and AU against what eventually became an alliance among Russia and United States had a major impact on weapons development. Along came a virtual mountain of weapons the world had never seen and all of them closely guarded secrets. The tanks that were imagined and finally built, the scramjets and F-37's and Bloodhound B's before them, the missile defense systems, and not to be forgotten the minute personnel weapons that so advantageously swung the war in the favor of the allies. But the best weapons were all developed by the U.S. and Russia where joint projects like The Fortitude tank crippled enemy morale to a shocking degree. When the U.S. and Russia pooled their knowledge and worked together to create weapons they were incredibly successful. Even Ben Wolfshiem who had created the first "termite satellite" to eavesdrop on enemy conferences lent a hand. The Russian Bloodhound B jet was thought impossible to build until 2035—in fact it was included with the five weapons Russia hoped to build by 2040 in a prewar top-secret memorandum released by the Russian Defense Department. U.S.A.F. Scramjets were heavily imperfect until 2019, but those weapons tortured opponents and destroyed irreplaceable enemy units. These technologies were too much for China to match at once especially when considering they were entirely on their own.

However, the most important difference—the major catalyst—was the average soldier whom no robot could replace, whose toughness nothing could match, and whose passion no machine could substitute. Men joined the ranks and died with unfamiliar consistency. It was every common persons way of doing what they felt was right, and in the process immortalizing themselves in the eyes of God. Those men had shaped the world, and the future belonged to them in every way except the tangible sense. Or as Thomas Powwer shortly stated referring to the feelings of every soldier, (repeating the words of Stephen Decatur), "Our country. Right or wrong."

These men were armed with other weapons of repute that truly integrated their forces through the most important facet of war—communication. Battlefield communications were done through the air, satellites, ground forces, and communication features installed in LW infantry (only U.S.). More information was available during World War III than any other conflict had previously provided. It was the first major war fought with wireless communications, the internet, and expensive satellites. Satellite technology progressed rapidly because both sides realized the critical importance they played in the war. Warfare in space over satellites became a top-secret activity that had a dramatic impact on the war itself. Satellites housed the Missile Defense Systems that secured the United States, while providing military communications, but also one additional benefit at least for the U.S.: At the outbreak of the 21st Century a new series of satellite was almost ready for launch. The American ESP satellite program had yielded the first series of satellites capable of pinpointing enemy movements around the world every second. In fact, the first pictures the Israelis saw of the Arab Union Army concentrating on their border came from these same satellites.

The ESP program was the brainchild from a war cabinet that needed reliable recon satellite for the next century. They also decided that longevity was a major factor as well if the investment was going to pay off down the road. So in addition the ESP's must be able to house missile defense technologies in the event of a war, and especially missile defense technologies that would stop the next generation of stealth missiles. All these specifications were matched to an amazing degree by an epic collection of scientists led by Jamison Browder. Browder was a pioneer in the introduction of lasers into warfare, and adapting them for use against nuclear missiles—even stealth nuclear missiles. Browder decided early on that the ESP's must use classified lightweight alloys that would make them invisible to the eyes of other nations. Browder went one step further, ESP satellites did not follow predictable orbits, and were kept far away from any other known satellites. If the ESP satellite detected anything coming into its own path—possibly a missile or enemy satellite coming to destroy it—a self-defense system was activated to remedy the problem and render the enemy useless. The ESP did not discriminate, it was given absolute priority over any other satellite, and a few worldwide companies reported losing satellites during this time for no visible reason. NASA was forbidden to speak about the ESP project and losses of some NASA satellites were attributed to mechanical failure. The ESP never destroyed one Chinese satellite during the war, but they were never discovered either. The Chinese took out numerous decoys, but overall never thought the ESP existed. The final part of the ESP proved to be one of the toughest questions science ever had to face.

Browder's chief concern was to develop a laser that was powerful and long-lasting enough to warrant its use as a missile defense tool in space. Browder added stable uranium materials to a hydrogen fluoride compound which produced a mass of volatile material. Browder's "nuclear laser" as they were called were the ticket to destroying ICBM's from long range. Now by just hitting an enemy missile Browder sealed the security of the U.S. homeland. He also formulated the start of a back-up plan by placing similar lasers on the highest points in the U.S. and Canada. These ideas supplemented by the Japanese advance in shooting down ICBM's with missiles erected a virtual steel wall around North America and Japan. Any nuclear missile shot was destroyed within three minutes—this was particularly important since after five minutes ICBM's naturally split into numerous numbers to strike their targets (many of them decoys to throw the targeted nation off). Browder's ideas had revolutionized lasers to an amazing benefit for the United States, but Browder doubted his legacy. Like all great inventors he was most disappointed to see his inventions used in the war because he had always hoped they would be announced to deter war. Nevertheless, Browder was the chief scientist of the United States at this time, and he alone had equaled the feats thousands of other men could not.

The spending on the satellite program was enormous—rumored at three-quarters of a trillion dollars!—but when the Chinese nuclear missiles came no one criticized Browder's inventions. The United States and Japan realized how important these weapons were to achieving peace. When the war started they were both online throughout both countries. Immediately after Chinese and Arab troops invaded India the United States began dispersing the ground mounted lasers to each ally. Only two nuclear detonations occurred on allied soil in World War III proving to the world that their salvation was saved by these systems.

The competing militaries of the world had never known so much about each other's movements. The real problem was to create innovative new ways to deceive and hide the dispersion of troops on the battlefield and flow of supplies that had to follow. The United States showed the aptitude to grasp this concept the best. The U.S. could both handle their troops through top-notch computer systems, and handle their equipment through the use of RFID (Radio Frequency Identification) chips. The same RFID chips that could cloak aircraft were used for their original purpose—tracking inventory. (There were obviously variations on the chips inserted to cloak aircraft these variations were still top secret while employed during the war). The RFID chips monitored where every piece of American equipment was located. Thus the U.S. lost virtually nothing in the way of foodstuffs, ammunition, or weapons. China also organized a massive logistics program whose only shortcoming was that in desperation they cast it aside. China utilized RFID as well, but had never developed the advanced chips that threw enemy radar through a loop. China's army was so enormous that they suffered from tremendous amounts of waste caused by the individual soldiers. Early in the war this was a problem because the Chinese soldiers moved so quickly they often discarded valuable war goods. However, as China became used to the idea of tracking everything they quickly learned how to put this to great use in the fields as well. Late in the war China moved men and material into the Middle East, and only a huge RFID system brilliantly coordinated could accommodate such a task as they did. China suffered from micromanagement as witnessed in the fact that their operations had to be planned long in advance. For example, to organize the opening campaign took over 2 years of planning. The allies won the war in less time after they took the offensive. China slowly began to lack the infrastructure necessary to conduct a war. As they tasted defeat they began to regress, and scramble to solve their problems through simplicity. However, the only solution that could have been forthcoming to save the Chinese army most certainly would have come from developing technology to limit waste. They had tied their own hands while looking for some type of super weapon to save themselves, and China's biggest mistake was they were never a military that developed rapid technological solutions quickly.

In time because of the shortened training period China began reverting back to the way they had fought past wars. When the AU surrendered China used guerilla style tactics and delaying operations, however, the masterpiece known as Land Warrior Infantry finally outmoded the long successful guerilla tactics along with the others. This was best witnessed when Odets led an army through India against a large Chinese occupation force. Odets's men—50% equipped with LW units—swept through the Chinese guerilla tactics suffering miniscule casualties. The Chinese had specifically put together a guerilla war strategy to defeat the English commander's force. Of China's 15,000 men over 10,000 surrendered in four days.

The United States had the most focused technological development before the war, and during the war devised even more creations. When one looks at the list of new equipment the US readied for war they must certainly agree it is imposing. The major weapons were: F-35's and F-44's, Firescout, Comanche, and Raven attack choppers, Fortitude and Powell tanks, MDS systems (satellite and ground based), chemical lasers, hypersonic sound, Poseidon Naval Missiles, Stealth Destroyers, various unmanned vehicles, and electromagnetic weapons that could cripple enemy communications. These weapons alone were too much for the AU and Chinese to match, especially when they began appearing in large numbers. America's weapons were the most efficient used in the war, and thanks to new special tracking procedures every missile, gun, tank shell, and vehicle was accounted for. It was this technology and efficiency the Chinese could not match as the war turned against their favor. There was also necessity when it came to this strategy for the United States. They could not afford to have any equipment go to waste. For the first time in a recent war the U.S. lagged behind another nation in manufacturing.

China's critical advantage over the United States dealt with manufacturing. China was the only country in the entire war that produced every weapon they used throughout the entire war. When the war started they had the largest army, and were producing more equipment yearly than the U.S. and Russia. This forced the U.S. and Russia into a frantic game of catch up, but it cannot be overstated that due to foresight the U.S. and Russians did not rush weapons into service. Instead they created weapons that were tactically unlimited for many years. The U.S. Defense Department expressed to President Powwer China's manufacturing prowess like this: "It would be like running a race, and when the gun is shot the best runner already has a one-year advantage." This was the major reason Zui felt he could achieve total victory in 18 months. As it turned out China needed an advantage like this in order to win major victories at the beginning. Their manufacturing strategy put them ahead and allowed them to dictate the beginning of the war with authority. However, it was stated earlier that China's army only used weapons made in China. But China never used a weapon built in a foreign land which became a major disability in an era of information sharing. The same could be said for the allies.

The allies relied on three nations to provide the weapons to fight: the United States, Japan, and Mexico. The U.S. themselves produced the technological weapons along with much help from Japan and Israel, while Mexico produced the assembly line vehicles like the Powell Tanks and Bradley Fighting Vehicles. For this reason Mexico and Japan were both protected immensely from invasion and cruise missile attacks. The United States retooled their industry effectively to produce the one-of-a-kind weapons only they could provide. The quality of these of weapons combined with the mass production numbers of basic weapons from Mexico and Canada drastically helped the allies achieve final victory. Despite China's manufacturing dominance before the war they could not produce enough to win. The most important victory on China's developmental idleness lay in one glaring fact. Their partners were not able to help them improve their technology. The U.S. worked with allies like Japan, England, Russia, Israel, Canada, Italy, and others when it came to weapons development. The bonus was the vast pool from which ideas for machines could be collected, and this factor led to Missile Defense, the Fortitude, and other advanced weapons and weapons systems.

There was a resource where the Chinese did hold the upper hand when they joined forces with the Arab Union. The quest for oil had become a priority for world powers in the 21st Century. The Arab Union produced enough oil to cover all consumption for their armies' and their friends. China had also been stockpiling oil from Venezuela for over a decade, and had built up a strong reserve in that department. The allies needed to find avenues to secure oil, and they did this in a number of creative ways. First, they cordoned off all major oil producing areas for military use: Alaska, Russia's Caucasus oil fields, Mexico, and Canada and even the Gulf of Mexico. These locations were critical in keeping the allied war machine intact, but there were numerous other ways the allies solved the oil problem. The hydrogen fuel cell was introduced making allied oil four times more efficient. The second and most ingenious idea was to install classified highly absorbable solar outlets in all vehicles from tanks, attack choppers, and aircraft. These solar shields saved the allies 15,000 gallons of oil per day! These solutions did not make fuel obsolete, but immensely changed allied strategy, and allowed war machines to move unhindered by gas constraints. Difficulties still existed on the home fronts as witnessed by a 2020 survey which found the average American drove only 600 miles that year! The American public found out as well that necessary sacrifices must be made during war footing.

However, the most startling technical occurrence of the war involved going backward, and this is the story of the Arab Union nuclear weapons program. While Annan was busy working toward sculpting the AU one issue could not elude him. Two nations he needed to secure his union possessed nuclear weapons, and were not interested in sharing them with the entire Middle East. Fierce U.N. delegations would not allow Annan to form his union and spread nuclear weapons to every country in the Middle East. Annan found grounds to compromise. He built up support for himself in Pakistan and Iran through the youth, and through them he became a national icon. In turn when the vote was offered for the two nations to join the Arab Union they accepted this invitation happily. When this was complete he agreed to dismantle all nuclear weapons in order to form the magnificent new Arab Union. He did this deviously though. Annan correctly figured he could restart the nuclear program at anytime. After all, he still had the scientists, all he would need to secure is the materials to build them. At the same time the seed of relationships with China for nuclear purposes was planted in Annan's mind years before the war. In the end Annan dismantled the nuclear program, formed the Arab Union, and received support from the aging leaders of Pakistan and Iran who were two necessities to build his "New Persia." The cover of this book represents the handshakes that took place between Annan and Iran's leader Mesa Shar Aqim. The act of creating the Arab Union drove the Middle East into each others hands. The way to power and nuclear weapons drove the Middle East to enjoin hands with China.

CHAPTER 8
THE TURNING POINT

The course of the war had not changed in any absolute way at the beginning of 2018. From every corner of the globe the news was nearly all bad. Turkey surrendered in late September, and Bakr had whipped the United States' highest-rated general in the same country. The Arab Union started their plunging drive into North Africa—surprisingly in the minds of a few—receiving support and no resistance from Egypt, Libya, Tunisia, and Algeria. This was the opening movement—the preface—to a European conflict, which by now everyone knew was coming. France and Germany were mobilizing forces to meet this new emerging threat trying desperately to race against AU divisions that had their sights set on their capitals. Russia had rebounded from the disastrous attacks throughout 2017, but was temporarily incapable of fighting such large well-organized forces like the Chinese and Arabs. The United States had suffered their greatest string of military defeats ever at Taiwan, South Korea, Wake, and Midway, while the Chinese had reached the gates of Hawaii with seemingly no trouble.

So why then was there optimism for a major victory? In most cases there was not, in fact, as stated before January 2018 was depressing for many civilians, as it was encouraging for the victors. But in spite of all this doom, for a small force hope and destiny was mounting on an island in the Pacific.

American Pacific Commander Nathan Moore gallantly continued to base his office in Hawaii. He favored being at the direct spot of the action, or at least as close as allowed by the president. Some pundits in the U.S. thought China would just bypass Hawaii heading straight for the shores of California. Quickly, Moore pointed out this was foolhardy for China. The United States Navy struck fear in the hearts of all, and it was the most complete fighting force he possessed. China could not afford to bypass the major U.S. naval base of Pearl Harbor. Moore would make sure Hawaii was the sight of a major battle with his navy. He had too. If Chinese forces had reached San Francisco there were precious little American forces left to stop them. In three months Zui could celebrate his stunning victory on the steps of the White House.

Adding to the dark times; for the first time in history the continental United States was attacked from the air. Chinese bombers leveled San Francisco on January 3rd, and over 500 were killed in this raid. The shocking Chinese bombing of San Francisco brought home a new element of the war never experienced by the American nation. In addition, Chinese bombers also destroyed the Panama Canal despite rabid defense by U.S. aircraft and air defense forces. U.S. movements were severely hampered, but the country was awakened. Powwer was furious and stepped up bombing China, but the scars of the Chinese raid reverberated throughout the United States. The sight of many Panamanians dying left an indelible vision in the minds of the U.S. citizens. The U.S. would now be ready to fight back.

By this time Nguyen had nothing more than a modest naval force at his disposal in the warm Pacific. The only Chinese Admiral, Ching Shan was dining with Nguyen on Midway Island in the General's personal headquarters. Nguyen and Shan were celebrating New Year's—five days belated—in a dark, boring room, enshrined in memory because it was so common.

"My congratulations to you General, you do the land of China great justice. How great you must feel about your accomplishments in this war." Shan was a man who had obviously been far removed from his prime, but in some ways he seemed immortal. The gray hair, which peaked from his cap, soon contributed to that myth. Hidden in this mortality was a man who was very well respected by the Chinese sailors. He had been a leader in the industrial movement throughout China, and he was a progressive who had urged Zui to continue the postindustrial movement even though some thought technology would threaten communism. Communism was eradicated by technology but Shan helped to launch a new carrier, submarines, and destroyer class ships. All of which were more valuable to fight a war than any ideology.

"Our job remains unfinished Admiral, we still have much to conquer, and I must recommence my offensive as quickly as our ships can sail." Nguyen was always careful about accepting compliments, and would not take credit for anything until the U.S. was vanquished.

"I imagine we should have all ships ready in a few days. I can promise 19 destroyers, 6 cruisers, 1 carrier, and around 100 frigates. "Although," Shan said with a pause, "our transport vehicles are especially disconcerting." Shan was not joking; the Chinese were still using a slightly spruced up DUKW—the landing craft the allies once used at Normandy. Their infantry platoons counted on the former and the Chinese manufactured PTS—Personnel Transport Ship. The only amphibious vehicle solely of Chinese design was the VTS—Vehicle Transport Ship. The VTS was the only landing craft capable of accommodating the massive Type-3000 tank.

"Your wrong admiral. You can promise me 15 destroyers of value, 6 good cruisers, an obsolete carrier, and frigates, which will suffer at least a 60%, sunk rate against the American Navy. If the Chinese Navy makes it within 300 miles of Los Angeles I will be shocked."

"I hold similar reservations as yours general, but under the orders of Zui I will obey with supreme faith. If we win we shake the American people into insanity. They could capitulate without us doing anything, and then the war becomes easily winnable." Very few Chinese commanders looked brightly upon the campaign, but their confidence had grown immensely during the opening of the Cluster Assaults. Furthermore, the U.S. looked unprepared at Midway giving the Chinese a tremendous confidence boost at Hawaii. "Zui knows what to do." Shan added.

"I worry about that sometimes." Nguyen said earnestly quiet.

"Say again, sir? I did not hear."

"No, it was nothing revolutionary." Nguyen said, he was laughing on the inside over how ironic his declaration truly was, if anything it was revolutionary. Nguyen took a long pause before ongoing with his oration. Shan was to be the first person to hear the plan for the Hawaiian invasion. It was protocol for Nguyen not to give Zui specifics because the news that traveled back to China could then become multi-governmental domain or read compromised. Besides even though Nguyen had drafted preliminary plans, he constantly had to revise them after each battle depending on what situation he was now confronted with. As a result, Zui only knew the first part of the Cluster Assaults that seized the Bonin, Volcano Islands, and Iwo Jima. Even though Zui had started the war—and controlled it—he steadfastly refused to interfere with his generals. He had seen Hitler, Stalin; interfere with their chains of command, and justifiably bring disaster to their soldiers. He had also seen Ridgeway, Marshall, and Bradley receive no direct stratagems from their political leaders and because of that prevail. Additionally, Zui felt a close affinity with his generals—he loved them. He loved his own agenda more, but as long as both agendas were the same—the increase of Chinese power (Zui's)—he stood by them. If they stood in conflict the general always lost.

Nguyen restarted his tête-à-tête, "I want you to be the first human with whom I discuss Hawaii in depth."

"That is a great honor, General."

"The Americans have at least 6 carriers, 16 cruisers, 26 destroyers, along with a massive number of smaller war craft. I remind you, those are just estimates, and these numbers could be wrong, but with the Panama Canal destroyed we will only be facing U.S. ships stationed on the west coast of the United States."

"It will be an imposing force, of that there is no opinion, just reality," Shan said solemnly.

"We have 800,000 men for use in this operation. But I imagine at a minimum we could seize and hold Hawaii with only

100,000. Now assuming we lose an astronomical and overestimated 150,000 men in the landing process, and 100 tanks—one-fifth of our total—we would then be left with a minimum 650,000 men and 400 tanks to invade the United States from a base on Hawaii. Knowing a minimum of 700,000 men must land on the American mainland in one day it is easy to see why the odds are stacked against us."   This basically meant that every soldier under Nguyen's command currently had to land on the U.S. mainland together. Nguyen currently had a little over a million men under his command. "Simply, I calculate it would take 4-5 months to bring all the equipment we need across the Pacific. Knowing how the Americans could bomb us, torpedo us, and hit us with missiles how much greater would that threat increase the difficulty we face?" Nguyen restarted, "Admiral Shan, our most logical scenario is to place every ship into the seizure of Hawaii. I plan to use our most premier forces, our best commanders, our best marines, and our most elite commando teams. We can provide them with adequate air cover, and we will have the opportunity to refuel our aircraft from the sky. Once we land on Oahu we can quickly commandeer airfields for our aircraft, ports and harbors to repair our ships, and build barracks to stockpile our soldiers. Holding a base at Hawaii will give us more than enough resources to begin a rapid bombing campaign on the west coast. If we get to the American coastline our air force will be as responsible as your navy."

Nguyen now asked a question full of moxy, "What I'm personally asking for Admiral Shan is your permission to use the entire flotilla you have arranged, organized, and brought here with my soldiers. But according to my plan you must understand this may mean the loss of every vessel under your command."

"General, I will gladly honor you with my life, or even more importantly my sailors, their ships, and everything else to carry out the orders of the great Zhen Zui and the Republic of China."

Nguyen immediately began talking again ignoring the last part of Shan's statement, "In six days—January 12—we will surge off Midway towards Hawaii in a perfect straight line. We will either achieve victory or defeat—but I warn: both will involve death on a heavy scale."

"Yeah get them there now, quite clearing everything with me, if it sounds good have enough common sense to carry it out, enough with the damn permission."

"More trouble Commander Moore?" A middle-aged punster chimed in.

"No Tommy, but all this time wasted. They call and ask me if it's okay to bring up five more artillery guns. What do they think I'm going to say? No we're being invaded tomorrow we don't need that. Plus the weather all over the islands has been horrible, I don't want much roaming around out there in the ocean. We need too many things done here now."

"If you don't mind me asking sir, what's the situation on the islands?"

"Hawaii, Maui, Lanai, Molokai, and Oahu all have as much as we can possibly give them. Unfortunately, General Edward has asked for 3 million men, and all the equipment this nation can spare to fight the AU if they invade Europe from Turkey so both us are in a jam. Now I'll tell you my biggest fear. If Nguyen can land on the islands there is a great chance he will conquer all of them. We do not have the manpower necessary to take on 300,000 experienced soldiers gathering momentum. They will swarm all over these islands, and probably to Los Angeles. Our standing army before the war is dwarfed by China's now, we need time to train soldiers and build weapons. But, if we can surprise them here, stop them with our navy, then we can send them packing back to China and make them wait for us. Nguyen must operate with his best troops, and send all his ships on a B-line at us. A victory here could paralyze their navy, and leave China in a catatonic state until *we* are ready to strike back. Not to mention his best soldiers would be eliminated for good."

"This is what I've decided. I will wait until Nguyen's forces are fifty miles from Hawaii, we can stop their air attacks with our aircraft, and we have enough Patriot IV stations online to make us immune to cruise missiles. Nguyen will have to outfight us to a spectacular extent to get a hold of this island, or get massacred to a spectacular extent. May God be with us."

January 12th, 2018 was a warm peaceful early morning in Hawaii. The tall drooping palm trees gave an everlasting peace that was about to be abrogated. It was one of the most beautiful days that anyone could remember, and Hawaii was nearly void of life. Civilians left for California, or shacked up underground. A terrific defense awaited the Chinese like a dagger waiting to swoop down upon a helpless person. The presence of the U.S.S. Arizona Memorial added an obsequious touch to the day, which would make it a rallying point 76 years later for an even more epic struggle. Perhaps it was intended to inspire future men, as much as to revere those who had given so immensely in 1941.

At 8 o'clock in the morning it began. Forty-four Chinese jet fighter-bombers had been spotted coming from the Northeast—had refueled—and now regrouped for the first wave of the attack. As soon as these planes appeared on radar two squadrons of Joint Strike Fighter II's (F-37's) immediately took to the air. Lieutenant Commander Joseph Knight was in overall command of Blackberry squadron. Knight's 11 planes succeeded in shooting down 14 JH-27B's, while only losing one themselves. The JH-27B's avoided missile fire and managed to hit a few forward communications stations doing little damage. The Battle of Hawaii had begun.

"What's the damage?" Moore shouted at one of his lieutenants. Moments ago he had seen the bombs explode.

"Just a scratch sir. I don't even think we suffered a casualty. It's likely this attack was just to test our defenses."

"No, Nguyen just sacrificed 14 of his best pilots and destroyed a few buildings. He wanted something special from this attack; he failed now it's our turn. Radio all fighters, I want to launch a strike as soon as possible aimed at Midway."

"General Nguyen we have the results of our first air attack. We have lost 14 aircraft, while inflicting losses of one enemy aircraft and hitting two radar stations."

"That's all?!" Nguyen was furious. How could his best pilots have been so careless? "They retrieved no information on locations of the American carriers, no information on missile defenses, and destroyed next to nothing. Regroup all of our aircraft immediately. Make contact with our subs, and launch a barrage of cruise missiles now. While our missiles are launching, fuel and arm every aircraft , then we shall launch all our carrier aircraft, and half of our ground aircraft from Midway. They must obliterate the American defenses all over Hawaii. Now our ships will have to protect our invasion force the entire way in, we have no other choice. The Air Force will have to be used to destroy American defenses and carriers and cover us from American fighters. Let the soldiers know they will not have aircraft cover during the landing."

Nguyen turned away then returned towards his subordinates quickly. "One more thing, immediately get aircraft over our heads because the Americans will appear on radar shortly. Gentleman all this is happening, and war is a very frenetic event, but carry out the given orders and adapt to meet this new challenge and we will prevail. We'll have to invade earlier than expected today."

"Yes, sir." Every person in the room responded emphatically. Nguyen was never afraid to take charge in any situation, even while he was infringing on Shan's command no one minded, they just trusted in Nguyen that much. And even though the Chinese had suffered their first loss with Nguyen in command no one seemed to notice.

At 10:18 a.m. on January 12, American F-22's located the massive Chinese armada 50 miles east of Midway. All the Chinese ships opened fire, combined with the aircraft umbrella above, but the F-22's struck with ferocity. First they engaged the JH-27F aircraft, and while avoiding surface to air missiles from below, headed straight for the troop transports. In 10 minutes the Chinese had lost 3 transports, 2,000 men, 1 destroyer, and six aircraft. The Americans had lost only 3 F-22's.

After witnessing the second minor American victory of the day, Nguyen reluctantly decided to continue onward—he still had a massive force—to Hawaii. Nguyen firmly believed it was China's turn to respond. JH-27F's from the carrier Great Wall and Midway, fifty in all, directly headed to strike the American shore defenses on Oahu—it was 11:15 a.m. Chinese forces were now about 150 miles from Honolulu, and Nguyen had to do a better job weakening the Hawaiian shore defenses or the invasion stood no chance. Before the jets arrived, Chinese ships—under the command of Admiral Shan—launched 200 more cruise missiles—fifteen of which got through. One missile actually landed a few hundred feet from Moore's Headquarters. But in actuality the Chinese were getting desperate.

When the fifty jets arrived they saw Oahu, Hawaii, and Lanai barely scratched. This time the JH-27F's accomplished a mission. They received little resistance because many American jets were busy rearming and striking the armada. Also the sheer number of cruise missiles temporarily crashed American radar—and Chinese pilots were able to hit radar stations, missile defenses, and artillery guns. The Chinese only lost 2 jets, but more importantly they had kicked the door open so an invasion force could now realistically be landed ashore. When the aircraft reported in, Nguyen still feeling bleak, felt much better about his chances of invasion after this attack. Philosophically, it was still amazing to Nguyen that the aircraft was such an amazing weapon where one strike was still capable of inflicting tremendous damage and affecting outcomes so extraordinarily.

All afternoon long, Chinese ships advanced slowly under a shield of air cover. All the while JH-27F's and JH-27B's continued to slog it out with F-35's, F-37's, and F-22 Raptors as the U.S. waited for the showdown. Neither side really gained a major advantage, but the Americans never sent the numbers that the Chinese were fighting with, and despite that being the case, stemmed them back. The Americans were winning the air war, but Nguyen forged ahead with still a largely undisturbed surface force.

Each mile closer Nguyen came to Hawaii gave Moore one more mile with which to attack him upon retreat. Moore was successfully drawing Nguyen in, and Shan who did not believe in caution vied to continue going forward despite having no idea what type of U.S. Naval Forces were out there. Moore was outsmarting Shan and Nguyen together because the Chinese commanders never obtained accurate U.S. Naval information. As a result they continued sleepwalking into a trap.

While the fighters were exchanging their murderous munitions another unprecedented battle was also taking place. Chinese cruisers and destroyers kept pouring out missile fire aimed at the Hawaiian Islands in an effort to weaken the defenses, and intercept anti-ship missiles. The U.S. made Olympus anti-ship missiles were the newest addition in naval vessel destruction. Olympus missiles were capable of becoming a torpedo mid-flight, and striking from above surface or under water. The only problem was the fact that the U.S. only had around fifteen of them, and at best they were barely tested. However, in the afternoon transactions the Olympus missile inflicted a loss of 500 men by sinking a transport, and another Chinese destroyer. Admiral Shan was shocked such weapons even existed, but seeing them only motivated his urgency to move forward. The U.S. had lost comparatively little, except for a few missile hits on Hawaii the bulk of U.S. forces were still untouched. But more importantly for Shan, where was the American Navy?

Chinese intelligence placed no less than six American carriers in Hawaiian waters. However, Nguyen had not encountered a single U.S. ship. In order to sympathize with Nguyen one must understand that he could not turn back. For what grounds would he explain there was sufficient evidence to retreat? At last, Nguyen decided to continue moving forward with the operation. The first soldiers were scheduled to land at 6 p.m.

"Give me some type of report! Now!" It was not until 4 o'clock p.m. that he knew exactly what was going on. For over 8 hours U.S. and Chinese forces had exchanged fire back and forth, but no invasion was imminent. Hawaii was taking hits, but was far from losing. The Americans on Hawaii still had a high—-undisturbed—amount of fight inside them. The army was ready, the air force fighting, and the navy laying in wait.

When Moore's cahier finally was brought up a subordinate announced to Moore: "We've suffered very little, 5 aircraft and countless missiles lost in the last hour, but we have sunk 2 destroyers and 2 medium troop transports"

"Approximately how far away are they?"

"We estimate about 22 miles, but they appear to be reforming placing the landing craft ahead of the warships, before heading in for an assault."

"O.K." Moore said coolly. "Wait until they are 15 miles out. Then have the Enterprise, Reagan, JFK, Washington, Stennis, and Truman send every last aircraft they've got. We'll catch all of Nguyen's pilots at the closing moments of a very lengthy day, and give them more than they can handle."

And just where were the American carriers? Moore had stationed them—in groups of two—completely behind the Hawaiian Islands under a perfected new form of defense—the radar jammer. Or in plainer terms a mountain of aluminum and chaff. As yet the Chinese had not developed any way of cracking these old tricks, as a result they never looked 40 miles past Hawaii for the danger, and traipsed into a trap clouded by thousands of pounds of chaff.

At 5:42 p.m. 358 American Naval aircraft attacked the Chinese flotilla in the most important air naval/aircraft battle of the war. They appeared so quickly on radar there was little that 20 JH-27F's could do. It was a spectacular moment to be an American! The aircraft plunged out of the sky like pure madmen; like freedom loving Americans. Nguyen was at the end of his aircraft strength, and did not have the numbers to compete with this enormous new threat. He sent the invasion force on a scramble after explosions lit up the scenery, or so one vice admiral described over the radio. Shan released the transports prematurely echoing the words of Bonnie Prince Charles, "Every man for himself."

In fifteen minutes 3 cruisers, 6 destroyers, the carrier and 15,000 men had been slaughtered. Nguyen sent his men to a cremation. He encouraged his forces to move quickly through the waters, but his ships were pummeled, running out of ammunition, and worst of all he could not help his soldiers sequestered so far away on Midway on the somewhat firm ground of Midway Island.

Despite all of this, Nguyen still had an opportunity to overcome the aircraft. It was still possible to land the rest of forces on the Islands, but it would have to happen immediately and miraculously. Nguyen wished he could be in the middle of all this action with his men instead of at Midway, but Zui had forbade it. Nguyen's hopes were dashed when across the radio came the last dagger.

A pincer of over 50 cruisers, destroyers, and submarines closed in on Shan's Grand Navy. Conversely, Chinese submarines had miscalculated, and were too far away from the battle to provide adequate help. The sizable American Naval force now would cast the final blow. The American Navy began eliminating disorganized Chinese ships one by one. Most Chinese ships were picked off before they had the chance to fire back. The western area of the Hawaiian Islands had become a flaming alley. Predominantly all of the ships ablaze belonged to China. The disparity of the victory can be found in the numbers. By 9 p.m. 5 Chinese destroyers began to limp back to Midway Island; they were all that was left of the invasion force. About 8,000 Chinese soldiers were able to land, but they were woefully short of support, and those that did not surrender were annihilated. Chinese casualties were incredibly high. They had lost virtually their entire navy: 1 carrier, 6 cruisers, 14 destroyers, 50 frigates, 67 aircraft, and most costly 95,000 men, or 95% of the total invasion force including 60,000 killed or missing not including at least another 20,000 sailors. The highest-ranking Chinese casualty was none other than Admiral Shan, who went down with the carrier "Great Wall."

It was a shattering loss, but with Shan had gone the entire Chinese Navy. The American forces put up a disinterested chase, but they had lost fewer than 20 aircraft, a slightly damaged cruiser, 1 destroyer, and sustained 82 casualties while winning their first major victory of the war and what became the turning point.

Nguyen started a rapid retreat to save what he could, but five days later with no significant naval force, and no ability to conduct further operations he limped back to China. Nguyen's ordeal did not come to an end at this point it only started again. Sorrowfully, the only way to describe the trip, Nguyen had chosen to sail back to China with his 700,000 men who did not participate in the Hawaiian invasion. Sorrowful because his forces were to be further decimated with the introduction of a brand new weapon of war.

In 1994 a joint project between Japanese manufacturers and the U.S. "skunk works" division had begun under the strictest secrecy. The outcome of this cooperation between the Japanese and U.S. governments was the new SD1 Poseidon 23 Titan E, or in simpler terms, the first stealth destroyer. Originally intended as a gift to the United States for help with missile defense systems the Japanese poured massive amounts of capital into constructing two of these highly disguisable ships. Instead, before they could be delivered secretly to the U.S. Navy war broke out, and Japan now used these two siblings of death on the returning Chinese forces. The two destroyers sunk 2 more Chinese destroyers, and when the force panicked, picked off 100,000 more Chinese soldiers (about 12 large transport ships.) The streamlined effectiveness of the SD1 raised the bar in naval technology.

Both of these terrible events coming right on the heels of each other dealt a one-two punch which severely crippled Chinese confidence in their leaders, morale, and equipment. Never did they imagine losing 250,000 men, especially after the first steps of the "Cluster Assaults" were so successful. But Zui and discipline would hold China together. The AU would land in Europe next month, but for the most part the one day Battle of Hawaii foreshadowed the probable outcome of the war for Zui. China was now impotent in the Pacific and unable to hit the U.S. with nuclear missiles. And now having no navy, meant the U.S. would not be defeated quickly or even at all. China fell all the way back to Taiwan, and when news leaked out about the loss an underground resistance began to gather steam. China was now totally restricted to landlocked battles. Zui's

Grand Fleet had forced a showdown with superior manpower and momentum, and was decisively beaten back. For the first time China assumed the defensive trying to hold what they had won 7 months earlier. This is why Hawaii has gone down in history as the turning point.

When the world heard the news of the first major allied victory during the war almost every nation except for the Middle East and Asia celebrated. In London, Berlin, Paris, Rome, Moscow people celebrated hand in hand shouting, "Long live President Powwer, the great general Nathan Moore, long live the great Americans!" The allies had put years of squabbles behind them, years of half threats, and were now unified all the more so by electric feelings of cooperation and victory. All the nations' leaders wired President Powwer congratulating him on his tenacity and the American victory.

Fittingly, at the highest end of the spectrum stood a resurrected Nathan Moore who had turned the tables, and now opened the door for a total victory. Although it would be many bad times and months away, Moore single-handedly hatched the plan that would eventually help subdue China. Moore, who at one point was a scapegoat, stubbornly pursued what his convictions were to force a showdown and found the skill and nerves to win. Another deserving candidate of respect was indeed Thomas Powwer. Many critics who lashed out when Powwer had not removed Moore after the Taiwan disaster now ran for cover. Powwer recognized Moore to be a man of rare talent, put him in a situation to succeed, and the rest as they say is history. Together they walked into destiny, exclaiming, "Ua mau he ea o ha aima I la pono," or "the life of the land is perpetuated in righteousness."

CHAPTER 9
A NEW EMPIRE

When Arab Union General Auda Bakr first heard the news that his allies had suffered a devastating setback on the shores of Hawaii, he felt two entirely separate emotions. Namely pro and con. Pro because his Chinese allies were now forced to guard their homeland and immediate areas meaning they could protect the underbelly of Asia—as well as protect the AU. Also China could no longer glide along the Ocean hoping to gobble up islands, but instead were now restricted to expeditions over land only. America was still short of men and equipment to confront China in Asia, but would obviously continue to conduct daily and nightly bombing raids. Bakr assumed China would now modulate all available forces and embark on a trip to the Kremlin. Russia was the only country surrounding the axis, and more importantly Russia was still weak. With China in Russia and protecting within the AU's vicinity this meant Bakr could wield a freehand in Europe attacking anywhere he wanted. Bakr could conduct a war free from the concentration of both Russia and the United States. The AU would not deal with any formidable military nations, and numerically could swallow up the European armies. Bakr had known Zui wanted to invade Russia ever since the beginning of the war, however it was now the only logical place for the Chinese Army to go now.

Bakr was an educated man who also knew physics—for every action there was an equal and opposite reaction. The worst tiding to appear from the U.S. victory—the con side—was the fact that the allies in a short time could now aggressively focus on the AU to a much greater scale. The fact that China—and all her dreams—were gone in the Pacific became a worrisome thought because soon the allies would possess vast numbers of superior weapons. This worried Bakr, but it would not negate him from achieving his dream of conquering Europe. When the Chinese loss should have been a warning, Bakr considered it an opportunity. When he should have rethought his strategy, he forged ahead unadulterated. Never second-guessing his dream, he relit the spectre of war in Europe for the first time in over three generations.

In late January 2018, after AU forces congregated themselves in North Africa, Bakr found himself in Algiers, as the honored guest of the entire nation. Algeria had opened themselves to Annanian influence, and had even thought about entering the war alongside the AU. The Algerians never entered the war officially, but did harbor almost the entire AU Army and Air Force for a time. By doing this Algeria never need proclaim they were neutral, quickly they became the nightly targets of the Allied Air Forces in Europe. It should be noted they did not discourage their citizens from joining AU divisions, and "lent" most of their army to help transport supplies. Constant bombardment rained down on clustered AU divisions, and as speedily as the bombs struck, Bakr ordered his entire air force to patrol the skies. The AU Air Force would do the same in southern France and southern Italy avenging their North African allies and fellow comrades on a regular basis.

But everyone knew that Bakr had not come to endure a hiatus in Algeria. By early February, Bakr had seen enough of the French, German, and occasional Italian bombings that were now an etched tautology in his mind. Unfortunately for the allies the repeated loss of experienced aircrews began to slow their momentum. Any war of attrition favored the Arab Union since they could afford to lose huge numbers of aircraft, soldiers, and equipment versus all of Europe. This resembled the reverse in military power that had taken place in a few short decades. The only Achilles Heal of the AU was food. The AU army marched on their stomach and only wavered when a shortage of foodstuffs struck them. Europe was a land rich in food, and Bakr planned to exploit their stockpiles during the invasion when he could.

The French suffered the worst in the air because they attempted to stop an invasion with their air force rather than attempt to stop the AU in naval or ground combat. The Arab Union now had fighters and pilots capable of defeating the French making it nonsensical for the French to think this way. Trying to force a quick outcome many young Frenchman climbed into their Mirage's, and Eurofighters to take part in the battle of the treacherous skies over the Mediterranean. Those same skies were constantly raked with anti-aircraft shells, surface-to-air missiles, and a large number of AU planes waiting for the enemy. Allied losses, French especially, began to pile up towards the end of February. Much the Battle of Britain this air war became known as the battle of Europe, and the success the AU had allowed them to invade Europe.

For an extended time period—January to April 2018—the skies of the Mediterranean were filled with jet aircraft of both sides looking to gain dominancy. AU soldiers traveling from the Middle East stuck close to the shores of North Africa all the while protected by a jet umbrella that would see the men and equipment safely to Algeria—the starting point for the invasion of Europe. Meanwhile, Egypt, Libya, Tunisia, Algeria, and everywhere AU soldiers roamed became the focal point of tactical allied bombing attacks. Some of the North African natives defected from neutrality to take up weapons in the ranks of Annan's Army. Even those residents who at first had been opposed to letting the AU soldiers cross their sands relished in feeding and taking care of the Muslim warriors. The bombing campaign in North Africa did not weaken an army or a nation, more importantly, it just gave private citizens the opportunity to become victims and provide care to Annan's army. After all, Annan had united the Middle East on the pretexts of Islam. It should come as no surprise that his North African colleagues in theology served him on this basis.

The array of soldiers that battled for ground supremacy did so under the tactical eye of the most advanced aircraft in history. The aircraft that took place in these actions were as numerous as the nations taking part in belligerency. By now the AU Air force was comprised of state of the art to long-in-the-tooth aircraft. Annan's pilots were equipped with Atlas Cheetahs, F-15's, Migs from 25's to 27's, and of course a large consignment of JH-27F's. The JH27F's shown themselves much more efficacious when fighting European aircraft and European pilots. Arab pilots versus Europeans proved a better proposition than Chinese versus American pilots did for the infamous jet. Arab pilots underwent rigorous training programs making them more than a match for the European equals. The Arab Union Air Force proved itself a strikingly successful tool of importance in the European invasion. It showed again in history that it is not the machine, but mainly the person operating the machine that determines outcomes.

Opposing the AU Air force was a collection of technological jets that stood in the way of AU from conquering Europe. Eurofighter 2015's patterned after the highly successful Eurofighters of the early 21st century were the best in terms of defeating the Arabs. Typhoons, Etendards, Mirage 2010's, Rafale P's, AMX's, F4FII's, Tornadoes, and JSF's were all used ranging in countries from England to Germany to France to Spain to Italy. Every night for 4 months AU fighters encountered allied fighters trying to destroy AU weapons and provisions while keeping civilian casualties to nil. The European pilots tried to fight a perfect war and inflicted little damage by doing so. A nation cannot fight a war to not do something. Had the Europeans inflicted civilian casualties they would have eliminated AU equipment and stopped the invasion, but because of their civilian parameters they failed miserably. This allowed the AU to say they were just looking out for the civilians of North Africa from the European powers, and used that as justification to invade. The idea was accepted virtually nowhere out of Africa, but accepted everywhere the allied enemies resided in Africa. This reflected another lesson of war the allies fumbled to understand at the beginning. When an enemy is your enemy it does not matter what is said or done by the opposition. They will forever remain your enemy. The allies had not yet caught on to this rule, but the AU had been exploiting it for nearly a year. Had they bombed civilian dwellings where AU men and equipment were World War III would have been kinder to Europe.

Annan even hoped to bait Europe (Spain, France, Germany, Italy) to invade Africa were he could count on the entire continent to rise up and support him. "It is always easier to be passive," he proclaimed. The best AU pilots went into the sky in the best jets and tore holes in French and Italian formations. The Arabs had their losses too. Over 500 jets in less than 4 months time, however the AU could quickly recover from these losses with sheer volume and assistance from underground Chinese production. Furthermore, most AU losses were inexperienced pilots in outdated machinery—both which their leaders considered expendable. The tables had turned manufacturing wise. The allies were stuck on bombing tactical sites, and could not begin a bombing campaign against the industrial underground cities of the Middle East. Annan took a page and had forgone the missile and bombing threat by producing everything underground where no missile not of U.S. creation could reach his precious manufacturing outlets.

While the allies took a different opinion about their fliers the AU Air Force leaders maintained a very cavalier attitude towards theirs. AU pilots were looked at as machines that flew machines, and in everyone's eyes the flying machine took precedence over the human machine. Conversely, French and Italian losses were staggering. Combined, over 1,100 aircraft were forfeited in 2 months. Many brave pilots had perished in the face of sheer numbers. Many of them died due to carelessness by flying into aerial traps combined with a temptation in the allied ranks to continually throw aircraft "to resolve the African front quickly." It was thought the invasion could be stopped by air attacks alone. It could not. By the middle of April it was apparent the AU would have the opportunity to land an army in Europe. Annan had succeeded in "playing defense" in order to invade.

The battle for air supremacy over the Mediterranean ended as an AU victory since they lost close to 200 aircraft per month while the allies lost close to 2,000 total. For all intensive purposes the AU took the initiative even though the allies had done a credible job damaging the AU supply train. The AU Air Force had inflicted just enough losses on the allies to begin bombing the southern coast of France—a prerequisite to invasion. Their aircraft could now turn their attention to cutting off the allied navies who loomed as the greatest possible threat to any AU invasion force. Of no importance were the AU squadrons; whether they were all shot down or not Bakr planned to continue onward. Do not forget when AU pilots were shot down over Africa they were given new aircraft almost immediately. The same could not be said for the allied pilots who were shot down over Africa, they spent time in prison camps or were killed immediately by AU soldiers or civilians. With the skies over Europe clear of enemy aircraft Bakr was now free to start preparations to land the bulk of his army in Europe, and more importantly to begin nibbling at their navy.

Ali Annan had given Bakr a general directive one-day before his general set out to North Africa on January 15th. Annan said, "You are to take our hardened soldiers, and like the last Arabs who rode for Mohammed, drive into the soft underbelly of Europe, and demonstrate to the entire continent that the AU has reached its Golden Age. Europe will digress into the vast unknown that is history. Follow your best judgments, and command through your instincts. Accomplishing victory will bring the Muslim race to ultimate dominance, bring the war near the end, and make the Arab Empire breathtaking. Know that every Muslim is with you, separate but apart, sharing, but Unis Toujours." They were stirring words, but Annan knew his army was in a tenuous position and needed more than words. If they were cut off they could be destroyed piecemeal, but the birth of the AU—when it happened—was even more tenuous, and it had already yielded an Empire. So why should this work out differently?

The coming battle in Europe would fall neatly into three separate parts: the landing, the drive east, and the importance for Bakr to force at least 3 decisive battles—all of which he obviously had to win. Bakr's plan was prodigious to say the least, but he saw it imperative to do two things before he could hit Europe proper. First win the skies over southern Europe, and find a way to offset the navel advantage that Spain, France, and Italy held. The AU had nearly no navy at all. Posterity wonders how they managed to even accomplish the landing. As far as surface ships, they had no carriers, cruisers, or destroyers. A few outdated frigates and amphibious craft made up the bulk of Annan's "grand" navy. They only true trump they owned was not even manufactured by them.

Long before the war the AU had bought 3 Chinese Han V submarines, a heavy arrangement of old Russian subs, and the crown jewel taken from the Israelis 5 Dolphin class subs. Luckily the subs had snuck through to Algeria unscathed. The main reason for this was the allies were less concerned with the submarines than with the air and ground forces. As a result little attention was paid. The loss of these few vessels would have postponed or possibly even canceled any invasion of Europe. The allies were punished for their carelessness while the AU was rewarded for their risk.

Bakr was willing to wait until doomsday—no pun intended— to launch the attack. On the night of March 8th, Arab Union Navy submariners inflicted the greatest naval disaster since Pearl Harbor. Over 20 submarines took part. The AU had waited until the allied navies relaxed comfortably in their ports, and at the French port of Marseille while French ships were moored won an audacious victory. The subs penetrated the French underwater radar defenses (inexcusably), and achieving complete surprise sunk the French carrier Charles De Gaulle, 2 cruisers, 4 destroyers, and over 10 other vessels, they also killed 3,000 French sailors. At the same moment a force further west hit the Spanish naval base off the Balearics. Spanish losses were not as serious—2 destroyers, and 2 frigates— but the attack had the desired effect. Spain's navy was now only to be used for defensive engagements pulled back to Spain proper. All at a time when French sea power took such a blow it temporarily hampered allied morale. A few squadrons of AU pilots could now lead the way to an invasion through an unprotected France or Spain. Bakr met with his general staff expressing to them the European invasion now was imminent.

Bakr's naval difficulties would best be overcome by landing his soldiers on foreign soil in the quickest time. Once on land the army would be immune to the naval power he felt the allied navies could still threaten him with. In landing quickly the allied navy could have a tangible affect on the success of the landing. The only real affect the warships could have was on his supply lines, but the AU planned to exist in Europe as they always had—hand to mouth. Supplies could also be flown in, and the allied navies could be hunted easily when a foothold on Europe was secured. With his intact submarine corps, Bakr knew he could bring his full force to bear on the European continent even with no naval force. He vowed not to let the allied warships frustrate his plans.

It was not until March 28th—three weeks after the naval battle—that Bakr felt comfortable enough to begin implementing the first part of his plan, one which would culminate in ashes in Baghdad. The opening attack was aimed not at a French possession, but at a Spanish possession—the Balearic Islands. The little chain of islands had not been looked upon as a danger for invasion, and Bakr needed a supply base closer to Europe than Africa. He preferred a step-by-step assault rather than a great single thrust because he desired to protect himself at all levels. In addition, Bakr found a suitable compromise to take an island between his North African bases and the enemy. Bakr was aware that these islands were also a fiesta's delight to the entire world something his soldiers enjoyed destroying.

The attack was postponed due to poor organization until April 2nd, 2018. On that morning for the first time since Mohammed's contemporaries fought wars in his name, Muslim warriors stormed onto European soil. It only took Bakr 5,000 men to end the Spanish grip on the islands. His troops had excellent coordination, air cover was complete, and the weather was cloudy, which helped keep the AU amphibious vehicles hidden from sight, but not allied radar. The Spanish thinking this was a feint responded minutely unknowing Bakr's best marines were headed for them. It is easy to consider that when Bakr had 2.8 million men in North Africa a mere force of 5,000 could easily be overlooked. In any event the Balearic's were now the property of the quickly growing Arab Union. The minuscule Spanish force surrendered on April 6th, and it was clear that a European invasion was only weeks away.

When the AU had subdued the Balearic Islands very few people considered it an important loss, and certainly not a sign that an invasion would turn successful. The nations of Europe had hurriedly rushed together to erect some type of synchronized defense securing each other; utmostly unconfident in each of their abilities to defend their country against Bakr. Frenchmen, Germans, and Spaniards all pledged security for each other; an attack on one was an attack on all. Italians were hoping that any AU attack would emerge from the south giving them the ability to control the mountains in order to tire and weaken the Arab soldiers to the point of exhaustion.

Western Europe was a very different place in the early 21st century. No longer were world powers preeminent within the continent. In fact, a rising Eastern Europe prepared to take a great leap forward, and attempt to pass their neighbors in dominancy. World War I sparked the rise of Russia, the second fueled China, and the lasting legacy of World War III was to be the rise of Eastern Europe. Western Europe still had great armies, but not armies that struck fear in the hearts of opposing soldiers (or were even capable of defending their territory against superior armies), certainly not the Arab Union. In 2018, amazingly, AU manufacturing had reached a point where manufacturing output surpassed everything that Western Europe currently produced except food.

Annan now pronounced the famous statement of Erwin Rommel, "The first 24 hours of the invasion will be decisive for the course of the war." If the AU successfully landed in the south of France a dangerous situation could ensue for the allies. The quantitative advantage of trained soldiers was squarely on the side of the Arab Union, they could fight their way recklessly to Paris. As of April 6th allied reports placed 2.7 million soldiers, 6,000 armored vehicles (including 1,500 Type-3000 tanks) 10,500 artillery guns, and 6,000 operational aircraft. The AU had at least 6 million more soldiers in Israel, Turkey, and scattered throughout the Middle East for the purpose of home defense. Bakr easily could have gotten 2 to 4 million more men if he felt the need or had the desire. It was an imposing force, but there were numerous ways it could be stopped.

After the siege of the Balearic Islands everyone knew what was coming next. In theory most military experts knew exactly where it had to come. The French Prime Minister Marcel Leclerc turned to his top general, specifically Jean-Paul Prumee. Prumee knew Bakr would attempt to land at Marseille, the major French port, and the one port the AU so desperately needed to bring supplies ashore. In perhaps the greatest folly of World War III Prumee asked his neighboring nations for help. It arrived in the form of Spain, Germany, and Italy. Prumee created an invincible wall 30 miles north of Marseille ready to crush any appearing military forces. The AU was now forced to fight a bloodbath if they wished to capture the port city. Soldiers, armor, artillery, and aircraft gathered in a plethora of numbers under the command of Prumee. A major landing aimed at Marseille would prove useless. But it had to come at Marseille?

Undoubtedly, Bakr's legacy as a general was decided in Europe. If that was the case he greatly outranked most who had come before him—much better than any previous Muslim. On May 1st, in a move of sweeping improvised genius, Bakr's army struck. He chose to land in three separate places: in the south of Spain near Barcelona, at Toulon, and at Marseille. With enough control of the skies Bakr was able to shield his spearhead for the trip to Europe. Bakr landed a modest force at Marseille of only about 20,000 men who gallantly fought there way ashore, but would not last long because Prumee's forces would soon sweep down to completely destroy all of them.

Toulon and Barcelona were much more carefully and easily negotiated. At Toulon 5 Imperial AU Divisions landed, and against a depleted French force moved forward to establish a beachhead in one day. Meanwhile at Barcelona 6 regular divisions were landed successfully, and drove forward, beating back the largely unprepared Spanish at every turn. In one day Bakr had established two unreliable but separate beachheads from which to bring supplies and men to his thriving army. Also he had locked an Allied force currently 7 times larger than his own in a cat and mouse game at Marseille. Prumee quickly struck but only engaged half his forces at the AU landing at Marseille. He threatened to drive Bakr's men at Marseille back into the ocean, but inexplicably stopped short to turn his attention to events happening at Toulon. Prumee was very confident in his ability to stop the AU landing at Marseille and Barcelona, but he felt Toulon was the greatest danger. This diversion gave Bakr a precious few days to reorganize and meet Prumee with a somewhat equivalent army. Events were turning Bakr's way.

By May 10th it was apparent to all parties involved that the AU was in Toulon and Barcelona to stay. Marseille despite becoming a meat grinder still held great promise for allied victory even with only half of Prumee's forces stationed there. Bakr moved his forces as fast as they could come ashore, and on May 15th claimed he had landed 2 million men on the shores of Europe. Quickly, Bakr began implementing the second phase of his plan; closing in on the heart of France. Prumee realized Bakr was trying to encircle him from the east, but what was Prumee to do, turn westward and attack Bakr head on, fight at Marseille, or retreat to a more favorable position? In effect, Prumee did two things. First he used his entire army to force a decisive battle at Marseille. However, Prumee's patient carelessness had now given Bakr over a week to land a substantial force capable of fighting the allied force at Marseille.

Undaunted Prumee launched his attack on May 20th just days after Bakr started moving. The Battle of Marseille was the largest battle fought on European soil since World War II. Prumee sent an entire division to act as a skirmish force, and as a result received the best of information. French artillery slaughtered AU divisions, but young General Abu Rahim held his forces together with incredible skill and grit. Rahim used his tanks, and held off Prumee long enough to have the AU Air Force provide his rescue, and eventually they did. Prumee's men were chopped up on the terrain, while Rahim's tanks continued to drive backward the disorganized French chewing them up in the process. The beautiful sights and high-rise buildings of Marseille used to be breathtaking. Now the entire city resembled a junk depot replete with nearly every building collapsed on itself. The sight of over 17,000 bodies massacred on level ground was too much for Prumee to take. The AU had suffered heavily, but had now bought time to regroup. Prumee decided to retreat north on June 2nd. He had lost over 7,000 dead, and tired his force considerably before they turned to meet Bakr's now steamrolling army. Rahim was hailed as a hero among the AU ranks for his mastery performance during the battle. Annan himself bestowed the Arab Star on his youngest, but most determined general.

Bakr had finally negotiated the rocky terrain of southeastern France, and was heading for his next objective of Avignon (why Avignon was an objective was the hidden fact that it was once briefly the office of the papacy. Annan was determined to take every historical site in Europe in an effort to blot out Western Civilization for eternity). Bakr reasoned that he could get to Avignon before Prumee could retreat past it. The dash to Avignon crumbled French military power for good. Bakr's advanced units raced ahead and attacked shocking Prumee's forces before they could react. At Avignon the Arab Union soldiers finally showed themselves as the most capable outfit in Europe. Simply by outfighting Frenchmen on their own soil the AU soldiers showed their prowess over their European enemies. AU tank divisions severed all of Prumee's communications, and then roamed the countryside to tear holes in Prumee's crumbling infantry. The AU Air Force constantly struck allied air bases and tanks while French air power shrank and waned. The French Air Force was incapable of defending the country and after the battle of Avignon French soldiers had to rely on foreign air support. Never a recipe for success.

By the night of June 8th Auda Bakr rested knowing he had stopped French soldiers for good. The French armies received no coordination, and were left defenseless without air cover and artillery. Prumee's outflanked forces scattered hoping they could fight their way out of the AU cauldron to Paris. Nevertheless, Bakr had eliminated his greatest inland threat at cheap cost. At Avignon, 50,000 Frenchmen were captured, and Paris was now within reach. Prumee eventually willed his forces to fight their way to Paris at a great cost to the AU, but he had forfeited 6 more divisions, and his air force was non-existent. Avignon had marked the probable end in France. In the Gothic Basilica of Saint Peter near (Avignon) 40 French citizens were found crying by AU soldiers who had come to destroy it. The work of art was destroyed with the citizens inside— half the citizens were Muslims.

Meanwhile, the AU Air Force was gathering strength at an awesome rate now the most feared utility Bakr had available in the invasion of Europe. During the Battle of Avignon, JH-27F's struck with regularity reigning death upon the gallant French infantry so far removed from safety. French soldiers had fought bravely, rabid in some cases, but their leaders had let them down by placing them in poor situations leaving them with little support and no ability to maneuver. Poor French command—a recurring theme since Napoleon—had sent many brave French fighters to their death.

For the third time in three World Wars the British landed an Expeditionary Force in France, although this time it was during the first week of June. Two weeks later they had met their withered allies 50 miles south of Paris in one last ditch effort to hold off the burgeoning AU from the French capital. Prumee began to rebuild a sizable force with help from Britain, Germany, and Belgium, but his own soldiers had already suffered a great decline in morale. Prumee was also drastically outnumbered at this point. Bakr had a 3 to 1 advantage in men, 2 to 1 in vehicles, and over 6 to 1 in artillery thanks to his vital blow at Avignon. These numbers can all be traced back to when the Arab industrial machine was awakened with much of the help coming from two other nations: China and the United States. The only true advantage Prumee had was in the air where the R.A.F. and the Luftwaffe were quickly becoming godsends winning major victories when they could fight in numbers.

Nevertheless, Bakr had already achieved the most difficult part of his plan and enduring the long trudge up the middle of France was tiring his soldiers and straining his machines. Allied Air Forces were also creating nightly headaches for Bakr's landed forces. The AU lost only 250 planes so far meaning Bakr could continue to sacrifice his aircraft in order to achieve short-term goals—for the moment. Bakr's whittling away of his air force would eventually be the straw that broke the camel's back. However, at the moment everything was proceeding perfectly for Bakr who brought his force to 80 miles within Paris on June 15th. The two sides exchanged artillery fire, while the action in the skies heated up through the day and night. Then on June 18th the end of an era—French freedom—came to an abrupt start. Bakr's best tanks lashed out seemingly bulldozing Prumee and his zombie-like allies backward. Taking a page from the Chinese philosophy some Arabs harassed the airfields (especially those who resided in France before the war), and fueled confusion to a retreating allied enemy. The allies had no match for the Type 3000 tanks, and Arab Union pilots found large pockets of Prumee's forces left in open ground inflicting devastating losses. Prumee began looking for another place to retreat, but in the process conceded the greatest city in the European Union to a new empire.

General Auda Bakr marched into Paris with his troops on June 20th, 2018. It was a deplorable sight for the French citizens who had only heard stories about what the Nazi surrender had done to their nation. Even more depressed were those French citizens (80 years or older) who had seen their country conquered for the second time in their lifetime. Some even committed suicide in yet another dreadful turn of the war.

Bakr's first act of victory was to raise the Arab Union flag from the Eiffel Tower a symbol of French pride. Curiously missing from the march into Paris was Ali Annan who was urged not make the trip because his security could not be guaranteed. Europe was still a dicey place for the AU army involved in Spain. Despite taking Paris there was still a massive part of the continent left unconquered, and a massive allied army that would counterattack. But while an underground resistance to the Arabs had begun the AU began pondering their next move undaunted.

Bakr had already subjugated the most powerful nation in the European Union at a very small cost. He had lost less than 16,000 dead, and planned his next strike at the powerhouse manufacturing city of Lille. Deep inside Bakr knew he had to get to Berlin as quickly as possible, from Berlin he assumed he could wait a winter and hit the Balkans, or even attack Europe through Turkey in the hopes of forming a tremendous (and disastrous) link up celebration in the middle of Europe. Either way Lille was the next logical target to lust. It was not until June 25th that Bakr summoned his undefeated army to the battlegrounds of Lille. The AU soldiers who had celebrated the most important victory ever won by a Middle Eastern power were drunk with joy. The Arab soldiers in Europe now numbered over 2.5 million, and when they confronted a diminutive allied force in Lille another AU victory was easily notched. Once again Bakr could do no wrong; he had eliminated any allied presence on French soil hopefully forever. Prumee's last remaining forces were destroyed, surrendered, or retreated into Belgium. The battle for France had come to a close on the last day in June and with it a resounding AU victory.

Never before had such a confident army been seen on the slopes of Belgium as the Arab Union. Led by their top officer Auda Bakr they glimmered with dominance. It was with great emotion that they waited to fulfill his destiny as the ruler in wake of Europe. The AU soldiers approached their next operation—a blitz through Belgium—with great vitality. The Battle for Brussels was over long before it had commenced. The Arab Union was a steamroller on the rolling hills of Belgium. Bakr was a student of military history; Bakr knew how to attack in this terrain. Combined with that, Belgium had sent a large part of her armed forces to aid the wavering French, and their soldiers with there French and British contemporaries were far from putting up a fight of any value. After a small skirmish the allies numbering 5 divisions retreated from Brussels and broke for Germany—their position was untenable—the Germans had mobilized fresh forces, and quartered them close to the Belgian border to aid there fleeing allies. Brussels was declared an open city on July 8th, by nightfall it had become the newest bastion of the AU Empire.

At this point Bakr figured (correctly) he had enough time to rest his ailing forces, and most importantly bring more supplies ashore to expedite this process. It was with great encouragement that France was the leading food producer in the European Union; something Bakr's troops—still the hand to mouth army of Israel in many cases—were quick to take advantage of.

Bakr now had the opportunity to move east again to take the most prized city in Central Europe; Berlin. However, he would have to face a brilliant young general who had hatched a plan specifically to destroy his army, Heinrich Schliemann. Schliemann had made a meteoric rise through the ranks of the German army, and was only 40 years old when the whole of Europe needed him.

Schliemann had created an audacious plan where he allowed Bakr to move east ahead of his ever-increasing supply lines. Schliemann had constructed an entirely German force of about 33 divisions around the city of Hannover. His force would be augmented with the addition of British, French, and Belgians. Hannover was the key, he planned to release all his strength, and annihilate Bakr dead-on at this spot. When Bakr's troops found themselves moving into Germany they encountered unnaturally light resistance. Immediately, Bakr halted his forces asked for intelligence, and waited an entire day before setting out again. By this time Bakr knew exactly what Schliemann had in store for him. In order to counter this new enemy Bakr consolidated his forces, drove to within 50 miles of Hannover, and cut them in half. His forward forces assumed a solid holding action, while his other half looped deviously behind to surround Germany's young genius. This they did, and on July 12th despite desperate attacks from the Luftwaffe, Bakr had cut another link from the chain. Germans, Britons, Italians, Belgians, and French soldiers surrendered, or were slaughtered by Bakr's deadly warriors. An all too familiar scene was playing itself out again Europe. Bakr was the most feared conqueror since Hitler.

Burned out German equipment littered the scenery of Hannover:

AMX's, Panzerhaubsites, Leopard 3's, and numerous artillery guns were rendered useless. Schliemann had made his entrance into the war instantaneously, and just as quickly he made his exit. Of his 33 divisions 20 were now gone along with 16,000 Germans dead. His plan had the right idea, but it was a dismal fiasco. Germany had signed themselves over to the AU in one battle because Schliemann had no concept of defeat. Meanwhile, Bakr who had lost a total of 26,000 men through casualties, deaths, or prisoners was definitely hurt, but not nearly enough to send him reeling back to the AU. Certainly not enough to accomplish Schliemann's plan of knocking him out of Europe for good.

The final curtain for the Germans came when what was left of their divisions trotted across the Rhine, and assumed defensive link ups with the Poles. Once again, Bakr had confronted a seemingly superior force and devastated it completely. On July 17th Bakr marched into Berlin, and found his troops had already installed all the comforts from their homes in the city. Many religious artifacts were destroyed, burned, disassembled, or looted. All that stood between the AU and European domination were a few schistic countries known as the Balkans. However, even the smallest in any endeavor are capable of producing a trump card, and the Balkans certainly had theirs

Thomas Edward had brought the American military to Greece after the fall of Turkey in 2018. Rumania, Hungary, and Yugoslavia had all been working together to prevent a situation such as the one now thrust upon them—direct attack on their homelands. Edward headquartered in Greece was waiting for Bakr. He constantly propositioned President Powwer to give him more troops, equipment, aircraft, something the President almost always did. Bakr decided to divide his forces and head straight for Rumania with the intent of destroying Edward before a vicious winter could possibly set in, but before he did that on the date of July 18th another critical event overshadowed even this move. On July 4th China invaded Russia.

CHAPTER 10
KREMLIN

In response to the American victory at Hawaii Zhen Zui ordered the destruction of Los Angeles on January 17th, which the Chinese achieved through their new wonder weapon—the stealth cruise missile. However, this weapon was only a prototype, and they had not yet made it into mass production. Twenty-seven of these missiles were strategically placed to destroy the entire urban area of the city. Los Angeles was deemed impossible to rebuild by many, but nevertheless these efforts were started immediately. It was a nice press story for the Chinese, but the impact of it on the war as altering the tide was negligible. The impact on the morale of the American public was severe, but it fell short of what China hoped because the Battle of Hawaii was now immortal in the annuls of this war. The destruction of Los Angeles though terrible in claiming 40,000 lives only stiffened the resolve of the American public. Everywhere American citizens united in outright hate of China, and developed a complete attitude that the destruction of China must be complete.

All this had been decided when Zhen Zui stood in his presidential palace thundering out commands, and screaming at his advisors on January 13th. The sound of displeasure was electrifying one day after the battle of Hawaii. The leader of China could not believe his powerful army had been vanquished in the enormous Pacific. How could the hated Americans pull off a victory of such magnitude considering their circumstances? Zui's anger grew by even greater strides a few days later when he heard the news that Japanese stealth destroyers relegated his navy and more soldiers to the deep abyss of the Pacific.

Upon stepping back Zui had cleared his mind of rational thought, vowing never to give in to the enemy again. The war had reached its first crises for the Chinese military, and the time for action was now, before momentum copulated with the allies. Zui's frenetic demeanor demanded an immediate reprisal in the form of two separate offensive strikes. One was the strike on Los Angeles. The other was a place China felt secure about its chances for total victory—Russia.

China had already succeeded in weakening Russia with their version of strategic terrorism at the outset of war with the idea of keeping them supine and unable to interfere with Chinese military matters elsewhere. Again, Zui realized that Chinese was the largest minority in the Russian Federation so he came to see himself as the great liberator of his subjected people. It should have shown the Russians something when Chinese Russians welcomed Zui's forces—the enemy within your borders is always more dangerous than the enemy without. Zui also built a new army entirely separate from the one that took part in the Pacific campaign. In Nguyen's absence he built a fresh new force 357 divisions strong, including 57 armored divisions. It was the largest one country army in the history of the world!

However there was a drawback to this dominating Chinese force. Half of the armored divisions were equipped with obsolete tanks with no chance of defeating brand new Russian T-222's. Also many of the infantry divisions were of poor quality and lax training. In fact, in some extreme cases regular infantryman were not equipped with anything else but wooden rifles! In retrospect a Chinese invasion of Russia was something many thought would eventually occur sometime in history—sometime when the world was at war.

The most questioned change in the Chinese military hierarchy was in its leadership. Zui in favor of General Sun Tran had sacked General Nguyen after his failures in the Pacific. Tran was the commander of Chinese forces when they moved through Pakistan, and helped conquer India during the opening phase of the war.

Nguyen had been publicly scolded by Zui, and Zui even remarked at one point, "I will not leave our destiny in the hands of failures." General Nguyen became the ultimate scapegoat, and rightfully so, at any time he could have said no to the Hawaiian operation and he was the mastermind. Whether or not it was justified was a different story altogether. Nguyen accepted this expulsion honorably. Chinese troops mourned, Nguyen, the half—Chinese, half—Vietnamese general retired to write his memoirs, and under the tutelage of Tran, China prepared to invade the Motherland.

The Russians had been receiving American help since Gorbachev tore down the Berlin Wall. The U.S. had around two divisions of soldiers in Russia during the Hawaiian campaign. Of course they were more of a police force to help suppress the Chinese funded rebels than to fight a war. These Chinese rebels who attacked manufacturing sites and military bases had run their course by June 2018. By that time Russia cleansed itself of their interior trouble, and began constructing weapons and defenses in the likely event of an invasion. During the year long terror the Russian population fell by 55,000, a small number from the attacks, but mostly due to hunger, and the inability to receive supplies from the outside world pressed into conflict. Despite being brutalized for an entire year— they are a resilient people—the Russian civilians moved confidently ahead. Remarkably, so did Russian Federations arms production.

The Russians had perfected a new series of weapon designs and structured training regiments. Soldiers were trained in Siberia—even Americans—on how to fight the coming defensive war in Russia in early 2018. American and Russian commanders exchanged ideas back and forth during these exercises. Brand new armored vehicles began rolling off the lines at Tula, and appearing on the ground, among them were the heavy T-222's and the magnificent new Tsar tanks. The T-222's were a massive 60-ton tank, while the Tsar's were based on the vintage T-34's, but up to date with technology. The overall design was the same but an Aveo power plant, heat reducing armor, a Christie suspension, and lethal 122mm main gun made this a terror. These two new tanks put strike back in the Russian

Army. Even though Russia had struggled economically since the early 90's, they had remained a powerful military force in the world. Their weapons production stood as a symbol of pride waiting to be recaptured by the Russian military.

Furthermore, the United States reinforced the Russian Army with Humvee's, Stryker's, and Bradley Fighting Vehicles—making it fully and <u>modernly</u> mechanized. The lack of Chinese ability to hit the industrial heart of North America was never more apparent than when looking at Russia who had most of their equipment constructed overseas. New artillery pieces came into production as well from ranges of 155mm guns to 250mm pieces. Also Multiple Launch Rocket Systems (MLRS) became a predominant weapon in Russia, while new models like the MS-55 or AB 42 were capable of smothering offensive advances by firing 100 rockets a minute.

However, the Russian military's cerebral excellence was outstanding when it came to the skies above Russia. There was a new jet available to the Russian military for the first time since the beginning of the war—the Mig 99. Also nicknamed Bloodhound-B the Mig 99 was an amazing aircraft, and quickly became the greatest terror in the sky. It rivaled the Joint Strike Fighters and surpassed every other jet that took to the sky. For its time it was *the* tremendous machine of this era. It utilized radio-frequency identification to many different degrees, and this technology allowed friendly identification from miles away. As a result, friendly fire accidents were nil. The Bloodhound could pinpoint enemy targets from over 600 miles away, and this aircraft could track 20 separate targets at a time. Once a target was identified one of the 26 all-purpose *Ungrund* missiles was fired and the target was scratched. This remarkable jet was also cloaked with RFID chips that would manipulate enemy radar and send fallacious locations back to the enemy. The Mig 99 was capable of manipulating any defensive radar system, which included even the systems of their allies. The Mig 99 occupied Chinese resources to a high degree as they hurriedly tried to construct new radar systems, defenses, and aircraft. A Chinese rule was that it took a varying rate of at least 15 missiles for 1 Mig 99 casualty.

The new weapons were not available in large quantities yet, but the Russian military and regenerated capitalist regime had achieved heights previously undiscovered. With a little help and money the Russian military had again reinserted itself as a first class power. In the annuls of history it is important to note, however, that Russia for all her interior problems had not yet taken the step toward war. Russian leaders and citiznes knew exactly what was happening, and the terrorist attacks they endured were traceable to the Chinese, but Russia had not yet physically declared war even though they were developing amazing new weapons to win it.

Despite having every logical reason to tie these attacks to China, Salaval was often hesitant to cast blame on the Chinese government. He never felt strong enough to attack China without help, and in 2017 could not risk a war when his country was in such dire straights. When the terrorist attacks continued recurring it was beyond a shadow of a doubt that direct Chinese influence was the culprit. But by then Salaval had tied up his soldiers policing the country, and getting them trained. Zui had originally conceived these attacks as a small holding action and got exactly what he wanted including more. By the time the AU and China had overrun India, Israel, Taiwan, and South Korea; Russia was still bogged down with their own "semi-domestic" problems. Zui's plan had achieved more than he could have ever asked.

The coming invasion of Russia restarted a single theme for China and the Arab Union. Cooperation. In March of 2018 Zui began moving 290 divisions into Iran, Iraq, and Syria with the consent of Annan. Annan was ecstatic to bring China into the AU because his best and brightest were away in North Africa busily planning the invasion of Europe. There was a feeling between the two leaders—Zui and Annan—that the upcoming battle for Russia was critical in the long-term affect of the war. At a positive extreme with control of Europe and Russia the Armies of the East could then compel the rest of world to anything through economics and resources alone—what little world was left. At an extreme negative failure meant extermination. Then it happened.

On July 4th 2018 Zui hurled against Salaval the largest army ever seen in the history of combat. Three million Chinese soldiers of the PLA barged into Russia from 3 separate points. The first was under General Chou Hu, which had the shortest trip to take the port city of Vladivostok on the east coast. The two remaining armies both departed from the Arab Union. One under Chiang Zu was to rush to Smolensk then onto Saint Petersberg. While the last Chinese army under Tran was to barrel straight to Moscow force a military surrender then finish what resistance was still alive in Saint Petersburg with Zu's force. The culmination of the armies in Saint Petersburg would finish Russia politically forever.

When Chinese troops crossed into the Motherland it brought an abrupt end to all those Sino-Soviet relations, which littered the last half of the 20th century. What started with Stalin and Chairman Mao ended violently over the Russian plains 72 years later. Zui's reason for attacking Russia was obvious; with almost no tangible navy left his only hope for expansion was over land in a country close to his own. He planned to attack Russia regardless he just stepped up the time frame. Zui chose the largest nation on Earth to invade, and elected himself the liberator of the Chinese civilians residing in Russia. The United States and Canada had actually warned Russia an attack could be imminent, but the Russian leaders were reluctant to rush their army to defend frontiers.

The Russian President Darius Salaval believeing in the words of Frederick the Great told his military staff, "If I defend everything. I defend nothing." Salaval had handed over the Russian army to a little known general, but a star nonetheless, Georgev Donskoi. Donskoi prepared Russian forces for the largest invasion they ever faced. He also sketched out a plan, which would keep AU forces that were driving through Eastern Europe from linking up with the attacking Chinese forces in Russia. In theory, Donskoi created an Eastern European fortress. He knew if Chinese soldiers in Russia met the AU soldiers from Europe complete disaster would befall him, and subsequently the world.

Donskoi did this by persuading the Baltic States of Estonia,

Latvia, and Lithuania to keep enough troops at their western borders, and fight only towards a western theatre. He also encouraged the not yet belligerent Scandinavian countries to ensure Baltic sovereignty if the AU armies in Europe attacked them. Donskoi also received divisions from the U.S., UK, and Japan. The United States troop commitment in Russia went from 42,000 troops before Hawaii to 310,000 after; it was still dwarfed by Chinese numbers. Powwer also sent one of his best fighting men to aid the Russians—Major Matthew Whitney. Whitney was another freedom loving American sent overseas by his government, but he was fearless and always willing to take risks. He was partial to the bottle and because of it his men loved him. Frequently, he would stop in the open field to tell his soldiers jokes, and enjoy a drink against army regulations. A common man at heart Whitney was the model of emotional stability and intelligence, which made him the perfect man for the job in Russia which Powwer recognized immediately. In time the Russians who originally thought of him as a clown began to love this man as one of their own. With Whitney the war in Russia was closely won, without it him, it may have been closely lost.

Whitney marshaled all his provisions, men, and vehicles in places surrounded by an umbrella of air defense. Across the Atlantic he brought with him the new American Patriot 3 missiles that were capable of stopping the cruise missiles that proved so devastating to the allies in the past. Whitney was uncompromising, greatly admired, and stubborn; all qualities he and the allies would now need.

Strangely enough, of the 3 Chinese army groups that attacked Russia, two of them departed from the AU or Iran proper. The only one that did not was under General Hu heading for Vladivostok. In ten days Hu defeated the entire Russian garrison at Vladivostok, but 60,000 of the 75,000 men there were able to escape to Japan, and thus redeployed in western Russia in early August. Vladivostok was the eastern port and fortress of Russia, but it was not a major victory. Supplies still came via the Baltic and Barents Seas from the United States and the UK. Meanwhile, Hu not celebrating his eastern glories recommended he drive north after Vladivostok to cut supplies coming from the Bering Sea, Zui agreed, but Tran felt contempt. An extra 300,000 men could be much more proactive when it came time to march on Moscow during its most tenuous moments before winter. The end result of all the Chinese debating, Tran got them too late.

Zu and Tran hit the ground running on July 4th and made their way towards Smolensk and Moscow. Thanks to the AU forces in Europe the entire left flank of the PLA was secure. Donskoi opted to send small-inexperienced forces into battle and draw Tran into a Russian, UK, and United States trap in time for winter. However, by July 28th the speedy Chinese had reached Saratov and not yet fought a major battle. Over three million Chinese were less than 500 miles from Moscow. The world began to wonder what Donskoi was doing by fettering away his resources.

Suddenly the smallest major battle of the entire war was presented between American and Chinese forces at Kozon. Whitney—tiring of Donskoi's evasiveness—took the initiative with a small force of 20,000 (15,000 Americans) men with the intent to fight at Kozon. Tran's forces were at least 15 times that number in the area, but the desperately shorthanded Whitney stealthily surprised the Chinese and knocked out 54 tanks and inflicted 6,000 casualties. Whitney's casualty count was 14! It was one of histories great juxtapositions—the American army fighting for the freedom of the Russians in Russia. It brought a huge wave of support between the nations, morale increased, and cooperation exceeded limits, but most significantly it showed the allies they could beat the Chinese despite the quantitative figures against them. After the successful battle, Whitney retreated to Novgorod where the allies had set their first major trap.

Tran took 13 days to regroup after Kozon and to march northward to Novgorod, and on August 10th he arrived. Tran halted his advanced troops and waited for the superior armored bulk of his army to join him. While this was ongoing the allies sprung their first major trap of the war in Russia mostly with the soldiers saved from Vladivostok. Donskoi employed 6,000 self-propelled artillery guns, and commenced to fire them all at the entrenching Chinese. Tran's advanced forces were obliterated by 155mm, 180mm, 203mm, and 250mm shells, including free flight rockets. Tran lost 4,000 dead in the first 10 minutes of the attack temporarily stunning him into a state of stupor. However, the allies followed this up with a major counterattack meaning Tran had still moved 500 miles in a month. Most disconcerting for the Chinese at this point was the fact that their air force was finally shown as suspect deep into Russia. JH-27's were a step behind the aptly named Bloodhounds and F-37's that controlled the skies. The Chinese who had won the air war over Korea, India, and Japan became completely helpless over the skies of Russia. In fact, allied pilots claimed a 7 to 1 ratio over their Chinese counterparts in July much to the credit of the Mig-99. In August that ratio climbed to 11 to 1. In the end the Chinese failure in Russia was due in large part to the failure of Zui's aerial force.

Zui would not rest while his army had a chance to take Moscow before the autumn rains began. Zui was frustrated over the direction of the operation and his frustration soon turned to worry. As a result he issued a proclamation that Zu was to break for Saint Petersburg and Tran for Moscow immediately. They were to proceed in the form of a pencil-like drive towards the two objectives looming in front of both their forces. This decree now made it easy for the confident allies to wheel around and attack the Chinese flanks, a strategy Donskoi encouraged Whitney to utilize. Whitney did, with maximum effectiveness, and bit the head off the invading Chinese pencil.

After recuperating from Novgorod, Tran set out on a diagonally straight line to the Kremlin following Zui's orders. Encountering light resistance Tran defeated the allies at Vladimir, while Zu had taken Kaluga. Tran was now within an ace of capturing Moscow itself, he could actually see himself doing it now.

It was during the first week of September when Tran led his army to within 100 miles of Moscow. President Salaval relocated to Saint Petersburg for reasons of morale and safety. But not Donskoi.

Donskoi had encased himself in the capital not only to stabilize command, but also to unveil his final spearhead in the direction of Tran. Donskoi thought it funny that the Chinese media reports of Salaval leaving for Saint Petersburg meant Russia was on the verge of collapse. Little did they know it was all part of Donskoi's plan luring the Chinese so he could release his fatal offensive. In addition, Donskoi had sent his most brilliant general the 40-year-old Mikhail Tukachev to lead the Russian army—Donskoi in overall command.

Tukachev's name is remembered because he became the Russian President after the war, but his exploits during and after the war have not been forgotten. Through a number of reforms and mandates he restored Russia to its former noncommunist glory. Czar Tukachev—as he was known—rebuilt Russia into a world power within a decade after the war. However, in the immediate Tukachev waited patiently to launch the largest counterattack the world had ever seen. With the Americans and Whitney on his left, and the UK under another 4 star general, George Odets on his right, Tukachev could not fail.

On the night of September 4, 2018 Tran's army was beginning to settle down and rest—they had traveled a long way in a short time. Tran's army was tired and in desperate need of fresh supplies and new equipment. At 8 o'clock in the evening 200 allied divisions—28 armored—bore down and bludgeoned the PLA and saved Moscow for at least another winter. Tran's soldiers fought bravely, but 2,000 Challenger, Abrams, Tsars, and 222 tanks along with an air force dominating the sky made it impossible for Tran to hold. Tran's soldiers were not expecting an attack. After all they expected one more difficult battle followed then an easy march into abandoned Moscow. Because of this attitude many Chinese soldiers were not even prepared for combat. The forward Chinese lines buckled and disintegrated. Droves of soldiers surrendered in the hopeless atmosphere, and the allies claimed 700,000 prisoners in two days. Chinese historians even admit to 500,000. More importantly, Zu's army, which was making great progress towards St. Petersburg was now forced to fall back and give Tran time to save and reorganize.

Tran, face to face with a frantic situation was now forced to make a choice: First he could chose to launch one final offensive using Zu's army to capture Moscow assuring complete victory before the winter. Or he could fall back to Novgorod and establish a winter line, thus trying to overwhelm the allies when the weather turned warm again. In effect he chose to do both having over 2.5 million men at his beckoned call. Tran would use half to attack Moscow and half to defend his interests in Russia. If prospects turned bright more forces could be sent north. If not he could retreat and defend what he had won. Herein was his greatest fault.

On September 28, Tran chillingly issued the same dictum Hitler had in 1941. "Today," he said, "begins the decisive battle of 2018. The Russians, Americans, and British have marshaled their troops to save Moscow the economic and political key to Russia. Our mission is to take Moscow before the winter sets in, and consolidate an impenetrable fortress to break the Russians—and subsequently the allies in Russia—once and for all."

Tran's army set out that day with a newfound confidence in themselves, their equipment, and their leaders. In one week of arduous fighting they had reached Nizhny. It was a sluggish offensive though, and Whitney committed all of his land warrior infantry at Nizhny. Whitney only had one division—specifically the 3rd infantry—but they absolutely slaughtered Tran's troops at Nizhny nonetheless.

Tran wrote back to Zui of the spectacle, *"I had never seen a conventional weapon more devastating than the US land warrior infantry. For every American I saw dead there were at least 100 of my countryman. I wonder if our soldiers even knew the enemy was in front of them until fire broke out. This new weapon makes it impossible for the Americans to commit tactical errors—even on a small scale—and forces us to suffer the consequences of near perfect coordination. You can only imagine how much deadlier they are when no errors are present. They have the ability to see where we are going before we do, and abruptly surprise and then disappear under air cover. I recommend we acquire this technology by any means necessary. ASAP."*

Even with the loss Tran refused to stop. Instead, in a move of pure insanity he pressed onward. Dodging Nizhny, Tran moved toward Kaluga creating an inviting salient where two Chinese armies were now dangerously exposed. When Russian and British forces staged a small testing attack between Kaluga and Nizhny, Tran's forces were left with two gashes. Now Tran recognized his position was hopeless, he halted, and fell back on Novgorod. And began somehow to think of a way to get through winter with the allies gaining power. The calendar had spun to October.

Donskoi now realized the opportunity to positively eliminate the Chinese presence in Russia was at an all time high. Holding the Novgorod, Ponzo, and Kozon triangle meant Donskoi could attack using a downhill strategy. Immediately after Tran had fallen back and quit his offensive, Donskoi had stopped building defenses, and by the end of October he had constructed a new allied army totaling 310 divisions. There was a great mix of nations and ethnicities represented: Americans, Australians, Lithuanians, Latvians, Scandinavians, Japanese, English, Scottish, Georgians, Ukrainians, Canadians, Mexicans, and of course Russians. It was a magnificent force assembled outside Moscow well equipped and waiting for the onset of winter.

The war hit a stalemate for three weeks in November. The allies waiting to strike, and the Chinese hurriedly constructing a new defense line. The allied air force had taken complete control of the sky. So much so that it is widely believed at one time in Russia there were as many as 17,000 operational allied aircraft. Just an amazing number! When the ground war settled into stability, Chinese troops felt flattened under the nonstop bombing of allied aircraft. Imagine the shock of the Chinese infantry when they saw fewer and fewer of their aircraft appearing, and only more for the allies. Then the ground war came.

Coinciding with the first large snow storm on December 10th all 310 allied divisions attacked the Chinese triangles. Blizzard like effects blotted out the white clad allies, while conversely the PLA was suffering from a decimated supply chain. The only aircraft in the sky were allied all weather fighters, and combined with the demons on the ground inflicted crushing defeats on the Chinese. The Chinese found out what Napoleon and Hitler had once gone through in Russia. A brilliant military position had been ruined in a matter of weeks with very few major battles. The advancing allied army hurled back the oppressors, and liberated countless numbers of towns and villages along the way. The diligent allied armies fought their way to Ponzo where their offensive began to run out of steam. Why? It must be said that the allies also ran out of supplies, they also felt the cold, and they became weary. But they had eliminated 500,000 more Chinese soldiers at a cost of 26,000 dead.

The battle for Moscow ended in unmitigated disaster for Tran. He now had lost one-third of his original army that marched with so much ease into Russia. Tran would receive new replacements in the winter, but morale was dead, and training now had to be rushed to accommodate the dire straights of the Chinese Army. Tran was in a world of hurt.

Tran did not believe he could take Moscow anymore; he lost all confidence in his subordinates and their ability to carry out his orders. He was determined to link up with the AU forces in Eastern Europe, but for that to work Bakr would have to start advancing from the west. Events had turned negative for the AU in Europe.

The battle of Moscow foreshadowed the probable outcome of the war for both sides. The Chinese generals saw an unstoppable force meandering before them, and knew it was only a matter of time before their homeland was threatened. Many Chinese soldiers wanted to return there in defense as soon as possible. The allies had gained confidence, cooperation, and were not only competent, but with their new weapons were extraordinarily lethal. All at a time when China's military was seemingly falling apart.

In Moscow two generals found themselves together in the aftermath of the allied triumph. The Russian Donskoi and the American Whitney. In the midst of their congratulations to each other Donskoi asked Whitney a poignant question. "General Whitney, do you know what the word Kremlin means?"

"Of course I do general. It means fortress. I was never worried about losing Moscow, or any battle for it," as that giant trademark smile appeared on Whitney's face. Whitney was hailed as a man who knew "what had to be done." Even if he was not the most proper character, he took much press away from Edward in Europe until Edward saved him.

In Baghdad it was a very different picture altogether. A somber mood had encased the entire Middle East on the heels of bad news from Eastern Europe and Russia. Ali Annan was outside his imperial palace with a young servant named Maccah. "Maccah, did you hear of the situation in Russia?"

"Yes, sir. It gets worse by the day."

"It is nearly untenable. Tran will be lucky to hold until the end of the year, he even requested Zui to relieve him of command, but Zui refused. I'm convinced He is on their side."

"Who? Sir."

"God, Maccah. I'm not saying who God is, whether he is different for every religion or any religion, but if he plays any role in this war he is on their side. They say it is one of the worst Russian winters since the Germans invaded in 1941. 1941! Is that a coincidence? We are going to lose this war. If the allies were smart they could attack from Russia—and with the majority of our army in Europe—could take Baghdad in a matter of months expelling us from power. I know they will liberate Europe first though. I should not have let Auda go to Europe. Victory disease has given ourselves no out."

"Couldn't we bring our army home, sir?"

"No, we used everything getting them their, there is no realistic way to transport them back. They would be crushed from the sea and the air even if we had the ships to save them. Plus the loss of material, and morale would be devastating to the war effort. I assure you that I would not bring them home unless they are victorious. More men would die retreating, I'd rather see them surrender, and hope they do the best they can in the postwar world. We are far better off pursuing victory. It will be all, or it will be nothing."

CHAPTER 11
THE ROAD TO PLOESTI

A battle was assembling in one of the most divided lands of all time—the Balkans. The Balkan nations were the only territories that stood between Bakr and an Arab Union empire in Europe. After shellacking Frenchman, Britons, Belgians, and Germans only the comparatively small armies of Poland, Rumania, Hungary, the Czech Republic, Austria, Yugoslavia, Greece, and a few smaller others stood in the way of an AU European Empire. However these small nations did have a trump card and it was the Ace of Spades—the American Expeditionary Force—led by 3-star General Thomas Edward. Since the close of the Battle of Hawaii the United States stockpiled equipment, supplies, and soldiers knowing that losing Europe was just as crippling as losing Washington D.C. Edward had over 200,000 Americans at his command looped in with all the Balkan nations. In addition, he also commandeered all of the retreating French, German, English, and Belgian Forces whom had been on the run since Bakr landed. Edward molded them into a new army to defend what was left of Europe. They would defeat the Middle Eastern forces even though their victory was measured in atoms. This is the story of how World War III was truly turned.

As Tran embarked on his trip to the Kremlin in July, Bakr sat patiently eyeing the final piece of the prize in Europe—Ploesti, Rumania. Bakr could not have asked for a better situation in Europe than the one he presently created for himself. He owned all of France, Belgium, almost all of Germany, and Spain as far deep as Barcelona. Bakr had shaped a war on two-fronts and in reality he was winning it. The Spanish were tough customers reinforced by the United Kingdom. Together they grudgingly gave ground, but gave it nonetheless. Bakr knew this front could not continue forever without a decisive outcome against his favor. He did not want to continue driving east while leaving a sizable allied force behind him in Spain, but a quick victory in the Balkans would make his life much easier. Ultimately, Bakr felt when he forced the Americans forever off the European mainland; all of his attention could be turned to make a vigorous Spanish army into a comatose Spanish army.

In the south, Bakr saw no reason to attack Italy so he simply maintained a defensive skirmish line, lobbed artillery fire at the Italian infantry, and figured his AU troops could wait them out much the same way as the Spanish. Once again, Bakr felt no threat whatsoever of a Spanish or Italian attack at his underbelly, and with a strong discount of this threat he kept moving east and winning battles. In reality these feelings summarized how the Armies of the East felt about most of the allied forces. Once upon a time the world looked upon the Middle East as a land of silly people, but the view had changed 180 degrees since then. So to did the view of the Italian military in the eyes of the Arabs. They sent nearly 70% of their military to Eastern Europe leaving very little to put against Bakr's skirmish line. They gambled correctly that Bakr would not attack, but had the mountainous Italian terrain to thank for that. The majority of their military had now joined the Americans where they became a deadly force in stopping Bakr cold.

And, finally, with the news of China's march on Russia from Turkmenistan, Bakr decided the time was right for a gutsier AU move. Arab Union General Abu Rahim had fought amazingly during this campaign—he single-handedly saved the AU landing in France—and Bakr assumed now was the time to reward the fine officer. Rahim would be given command of 1.1 million men and sent east to subdue Poland. Afterwards he would drive into Russia linking up with Chinese soldiers ensuring a massive total victory celebration. Bakr on the other hand would destroy Edward, and the

Americans as soon as possible with his remaining 2 million men before the winter. Bakr even had visions of attacking from Turkey to envelope the entire Balkan continent—the allies were running out of breathing room.

Unknown to Bakr, Thomas Edward had been planning an offensive since he was exited from Turkey near the end of 2017. Rumania immediately asked Edward if he would place his headquarters in that country, and they also guaranteed the safe flow of supplies from Greece. Edward agreed delightedly, and with his time spent in Eastern Europe actually mapped out the exact plans Bakr implemented from France to Russia. The fact that Edward was pressed against a wall bothered him little because every mile Bakr marched would weaken his army just a little more until an audacious attack could launched. When Bakr took Berlin his supply lines were overextended, when he got to Rumania his supply lines were hopelessly overextended.

Sperneac Bogdan was the top Rumanian General and the Deputy Commander to Edward in Europe. After the fall of Berlin he and Edward spent a week together to formulate the plans that would bail Europe out of the mess enveloping them. "The situation has now reached its most desperate hour, General Edward, in a month the world's landscape could be drastically changed." From his words and demeanor, Bogdan did not share the same amount of confidence as Edward. Bogdan had taken this as an opportunity to reflect on the past, but much more to prepare for the future worse.

"General Bogdan," Edward said tirelessly, "The hardest part of our offensive will be negotiating the terrain of this area. If Rahim can be stopped in the north, I'll stop Bakr here, and then we'll trap both of them somewhere in Germany. The entire AU Army in Europe will surrender to us."

"But sir, if Rahim is not stopped then what will become of us?"

"Quite frankly General, if Rahim is not stopped in the north we'll have to transfer whatever forces will stop him, and then move the entirety of our forces here into Russia and fight the mother of all defensive wars. General Bogda, let me show you something. To the south is North Africa AU territory, occupied Turkey to the west, and to the east and north the best of the AU Army. We cannot get into a worse situation than this other than defeat. There is nothing to fear right now because not all is lost, but if 3 things happen then we will win this war. Number 1: Rahim must be held by our combined forces in the north. Number 2: Bakr must be stopped by us as quickly as possible because if Bakr is stopped Rahim will be forced to fall back and protect him. And third within the next three weeks an attack must be made from Bulgaria or Greece to eliminate the threat of a Balkan invasion from occupied Turkey."

Bogda sighed uneasily; he knew the scenario was much easier mapped than done. "Do you think Russia will hold on its own?"

"Yes, the land warrior infantry divisions we have here, are the same ones Whitney will be using soon. The Russians will find a way to stop Tran, they always find a way to stop everyone who invades their country. The most difficult problem will be keeping such a diverse force coordinated, but the men there are the best of the best."

As the evening progressed the conversation took more of a personal tone between two of the greatest generals of the day. The human side of both men began to emerge, lost in this titanic battle the simple pleasures and ideas of both men began shining through. Then Edward changed the subject; "I saw a horrible event transpire in Turkey, while we were falling back. I saw a wounded soldier on the side of the road moments away from dying; his face was contorted with pain. I walked over to honor this young man's sacrifice, and he said to me, almost whispering, 'get them for me general.' He did not want to die. As I saw his eyes close finally over his lurid face, a feeling of anger welled inside me. In the midst of it I realized how many people it took to bring that soldier here, and how many people depended on him up until his death. God help me Bogda I wanted to murder every enemy. An anger which emerged in me has now finally emerged in our nation. This war will get much worse the closer to the end it gets. But the thing is, the other side feels the same way about their men and my instincts. I know Annan and Zui must feel the exact same way about their men; the enemy is not devoid of compassion for their own. How many men have loved their lives, which have been wasted here? How much greatness is strewn from Hawaii to Madrid? Though a difficult task lies before us, it must be undertaken until every evil, every disutility, and every wretched creature is removed from the Earth."

"I too have seen enough dead men," Bodga replied. Bogda supplied a noticeable pause before provoking another answer from Edward. "General Edward, why did things become so difficult with America and the rest of the world this century? This entire mess could have been so easily avoided if we all would have been on one side."

"Looking back, many nations throughout the years were on our side. The countries that stood against us just happened to be the most vocal. The United States became a lot weaker not in military terms, but socially. My nation forgot its history and we became vulnerable in the eyes of the world. We lost our will to fight for what we believed in, and to make those our sacred priorities. As far as my nation losing the support of the world it is life. Taking sides and remembering past injustices will always be the past times of many, but truly the best among us work towards the future. The people who are with you never feel the need to constantly reassure you so you never hear them vocally. People will always stand against you challenging your thoughts and ideas. However, when you realize there is no more room for indecision an adequate person calculatedly reacts. We—the American—are now faced with that decision and we will respond the only way we know how. After this war problems must and will be solved."

"Do you think the world will ever tire of war?" Bogda was enjoying his chance at picking the brain of the most extraordinary man he had ever met.

"The world will never completely tire of war because it is not something that can be experienced and understood second-hand. If war took a 200-year hiatus, then people would forget what it is like;

therefore there would be no recent memories of the carnage, and somebody, somewhere will wonder. Just like I said about forgetting history it is the same idea. There is another tremendous caveat that applies here as well."

"Which is?" Said Bogda.

"One renegade leader can plunge his nation into a war at any time that can affect everyone in the world and subsequently destroy it. This was not possible in the past. However, one of two things will happen at the end of this war. Either, we the allies will win, or the AU and Chinese forces will emerge victorious. If the latter happens an age of discontent and rebellion will span the globe until these new empires begin to fall apart. In this case, the death we have seen in this war will be but a trifle compared to what will ensue. If the former comes to pass the world will finally have a chance to fix all of its problems, and this war will be an example that greed, hate, and weapons shall forever be put down. We have caught the world in flux Mr. Bogda, and all we need to do to change it is win a few random battles. Then an impact that will never be seen again can be left behind." Edward raised his head and said, "May you live in interesting times."

As the evening faded away the men continued to talk about the world, war, but most importantly how it affected everyone they knew. Bogda's son was a major player in the Rumanian war effort as he was an undersecretary for the economy. Indeed, much of Rumania's capitalistic growth, originated with thinkers like him. As for Edward, he spoke long and adoringly of his sickly father who he kept in contact. Edward being an only child with one parent still living meant he did not have much human connection. But he was highly reflected through them. The night concluded with Edward saying, "This is it for me." Both men foddered off to bed in the dark Rumanian summer night and it ended abruptly.

Bakr was a few short victories away from doing what no one thought possible. When an Arab newspaper reporter asked Bakr in June, "How did you accomplish this miraculous effort?" Bakr answered, "Because everyone was so sure I could not."

On July 16, Bakr began moving his forces after the successful capture of Berlin. His main enemy the U.S. Expeditionary Force, and the armies of the Balkan nations stood steadfastly before him. General Rahim began moving the Arab second corps on the same day to take Warsaw, after which he would drive past Belarus into Russia and attempt to link up with Tran's forces in Russia. Luckily for the Poles they received the bulk of retreating French and German soldiers, and also received a boost when Ukrainian divisions began assisting them. However, Bakr was the real story on the European front, every mile further he moved tightened the noose around Edward's. Originally, Bakr was aiming for a drive at Istanbul, and with this a link-up for AU soldiers towards Turkey. Further, an attack from Istanbul was also scheduled, thus shredding the allied armies between two tremendous forces. Ironically, in midstream Bakr became obsessed with the idea of eliminating the American presence in Europe, and on July 17 just one day after he strived for already held Istanbul, Bakr issued packets titled: Operation Eminence Grise: The Road to Ploesti. The link up was completely thrown aside in favor of this plan. When his troops first heard of this news, they were indifferent, and were not at all bothered by this change. In fact, militarily speaking an attack aimed at Rumania shortened what would have been an enormously large front in Greece.

When the bulk of Bakr's army began moving again on July 20th, his 1st Corps sledge hammered into Austria and met unflinching resistance. Austrians with Czechs, Hungarians, and Slavs met the AU outside Vienna, and slowly started pushing Bakr back. It was refreshing to see these nations, which had always struggled against each other in the past combine forces for the greater good. Many nations began saying to themselves, "If that type of cooperation is possible in Austria, then it is certainly possible here as well." Much of the future groundwork for revivals after the war was definitively laid by circumstances like these.

It looked like the Balkan nations could turn the tide of the war decisively, but on July 29th tiring of little progress Bakr threw in 90,000 trained reserves. Fighting developed heavily, and the AU Air Force had come to the rescue to thrust the Austrian forces backward. Finally, by August 5th, Vienna was taken while Austrian troops refused to surrender. Their soldiers moved into Bulgaria, and continued to construct defenses searching for a way to halt Bakr. Much to the credit of their tenacity the Austrian troops and their commanders forced Bakr to use troops now he wished to use later. This put a restraint on the time he had to complete his campaign before winter. Those brave divisions who fell back had as much to do with keeping Europe free as anyone.

A couple hundred miles north of Bakr, Rahim moved his forces through a dense Polish forest. It seemed to Rahim, and he wrote this to Bakr, "That every 30 feet the Poles put up another defense. Some of them well entrenched, and some of them pathetic. But each second brings more Ukrainians, Belarus, and Baltic soldiers who are out for blood—mine." Rightly speaking, Rahim was tired of crossing fanatical defenses, and seeing his men killed and their blood spilled. So on August 10th while the Chinese were commencing another offensive in Russia, Rahim stopped at the Polish city of Kutno to take up defensive positions. For the first time in Europe the AU Army was explicitly showing they were on the defensive. Rahim had virtually given up all initiative to wait through winter. Annan had stripped Rahim of air cover and tanks sending them southward to prepare for battle with the Americans. Knowing he had so little in both categories Rahim decided any advance was hopeless, he halted and hoped Tran and Bakr could achieve critical victories elsewhere. At this crucial moment many allied soldiers were redeployed to Russia or Romania giving them one more boost to morale and efficiency. Rahim had no other choice but to pull up and depend on his friends.

On August 8th, U.S. General Thomas Edward engaged in a substantial dialogue with Philip Poponea, the leader of the Greek military. Edward quickly realized with Rahim stopping, the northern front had finally been stabilized. At this point Edward proposed a joint United States and Greek assault on Turkey.

Poponea was excited to join such a daring operation, and the raid was scheduled for August 20th. On that evening 10,000 Greeks and 8,000 U.S. Land Warriors with air cover from the USAF and naval cover from the Italians and Greeks disembarked on the strategically important Dardanelles Straight in northwest Turkey. U.S. bombers targeted AU divisions and poured hundreds of thousands of pounds in bombs on top of them. Naval fire was directed at radar and communications stations, while F-22's cleared tanks and vehicles. The assault was frighteningly well planned despite the narrow terrain, which confined the allied soldiers and tanks. Nevertheless, in 4 days the allies—diverting their main attention away from Bakr—continued to drive wedges into Turkey. On August 25th, Edward hesitantly pulled his mitigated forces out of Turkey having inflicted over 40,000 casualties on the AU in large part to the air campaign. Operation Sabre was a complete success.

The raid envisioned by Edward was meant to stabilize the Turkish front. In basic terms the attack made it impossible for Bakr to launch an attack on Eastern Europe from Turkey, especially with no navy. The AU forces in Turkey became greatly disorganized and desperately in need of time to rebuild. They were in no condition for an offensive. The entire allied force in the Balkans was now secure. Secondly, it gave Edward's troops their first taste of combat with land warrior infantry systems and tactics. It was their first chance to use the system and weren't they a proficient bunch! The allies suffered only 1,400 casualties.

While all this was going on Bakr did not imitate Nero. Between August 5th and 25th his armies battled their way to the heart of Hungary. In defense of Budapest, a multinational coalition opposed Bakr. Karoly Koestler led the small but hardened Hungarian infantry as they fought demonically through the Kisalfold (the narrow plain in northwest Hungary). The primarily Hungarian forces put up a masculine defense, and held Bakr for over a week before falling back to protect their capital.

Undaunted, Bakr kept marching his forces slowly onward determined to make up for lost time in his inflexible timetable. At

Budapest a historic struggle was destined to occur as Koestler literally emptied all of his guns. Bakr made the opening move August 27th by sending over 16 divisions in a direct assault on Budapest. The USAF—after attacking Turkey—once again focused their tactical attention on AU tank brigades. Koestler put all he had left, around 12 divisions in a well-assigned defense around Budapest. Air Forces and artillery guns turned the beautiful rustic city of Budapest into rubble. Soon after the Hungarian soldiers assumed positions in the scrape, and in the aftermath turned Budapest into a deadly ring of fire.

Budapest became the Stalingrad of World War III. A giant meat grinder ensued as over 23,000 Hungarians, 9,000 allied, and 52,000 Arabs died in the 10-day battle. Koestler realized his position had become hopeless—Bakr was still over a million strong—and literally galloped back towards Rumania. The end culminated on September 10th when Bakr finally took control of Budapest. The Hungarians following the lead of Austria refused to sign a surrender document, but vowed to prolong the fight. Bakr had become increasingly aware of the fact that the European campaign supposed to be easier during this phase, had become infinitely harder each mile he moved. As for the Hungarians the time they bought for Rumania's defense proved crucial throughout the rest of the war. Had their resistance been weaker, Bakr would have had a great opportunity to conquer Europe. The Hungarians have become immortalized in the postwar world, and Budapest remains their Alamo.

It is worthy to note that during the time—while many people saw it—it had not yet become obvious to all. By this point Bakr's forces had been on the move for one calendar year. In fact, Bakr hinted that the 1-year anniversary of Turkey would give his weary soldiers something of substance to cling too. On the contrary, Bakr's troops were completely exhausted, and his forces—especially the air force—overextended. Furthermore, his air force had lost the punch that once carried him through France. The USAF had neutralized and began to control the skies of Eastern Europe. However, in the grand scheme of history, Bakr felt he had to keep going. He had come so far in one year, he could not stop now. Despite his dispassionate character, he had begun applying his emotional principles to the situation, and there is nothing more devastating to an operation than committing this error.

Finally, on September 15th, Bakr moved his forces forward for the last time. As they crossed the Rumanian border Joint Strike Fighters F35's and F37's swooped down to prey on AU infantry and tanks. Edward was lying in wait making Bakr's fatigued soldiers march ahead. With the Carpathian Mountains to the north Edward gleefully waited as Bakr's forces plodded through Rumania.

Bakr's air force was shattered and was nonexistent because superior trained USAF pilots controlled the sky with better skill and machines. However, Bakr amazingly continued pushing ahead—it was an extraordinay feat—and by September 25th had arrived at Cluj-Napoca in mid Rumania.

Six days later Bakr's front suddenly came crashing down. On October 1st Edward released one of the best-planned offensives in history—Operation 7, named for the seven major participants. Commanding over 1 million Greeks, Yugoslavs, Bulgarians, Rumanians, Hungarians, Italians, and Americans 74 divisions confronted Bakr's ragged army. From Iasi in the north, Rumanian General Bogda led a further 25 divisions of Rumanians and Italians to spring a pincer like trap. Finally, at long last, Bakr's own men felt what it was like to be encircled. Superior armored formations like Italian C2 Ariete's, Abrams, Abrams II's, Stingray's, and the new Deterius stealth tanks slaughtered AU divisions. Land warrior infantry eliminated Arab soldiers at a rate of 12 to 1. It seemed technology had once again offset greater numbers thus crippling the AU.

Bakr favored an immediate pullback, but lack of communications made this an impossibility. On October 6th—5 days after the offensive—the pincers snapped shut when Edward met Bogda at the heavily actioned city of Cluj-Napoca. Arab Deputy General Mohammed Al-Amin put up a maniacal resistance, but eventually was forced to surrender. Al-Amin later wrote, "There were weapons we have never seen before. My troops had come to far too fast, and were out of energy. When they began seeing these new vehicles we could not inspire them to fight. Surrender or wholesale death was the only alternative. I did not show my men death, but a new appreciation for life."

In one fell stroke the war in Europe had changed dramatically. Bakr had lost 350,000 of his best men—95,000 of which were killed in action. With little air power his situation in Europe had gone from promising to now in doubt. Such a brilliant position had been bastarded up in 2 months! Bakr fell all the way back to Budapest. Ploesti was saved. Rumania was saved. Europe at long last had hope!

Without delay Edward launched the second assault Operation Caracara and his troops moved as fast as the birds for which it was named. Ever so promptly Edward's troops began partitioning Bakr's forces, and subsequently chopping and dicing them like a set of cutlery. Caracara's ultimate objective was Munich, Germany as Edward reasoned getting to Munich would give him an opportunity to trap Rahim's corps in the north still muddled in Poland. Suddenly Rahim's conservative approach in Poland did not seem so foolish as it once appeared. Rahim was now the only man who could save the situation. Bakr rightfully knowing there was still a lot of fight left in his men decided to use it at Budapest.

By November 1st, Edward had rested and taken his mighty host outside Budapest. This time around Arabs were dug into the rubble and constantly hit by bombers, artillery, and frequent rocket or MLRS attacks. Bakr's men were annihilated by American weapons. Much AU equipment, especially their artillery and mortars were strewn between Hungary and Rumania in wrecked piles of masses. After 3 nonstop days of shelling infantry rolled straight through Budapest and reclaimed it. Many Arabs committed suicide taking Hungarian civilians with them. A few Arabs had reverted back to what they knew. The actions of a few gave all of them a bad name and complicated prisoner treatment. In any event Budapest—the much-exchanged city—was liberated for good on November 6th.

The conditions in Eastern Europe now became a factor as dustings of snow fell on the landscape determined to cease war. However, Edward refused to grant the enemy any respite. He realized the Arab soldiers—short of supply—would have a tougher time handling the cold than his own troops. Rahim and Bakr had both fought brilliant rearguard actions, which only cost them 10,000 prisoners. Suicide bombing had become more prevalent the further the allies got, and did more to slow down their advance than AU equipment. The AU had started recruiting them. The horrors of fighting a war circa 2018.

Now the situation had become less transparent as the allies moved westward. Before the outbreak of war France, Germany, and Spain wanted nothing to do with America or her military forces. Petty disputes had allowed the allies to nearly forsake their way of life. It is a good thing they did not allow these idealistic or illogical feelings to continue now when the diverse allied force marched to liberate them.

Despite horrendous conditions, Edward continued Caracara and took his soldiers to Germany. Bakr had withdrawn from Vienna leaving it an open city, one the allies especially the Austrians took back with wild excitement. Likewise the German people welcomed the allied forces as much as their leaders did. On November 25th Edward started his assault to liberate Munich. Bakr and Rahim had assembled a conjoined line from Prague to Munich intent on holding through winter until they could regain the initiative in the spring. Allied intelligence—led by a man named Ben Wolfshiem—estimated that 3 million more soldiers, 10,000 artillery pieces, 2,000 MLRS rocket systems, 4,000 tanks, and 6,000 aircraft were promised to Bakr in early 2019.

Needless to say, Edward gave no comprehension on waiting for these variables to arrive. Therefore, he had to step up his offensive immediately or risk fighting a costlier war over Europe. Quickly, Edward took his army out of the importunity stage, and hurled them against the AU at Munich and Prague. At Munich infinite forces were gathered to bulldoze Bakr toward the English Channel.

For two weeks the Arab soldiers—against countless odds—dug in and fought the allies day and night in and outside Munich. Bakr dogmatically believed in his soldiers and threw high numbers of reserves in the lines incessantly. On December 9th, Bakr committed the last of his infantry and armored divisions and struck Edward in his interior.

For three days Majnun and Type-3000 tanks tore pernicious holes in the allied ranks. But by December 13th Abrams and Deterius tanks absorbed the AU and contained any possible breakthroughs. At this time Edward pivoted and recursed his forces at Munich for the second time. This time untouchable allied forces overcame the hardened AU divisions. Bakr had stung Edward as the allies suffered 8,000 casualties, but at least 15,000 AU infantrymen surrendered on the last day of hostility at Munich on December 19th. Bakr's pinprick was finally healed.

After the Battle of Munich it became apparent to all parties that the short but devastating war in Europe was over. On December 22nd, Annan canceled the list of materials Bakr was to receive. On December 23rd Bakr began planning an escape to North Africa for himself, Rahim, and 500,000 of his best troops.

Edward's speed was greatly decreased in the winter, and this allowed Bakr to evacuate more troops than he once imagined. Edward's army kept attacking with no intention of letting Bakr get out or get off light in Europe. Eventually Bakr did evacuate with much more than he should have because of the poorly carried out Spanish and UK campaign in the west. Their offensive achieved no objectives they originally set. Bakr's men stopped it easily creating a comfortable fold to evacuate to Africa. On January 15th 2019 exactly one year from his start point, Bakr was back in Africa hurrying his way back to Baghdad. Surprisingly Bakr had enough ships, mainly frigates, to transport 800,000 of his soldiers back to Africa where they could expect to return home. All hostilities in Europe ended for good on January 25th when Edward's 1st division, pursuing at a rapid pace, retook Marseille and cut the major jumping off point. The final tally concluded that Bakr had forfeited 2.4 million men and 22,000 vehicles in Europe, while the allies sustained almost 2 million casualties and damage in the trillions.

On January 26th, Mohammed Zqin—the highest-ranking officer left in Europe signed a formal surrender sheet in the presence of Edward in Marseille. Edward took the American copy and subsequently tore it up, then threw it away. He made it clear a piece of paper would not settle him. The Europeans who had suffered so terribly under the AU invasion looked at themselves and wondered how it had come to this. Edward simply told them, "In every countries history there lies events that are indefensible. But you must live with them and the consequences." Western Europe was in chaos, and in essence a fourth world nation. A long period of subsistence was beginning. The European Union had died miserably in its own backyard. Throughout the rubble of France, Germany, and Spain vigor had faded. Only one noise permeated through the continent—silence.

CHAPTER 12
DEATHGLEANER

On December 10th, 2018 a massive allied offensive was ordered to remove the Chinese Army from Holy Russia. The success of this offensive eliminated any last hope General Sun Tran ever held to capture the historic city of Moscow. By Christmastime all territory to the Ponzo/Kozon line in southern Russia had been reclaimed by the four allied generals. Once the Ponzo/Kozon line had been reached a period of inactivity thrust itself upon the allied army for good reason. Their success in December had greatly depleted their supplies and weakened their soldiers; they needed time to convalesce. The four main allied generals fighting in Russia—Odets, Tukachev, Donskoi, and Whitney—did more than just sycophant each other with stories of their victory during a stagnant winter. Both lines had finally stabilized, and the allies began planning a mid-winter offensive that would culminate in a summer invasion of the Arab Union—Operation Deathgleaner. The Arab Union reached its lowest ebb of power in December 2018. They were losing Europe to Edward, and were offering the Chinese very little to support the faltering Tran. The Arab Union had gambled too much and was now in danger.

An unprecedented invasion of the Arab Union was a difficult venture for even the allied side. They had to find a way to fight a multileveled war involving open ground, city streets, suicide bombers, and quickly change when the circumstances determined. Invading the Arab Union was not simple enough to just take a city, or capture a group of cities to force an unconditional surrender. The Arab Union put no real value in capturing cities because they would continue to fight whether Tehran, Islamabad, or Baghdad was theirs or not. Resistance from the Arab Union citizens and soldiers would be formidable in any case. At a low extreme it would be fanatical, and at a high extreme ferociously fanatical. Traps could and would be sprung from anywhere, attacks initiated at any point, and with these realizations all the memories of the American war in Iraq—15 years earlier—came to the forefront. Nevertheless, the battle plan must be carried out, by as Whitney said, and Marcus Aurelius before him, "the soldiers in the breach."

Deathgleaner began with some delay on February 1st, 2019 as all weather Russian jets torridly hit Chinese communication posts and separately airfields in China. After the air assault in near deathly silence 362 divisions—108 armored—rammed the Ponzo/Kozon line. The million-and-a-half Chinese soldiers left in Russia were slaughtered by fresh, warm, well-trained tank outfits and infantry. Chinese Type-3000 tanks outnumbered 14 to 1 were helpless to stop the plethora of allied tanks like the Abrams, Deterius, and T-222's. Tran's casualty lists were outstandingly high—over 70,000 Chinese soldiers lost their lives in the first week of Deathgleaner. Once again, Tran found himself in rapid retreat sending less experienced divisions to fight uselessly in an effort to stall for time. Eventually, Tran reached safety in a former Soviet Union republic—Kazakhstan. Kazakhstan had accepted the Arab Union at the beginning of the war spurning Russia. For better or worse Kazakhstan was now controlled by the Arab Union. Soon destruction would define Kazakhstan.

By Valentine's Day 2019, Tran had moved his army southeast where he held Orsk the last major Russian city in Chinese possession. In a cooperative move Annan had sent the largest piece of the AU Home Defense Army to Aqtobe in Northern Kazakhstan. Four million AU soldiers awaited invasion across Kazakhstan to cover the Chinese withdrawal against the allies. Annan, encompassed in the process of mobilizing as many men as he could—fit or unfit—fielded a humongous force to protect his faltering Chinese allies in Kazakhstan. They were second-rate soldiers to the ones returning from Africa, and few aircraft could be spared from protecting those soldiers returning from Europe. Abu Rahim had returned from Europe and was enjoined to take over this host noticed one fact straightaway. Rahim knew even despite these weaknesses he held a frighteningly significant presence on the arid yet fruitful terrain of Kazakhstan—the ninth largest country in the world.

On March 1st 2019 Deathgleaner was restarted for its next purpose: the recapture of Orsk and invasion through Kazakhstan. Weakly defended Orsk was in Russian hands by March 6th, but Rahim springing to Tran's defense overloaded the allies north of Aqtobe with Majnun tanks, infantry, and kamikaze style suicide attackers (a new unit in training in the AU). The UK force under Odets was aggressively hit by Rahim's men on March 8th. The United Kingdom lost 14,000 dead in the two-day battle of Aqtobe. A number so large it calculated nearly 5 percent of Odets' total force, it remains what Odets called, "The greatest English military disaster ever Europe." The allies turned meek with caution, and canceled Deathgleaner tentatively "until a much later date." Shocked by the allied paucity, both Zui and Annan used the time to reunite their forces during a two-month hiatus of World War III. The two-month hiatus only helped to extend the war as the Chinese were able to concentrate on building weapons and finally training divisions up to their standards.

Stabilization and minor skirmishes set in from March 10th to May 23rd with nothing of a decisive nature happening. While this recession was going on all Arab Union troops still in transit from Europe—about 1 million were ultimately able to return home. More importantly, Zui with much faith still left in Tran issued him a new command and inundated him with new material. Underground manufacturing yielded Tran 10,000 Type-3000's tanks, over 100,000 artillery guns and mortars, 9,000 armored vehicles, and a much needed 15,000 JH-27F's with trained pilots. There was also another matter of the movement of over 4 million Chinese soldiers to defend the Arab Union. Historians have rumored that in May 2019 the combined infantry total of the Armies of the East in Kazakhstan may have been as high as 11 million! This pause lengthened the war considerably for the allies in addition to leaving it in doubt. Edward's command in Europe received top billing over the offensive in Russia making it especially tough for the allied situation in Russia. What they needed was a second front where the entirety of Edward's divisions could be brought to bear.

The allies despite their caution did not sit idle on the issue of military buildup either. A massive program of production was put into action as soon as further continuation of Deathgleaner was postponed. The allied buildup, however, did not involve the sheer volume of men as did the enemy effort. Fighting on the north (or Russian Front as it was known) were Russians, Britons, Japanese, Australians, South Americans, American GI's, Canadians, Finns, and Norwegians. The allies built a force of 6 million men in southern Russia, but they were well supported with tanks, American mobile stryker vehicles, and aircraft thoroughly of the latest design. They also had created another prodigious force during the winter of 2018-19. Many top soldiers from Japan, Russia, and Brazil were trained in the U.S. and given the amazing new land warrior infantry specs. Only around a 20,000 of these allied soldiers had this equipment, but when Deathgleaner was restarted on May 24 they dominated the push through the AU/Chinese front lines.

On the morning of May 24 the allies under the overall command of General Donskoi began moving for good into the Arab Union with a chance to knock out half of the enemy punching power. Donskoi stressed that Ashgabat; Turkmenistan would be reached in as little as 6 weeks. While he spoke the most abhorrent sights of war stood out glaringly in Kazakhstan a country many never heard of before. The sights would only get worse, but still far away from Turkmenistan and the swarming den of the Arab Union a question rang. How much worse could it get? Mutilated bodies, miles of stretches of dead, and some corpses hardly recognizable to the corporeal body were par for the course on the allied side, and on the AU side it was even worse. Some of this happened in hand to hand fighting while some this happened when civilians tried to attack the allied forces. The Arab Union was much more heinous because they would execute civilians—even there own—if they refused to fight.

The Arab Union was eventually entered by three allied armies led by Odets (Western front), Tukachev (Central front), and Whitney (Eastern front) organized and poised at Aqtobe the first major city of battle. Gruesome sights already mentioned precluded the entire landscape, as it was clear that allied aircraft were surely winning the air war. A full-scale attack mounted on Aqtobe on May 30 gave a glimpse into what the rest of the war in western part of Middle East would resemble.

Tukachev's 2nd corps with 100,000 men and 4,000 tanks opposed a defending force of over half a million Arab soldiers. In what turned into an unusually feeble fight Aqtobe fell on June 4th, and the allies estimated 15,000 of the enemy had died. The allies themselves lost 3,000 men, and territory was being traded for lives at a disturbing ratio. Nevertheless, the first city on the Deathgleaner docket had been successfully invested.

Donskoi granted Tukachev one-day of respite to reorganize his troops, but lashed him to continue on June 6th. It was a short trip to Emba southeast of Aqtobe, but fighting proved fierce. This time Whitney was delegated responsibility to seize Emba primarily because Emba fell in his armies' sector. Emba was defended mostly by Chinese soldiers under Tran—who still had his horrific Russian memories on his mind.

Whitney received a massive air strike as aging F-22's devastated Emba with pinpoint accurate weapons, which left many buildings still standing—how war had changed. Pinpoint precision weapons negated the Chinese ability to dig into heaps of rubble and create a stiff defense. In some cases Chinese soldiers demolished buildings for refuge. However, even with the success of the air strikes a Chinese force 3 divisions strong emerged to confront Whitney at Emba the next day. Whitney's two divisions of Land Warrior Infantry and his Abrams II tanks turned Emba into a bloodbath by June 11th. U.S. forces estimated the Chinese figures at 8,000 KIA's, and 10,000 prisoners—Whitney eliminated an entire division—but Whitney also suffered 1,000 casualties—all LWI. It showed Whitney and America even with this incredible technology there was no easy answer to win this war or any war. The price of victory is never cheap.

Throughout the month of June ferocious battles were fought all over Kazakhstan with losses piling up on both sides. The allied forces finally took control of the skies over the Middle East, but dared not use the airfields in the Middle East. Allied airfields in enemy territory became sought after targets to partisans on the ground. Cruise missile silos, communication stations, and tanks were targeted in that order after airfields by suicide bombers and civilians. However, the one action air forces stopped and controlled were offensives launched by the Armies of the East. The combined air forces did not prevent a stiff resistance on the ground. As the allies found out suicide attacks and partisan activity in the forms of children and civilians brought from all over the Arab Union slowed progress to a standstill. But with overwhelming dominance in the air because of quality throughout their ranks; the allies prevented any offensives launched by Tran or Rahim since these attacks would have met certain disaster from the aircraft above.

Because of massive increases in surprise attacks—fully and openly sanctioned by Annan and Zui—Donskoi's operation quickly fell behind schedule. It was June 28th when Tukachev arrived at the city of Aral in the southern heart of Kazakhstan. Odets and Whitney were at least 3 days behind Tukachev who was still mopping up professional soldiers along with pesky partisans. The wily General Rahim saw this opportunity and began to author a trap to destroy Tukachev's Central Front in Aral. Rahim initiated a headstrong movement with his soldiers to get to Aral as quickly as possible. While this was happening other loyal Arabs blew themselves up against columns of English on the left, and the Americans and their armor on the right causing indefinite delays. The fanatics actually achieved much better results than Rahim's defense earlier in the month, and these attacks forced Odets and Whitney to stop dead in their tracks leaving Tukachev exposed from all sides. At this point Tukachev had begun skirmishing over Aral, and all other allied ground forces were tied up for at least a few days. While this happened Rahim finished his preparations and snuck his force of over 20 divisions (3 armored) to attack Aral.

Tukachev was outnumbered 2 to 1 in manpower but had better tanks and equal artillery, plus he could consistently count on allied air strikes. He called for the latter constantly to break up AU movements, and on the night of June 29th positioned his armor in hedgerows all along the perimeter of Aral waiting for Rahim. There was no one coming to save him and the fact he was surrounded forced him to fight or surrender. His action was predictable by all Russians. He chose to fight.

All through the night of June 29th Tukachev faced violent assaults from Rahim's divisions. First, they were shelled—artillery and rockets—then AU soldiers and tanks came in droves, and every time for over 8 hours Russian T-222's and 200mm howitzers turned them away. By the afternoon of June 30th Rahim called for a fire bombing of Aral, but few AU jets got through due to allied superiority in the skies. Immediately afterwards Rahim came again with his last and largest attack; one more time Tukachev dangerously commanding near the front lines stopped a breakthrough. Tukachev was holding on by his mere fingernails, but when Donskoi contacted him, asking for a report, Tukachev sent back a one-line message from his men, *"All is well, no assistance needed."*

By nightfall of June 30th, Russian soldiers emerged from over a day of nonstop fighting completely exhausted. But their spirits soon rose when aerial recon units confirmed Rahim had withdrawn to Uzbekistan. Tukachev suffered 10,000 casualties almost ten percent of his force, and lost an unheard of 73 tanks. Conversely, Russian forces inflicted over 35,000 casualties and most importantly held Aral, which placed the allies in Kazakhstan for good, while guaranteeing Rahim would back peddle to Uzbekistani borders. From Kazakhstan, China and the entire Arab Union could be confronted. The favorable terrain of Kazakhstan and vast size was soon able to support an even more significant allied buildup on the doorstep of the AU.

But Deathgleaner was far from over, its goal was Ashgabat, Turkmenistan and so it remained. The UK forces under Odets had become a weakened force after Aqtobe, and Tukachev needed time to recuperate after Aral. So by default Whitney and his American force were forced to carry the allied torch. They did to resounding allied victories. Whitney's newly formed 1st and 14th Armies reached Uzbekistan borders by July 13th. They did this with technological effectiveness possessed by no other army. Whitney's forces were escorted by the regular allied jets except there was one introduction in the allied fighter arsenal—the F-44 Scramjet.

The F-44 was the U.S. answer to the Bloodhound-B, and the first fission powered jet aircraft. It remains the fastest jet fighter ever built, laughingly capable of outrunning missiles, Mig's, and most importantly anything the AU could put up against it. It was nearly a telepathic piece of machinery, which updated events every trillionth of one second! It devised a new radar schema that could instantly recognize enemies based on model, occupied space, material, and outline. The aircraft would also identify the weapons necessary to destroy the target and carry out the operation. Unique features also let the F-44 fly anywhere from 500mps to Mach 6. The pilot was only needed for air combat and due to the speed could suffer greatly unless protected in the simulated cockpit. Every other imaginable function was incorporated into the jet's computer system. To paint a picture: the dimensions of a Type-3000 tank were loaded into the main computer, once recognized on the ground the armament system would launch Crusader missiles from as far as 30 miles away destroying the target all on its own, leaving the pilot little to be concerned with other than flying. Also shielded in RFID and radar destroying technology it overloaded AU radar stations with false locations causing them to temporarily black out. It also developed countermeasures on its own, and counted only on the pilot to activate them. For what it's worth the price tag for one F-44 was approximately 20 billion dollars U.S. Where should we deliver yours? These aircraft struck terrible blows in the Arab Union Army as there only hope was withdrawal to condense the airspace they had to defend. It was the first time in history any aircraft had accomplished a ground retreat solely based on threats from said aircraft. The F-44 was a super weapon that scared the world stiff. There was virtually no defense at the time for this piece of machinery.

The key aspect of the F-44 and Bloodhound B was that they rendered all Arab and Chinese missile systems useless overnight. Much like the French 75mm cannon did in 1897 to all other artillery at the time. The computer systems were able to manipulate the traditional missiles the two nations produced. These jets forged a new principal in the air, and it was unknown they were even there for a long time. They greatly offset the superior numbers of Chinese and Arab forces, as Annan said later tongue in cheek, "We should have attacked Israel with U.S. help."

The allied priorities had been decided, they were bent upon conquering the Arab Union to knock them out of the war, and then pivot to confront China. With this in mind the allied forces remained in their grouping of three and continued advancing towards the heart of the Arab Union. While the allies kept going forward they were bound to make mistakes. Odets' UK force made a blunder attacking stronger AU forces in the narrow path between Kazakhstan and the Caspian Sea. Odets' job was to keep Tukachev's passage to Ashgabat safe from any large-scale flank attack that Rahim could launch. Tukachev drove straight to Ashgabat, while Whitney performing duty over glory supported his left flank perilously staring at Afghanistan, Pakistan, and most frighteningly of all China.

On July 16th the allies broke for Ashgabat finally they were closing in on their target. Tukachev and Whitney encountered heavy fighting, but advanced steadily with what they deemed acceptable losses. However, AU divisions who turned Odets' back to the Caspian had bottled up the allied Western Force. Odets' force quickly went from innocent blunder to minor disaster when they began suffering appalling casualties in the face of Rahim's deathly attacks. Knowing they were in danger British troops tried to race away from the narrow corridor of the Caspian before larger AU forces arrived to crush them. But on July 20th, 12 AU infantry divisions led by Rahim sprung another attack and reaped egregious casualties on the British. The Arabs suffered 8,000 casualties before withdrawing, but Odets's losses were enormous and hard to replace. Close to 13,000 allied soldiers lost their lives and an additional 10,000 were taken prisoner—of which only about 200 ever survived to come home. Forfeiting over 20,000 soldiers after an already rough campaing meant that Western Force was now inactive.

As if that was not grievous enough for the allies Odets's was trapped with no room to maneuver, and not nearly enough manpower to fight his way out. Immediately Tukachev and Whitney diverted their offensives to save Odets and possibly trap AU forces gathering for one final demolishing surge. For the first time in AU territory the situation became packed with trepidation and worry. Tukachev's and Whitney's forces moved at top speed through Uzbekistan and Turkmenistan, and inflicted dreadful disasters on AU troops— rumors swelled to over 40,000 enemy casualties in Rahim's two army groups. However, Tukachev and Whitney suffered their losses too. To save Odets and the British all allied columns had dangerously exposed themselves to AU attacks. But in a stroke of luck Rahim was temporarily short of manpower to counterattack the disorganized allied advance. This was one of the critical blunders by Rahim, which in the end cost the Arab Union the war. If he would have reorganized his tanks to attack Tukachev and Whitney's main drive to save Odets, he could have won a great victory just outflanking them. Instead Rahim continued fighting Odets for no good reason while Tukachev marched towards the Caspian. Perhaps it was the abashed feeling Rahim felt, or maybe it was his defeat at Emba, or maybe he thought he could eliminate Odets for good, but regardless of all that he did not think he could defeat the Americans or Russians in battle. He felt so certain of this even if he was attacking from an advantageous position.

By the end of July, Whitney reached the outskirts of Ashgabat. Tukachev had finally broken through and liberated Odets who limped to join Whitney at Ashgabat. The seizure of Ashgabat was a story that remains in posterity as nearly impossible to believe due to the incredible number of battles. The AU force that crushed Odets returned en masse and hit the allies often. Allied soldiers were exasperated and parched against fresh AU soldiers fighting for their own homes. The USAF stepped up massive tactical air strikes in and around Ashgabat, while Tukachev surrounded the city preventing any re-supply or relief attempts. No less than 24 separate battles were recorded for Ashgabat—the allies won them all—but after one month (Aug.1st to 28th) the dazed and tired defenders—what was left of them numbering 12,000—emerged and surrendered to the dazed and tired allies. It was the first large scale AU surrender made with the full volition of the army entirely without the consent of Annan.

It had been a grueling first phase of the attack on the Middle East, but eventually the allies had achieved their objective. There were numerous and scattered infitadas in Turkmenistan that resulted in delays, but for the time being the allies had bigger problems. The allied force in the AU was crumpled—for the time being. They suffered 9,000 deaths at Ashgabat while eliminating 22,000 Arab Union soldiers. Each of the three major armies had participated in dynamic grueling sieges leaving them dazed and discombobulated. Add that to the fact that only miles away in Iran stood well-fortified battle hardened Chinese soldiers ready and waiting providing an ominous reason for caution. Deathgleaner ended in posthumous success, but any continuing offensives were halted indefinitely. For the moment air power became the only allied weapon on display in the Middle East.

In military history the battles of southern of Russia and the northern AU could have been fought much better on the scale of theory. But the major difference between theory and what was happening were the numbers of uprisings, suicide attacks, and hurriedly flung together offensives by the enemy that made any amount of planning curt. Donskoi did, however, keep one principle of old military logic in tact. Flanks. By putting the Americans on the left against nearly all of Asia and the Middle East he forced a showdown against them. Putting the strongest forces on the sides allowed him to control the perimeter of the battle, and the sheer amount of material he could concentrate in the middle broke the backs of the Arab Union.

For the moment the allies were stopped, but salvation appeared and was apparent. Hundreds of miles away a new victorious force had assembled against the Armies of the East. They defeated the AU in Europe, and were poised at the doorstep of Iraq. The newspapers later referred to them as the "Kings of the World." Their coronation started in Israel.

CHAPTER 13
INVADING THE ARAB UNION!

O n January 26th, 2019, 14 representatives of the Arab Union Army and Air Force—the highest being General Mohammed al-Zqin—had signed a formal unconditional surrender document in the presence of Allied statesman and generals in Amiens, France. It marked the first time the Arab Union surrendered en masse anywhere during the war, and cracked an invincible mystique their fragile army desperately needed to sustain. The war in Europe was now over. The once beautiful landscape of Europe had forever been broken, now standing as an inveterate distressed place of inhabitance. In time it was rebuilt, but not at this time.

Presiding over the allied garrison at the surrender ceremony, Thomas Edward was now the unquestioned leader of the entire allied coalition. Surprisingly—or perhaps not—the Western European nations of Spain, France, and Germany were prepared to let what was left of their armies be led by an American commander. But along with all this responsibility came the most important duty now resting itself upon the Allied High Command: Where to go next?

Right away, Edward issued orders to his newly named Deputy Commander—and good friend—Spearnec Bogda that he wished to invade the Arab Union and conquer them first, "with all urgency."

The allied policy had therefore been decided, and it was the defeat of the Arab Union first, and China to deal with second. A number of reasons contributed to this decision. First, the sheer size of the Arab Union—which was formidable—could be undone by the death of Ali Annan in Baghdad. The allies had no desire to traipse across the entire AU in search of their leader. It was anticipated that resistance inside the AU would not end, but from the reasonable citizens of the AU a lasting piece proving more desirable was a better option. Edward felt there was a distinct portion of the AU population wishing only to enjoy their new prosperity. He thought by exterminating the radicals peace could be paved with the reasonable citizens. Edward also wanted to cut off China's raw materials, especially oil, which would dramatically drain their ability to produce weapons and wage war.

Second, the war in the Middle East that was being fought would be the most fanatical and furious possibly in the history of warfare. If China would be defeated first the war may get to a point so terrible the volume of lives lost due to Middle East fanatics may be enough to force a peace agreement. The one class that could not survive were the radicals; Zui was merely a government that could be changed. Annan had control over men who would fight until the world was gone. The best-allied minds calculated that AU resistance would be less extreme if China was to *remain* in the war. As long as China kept fighting marauding Arab fanatics may find solace within their borders, and then all the enemies could be dealt with in one spot.

Thirdly, the terrain of the Middle East favored a more wide-open heavily mechanized force to participate in large-scale battles, exactly what the allies had built. These large-scale battles would now employ superior allied weapons against AU tanks, and the now vulnerable Type-3000 Chinese tanks. Even better and faster allied weapons like the Stryker vehicles, Deterius tanks, and new gunships were in, or coming into mass production drastically tipping the balance of weapons to the allies. Having a million more soldiers from countries like France, Germany, and Spain meant that American weapons had to be produced in order for these men to be ready to fight in these dynamic vehicles. And were they ever in the retooled factories of America!

The last and most decisive factor to destroy the Arab Union

first was ironically the fear factor in invading China. Even at the current upswing in allied momentum a giant question mark still hung firmly over the People's Republic. Their land mass (especially the terrain), weapons, and ability to draw forces from all over Asia caused the allied planners grave concern. In terms of training, organization, and ability of the entire officer corps China still stood supreme, possibly falling a notch below the U.S. and UK. In short the reason the AU was bludgeoned first can be boiled down to the fact that though difficult and costly, the AU invasion was considered easier. Also President Powwer remarked to the Prime Minister Bollingworth that after the AU was defeated, "Situations could drastically change in regards to nuclear weapons."

The final interesting note from the allied policy concerned Generals Edward and Odets. When Edward consulted Donskoi, Whitney, Odets, and Tukachev in February he urged the fact that their forces must cut off any retreat by the leaders of the Arab Union. Edward also stressed the fact that this campaign if conducted in a "knightly" fashion may end up getting allied soldiers killed. Therefore Special Allied Services created a new branch code-named: Project Shadow. Shadow's objective was to stop forms of vandalism, uprisings, and terrorism before they happened. Shadow utilized Americans of Middle Eastern descent to infiltrate organized enemy groups. They were close to if not actual traitors/mercenaries but they were paid well, and the information they funneled to allied intelligence saved countless numbers of lives. Once suspicious activity was reported in a city, town, or human that object became an immediate target, and was relayed to allied communications. Eventually an air strike or Special Forces Unit would terminate the problem. Odets, upon hearing of Shadow's existence, responded like no Englishman before him, when he said, "We will and must speak to terror tactics in the international language of the 9mm to the back of the head." There was to be no war of brotherhood in the Middle East—even from the civilized.

Originally, Edward estimated that it would take him 3 months to reorganize and prepare for an assault on the Middle East. In reality it took him double. Training was extended to ensure the finest fighting force in the world would march through and over Baghdad. A suitable place to embark from was as disagreed upon as much as an appropriate place for the allies to land their initial assault. Many numerous factors clouded the landscape. The allied navies could nearly ensure safe passage wherever Edward considered the best possible place to invade. Turkey was considered a particularly inviting target since cooperation from Turks loyal to the allied cause could be counted on, especially, coupled with the fact that Edward desperately wished to return there the site of his worst defeat. But another factor weighed heavily on the minds of allied leaders—some more than others. There were suspected atrocities taking place against Israeli citizens throughout occupied Israel at the hands of radical Muslims that were largely ignored by the leaders of the Arab Union.

When Annan celebrated the annexation of Israel into the Arab Union he placed Rabat Sakr as Executive General of what was now called Palestine—The Free Republic of. Sakr was an unstable man, and required a watchdog to keep him on his toes and to make sure he was doing his masters wishes not his own. A presence Annan was capable of delivering at a time. At first, Annan ordered no unlawful killings, no murders, and no infringements upon the lives of the Israelis without provocation. Annan would not allow a rebellious Israel to became his "Napoleon's Spain," Annan also intended to deal with the Arab-Israeli problem after the war. Now though, with the sudden invasion of the AU by Donskoi, Annan had now to devote himself to defending the empire and Israel was forgotten. Sakr was now able to begin violating certain rules Annan had given him like the definition of Israeli provocation. Sakr kept all of his deeds very quiet within and outside the Arab Union, but the rumor was he allowed his soldiers to perform any act "in the best interests of the Muslim religion." First, he began punishing Jews who formed the extreme right wing party steadfastly against the AU, and eventually began turning his attention towards those who had relatives in the Israeli military. At no time, however, did Sakr show contempt for just those citizens; his favoritism where Jews were concerned extended to nowhere. The allied landing—at least some form—would take place in Israel. In Edward's mind, it had too.

Therefore, it was decided that an independent attack with all forces from Europe would be launched against the Arab Union ASAP. The question now was where, and Edward had that answer to be sure. Before driving Bakr back from Romania the previous year he had launched a very small offensive engagement in NW Turkey. About 20,000 men took place in this assault, and beat an unprepared army of many times their number. Those men who took part in the attack knew the land, terrain, and the entrenchments, they could inspire the rest of army that an invasion in the same area could be carried out effectively. If the soldiers could not inspire their allies, Edward could. The Turks loved him, and the time he spent in Turkey during the opening of the war vaulted himself to endearment in the hearts of the Turks. The primary assault would embark from the port rich Mediterranean aimed at Bursa, Turkey.

But what was to be done in order to save Israeli citizens? Edward found an agreeable solution for the allies here as well. On the same day as the Turkish landing a much more daring assault would take place in Israel one the Americans lobbied hard for, and eventually convinced the allies of its necessity. An entirely American force would invade Israel and consolidate their gains while pushing the AU out. The Israeli landing would occur with much smaller numbers, but would comprise the best American Rangers, and Elites as well as the best equipment. In every sense of the term Israel would be given top priority in everything but numbers.

The landing sites were finally set at Bursa, Turkey—a location far enough away from the bulk of the AU Air Force, and nestled now by three corners of allied strongholds. In Israel the objective after the successful landing would be Tel-Aviv. The two forces were expected to link up in Amman, Jordan, then weather through a brief reorganization. The next and final goal for the allied forces was the Imperial Palace of the Arab Union in Baghdad City also known as the residence of Ali Annan. With all the difficulties in preparing for the invasion Edward's first calculation that it would take three months to organize proved impossible.

Thousands of hours of preparation went into Operations Jupiter (Turkey), and Pluto (Israel). Supplies were stockpiled in enormity throughout Greece, while material was stockpiled from Italy to Spain. Allied cooperation reached a maximum—finally. Satellites, spies, and recon flights marked nearly every enemy threat between Turkey and Israel. Immense air raids were carried out against communication stations, airfields, and tactical units—stationary targets never lasting long. The allies were in complete control when the invasion began.

The coming invasion was referred to as little D-Day, but still had just as great of an importance factor teetering upon it. However, there was in the form of the island nation of Cyprus a necessary precursor that would first need silenced. After Bakr had finished signing his Turkish victory he campaigned for a lighting assault on Cyprus just before the end of 2017. Bakr needed a held Cyprus in order to move the massive forces he envisioned enthusiastically marching through North Africa without harassment from Allied bombers and British warships. Bakr had the foresight to know his columns would need to be free of such detriments if Annan would ever ok the European invasion. So just as quickly in 2017, while the allies bantered around disorganized in December 2017, Bakr scooped up one of the major islands in the Mediterranean with seemingly no trouble. Now it was time to win it back.

As a result, in order for Operation Pluto to be safeguarded to the highest extent, Cyprus was a nation too critical to the allied effort to be left in enemy hands. Cyprus could also support the landings in Asia Minor at any point, supplies could be stored, and if necessary, homes could be requisitioned for the numbers of Jewish refugees who needed safe haven from Sakr's atrocities. So on June 2, 2019 Operation Cascade was launched against the inexperienced defenders of Cyprus.

Cascade was the second large-scale entirely airborne invasion in history (Crete was first in WWII). It achieved success mainly due to its utter surprise and clockwork efficiency shown most brilliantly in the magnificence of the F-22's, and F-35's that precisely combed Cyprus free of aircraft while establishing AU units into ineptitude. Bakr had never reinforced Cyprus to any extent, and the five allied parachute divisions (2 American, 2 British, 1 Greek/Polish) that landed there realized this fact quickly. Each drop centered around the capital city of Nicosia leaving the shore defenses virtually useless. Within hours of triggering the invasion the key airport at Nicosia was captured allowing additional reinforcements mainly tanks and heavy artillery to be flown in from Greece. The AU garrison of about 9,000 soldiers collapsed quickly when tanks and artillery began firing on them. The defenders succumbed to over 21,000 allied troops in 4 days. Allied casualties totaled a pinch over 300.

After Cyprus was back in allied hands the "all go" was issued for Jupiter and Pluto by the allied political leaders. Allied bombers returned their attention to the shores of Turkey, including Bursa, and to handpicked targets in Israel. The invasion was tentatively scheduled for July 17. Auda Bakr was back in control of what was now called Western Sector, which extended from Iraq outward to Turkey, Syria, and Israel. It was now his alone to defend. Bakr was determined to stop any landing immediately, but secretly wondered if it could be done. Was the allies' next landing assured to work because of the swing in momentum alone? He wondered. Not withstanding he incredulously ordered his troops to take up defensive positions at Eskisehir, Turkey. This put them within support of the two likely places he would be attacked Bursa or Izmir. His best waited at Eskisehir wondering to which part of the coast they would be deployed, while the newest AU jets patrolled the skies weakly avoiding dogfights to protect these vital soldiers. Bakr confronted the allies still in shock from the allied air raids, but it was a funk the AU came out of quickly. Bakr always had his men prepared to fight.

Finally, the time had come for the two prolific military minds of their respective nations to meet each other the third and final time. During the night of July 20th 2019, 36 allied divisions landed in NW Turkey while 6 well-equipped American divisions landed in the vicinity of Tel-Aviv. The landings were supported by 3 navies the United States, UK, and Greece (the United States represented 70% of the naval presence). All told their were 10 aircraft carriers, 28 cruisers, and over 200 smaller warships. U.S. built light Stingray floatable tanks provided support for the infantry landing ashore. Quick to follow were the heavier tanks landed by boat and artillery which arrived to push elongated holes in Bakr's Turkish defenses. The landing in Turkey was assured success in the fact that aircraft and naval forces were in themselves overwhelmingly deadly. The agglutinated allied force in Turkey took Bursa in 6 days, formally celebrating on July 26th, when 20,000 AU prisoners had been claimed and a beachhead created.

Bakr had seen his shore defenses blasted in Turkey, but he still had one move of recourse in order to shell shock the allies. The amphibious landing in Israel was by design supposed to be a holding operation of sorts. It was a holding operation that attracted heavy enemy attention, but did accomplish what it was supposed to do— save Jewish lives. The allied force was entirely American equipped with Land Warrior infantry that arrayed the most advanced small arms weapons. No one had more sympathy for the Israelis than the United States; these "brothers-in-arms" had suffered together, questioned each other, and now would win together against the evils of the Arab Union. However, Israel would still lose unimaginable numbers of life.

Bakr saw the chance to trap and eliminate the allied 4th Corps within Israel considering 6 divisions could not possibly last long against his force of 800,000. But he had to do it now. General Sebastian Bramley was commanding 4th Corps, which invested Tel-Aviv on July 30th. Bramley was to hold Tel-Aviv, assess the situation for advancement, and provide safe haven and evacuate Israelis who could escape to the western border of Israel now in allied hands. Bramley's contribution would also make it easier for Edward and his enormous newly formed 23rd Corps to move through Turkey to Damascus and Amman. Edward's divisions in Turkey began chewing up everything the AU threw at them needing time only to negotiate the elements and terrain. However, Bakr cutting his strength by nearly half in Turkey drew troops in from all over the empire and prepared to destroy Bramley in one swoop. Foregoing Edward's 23rd Corps to difficult mountainous terrain, and token resistance Bakr made up his mind to attack the best in Israel.

On August 3rd he counterattacked. Bakr sent disorganized, newly comprised regiments at Bramley in order to deceive the allied general and test his strength at the same time. Then the veterans of Europe came outnumbering Bramley and his 30,000 men at an astounding rate. Nevertheless, Bramley had important advantages such as all 30,000 men were LWI and had the finest weapons, best training, and excellent air and artillery support. Bramley added more pieces to an increasingly technological military as well including 500 Deterius tanks that were virtually indestructible by anything the AU employed. Two brand new weapons used for the first time were introduced in Israel. The first was the MM4 self-propelled artillery gun, which was basically a cruise missile launcher on wheels. The gun had radar reflective fabric making it invisible to enemy radar, and could fire a smattering of rounds including tank buster missiles, anti-personnel cluster mines, or destroy communication stations or artificial defenses. The MM4 also was looped into satellite control, and was virtually 100% accurate; all mounted on the mobile Stryker body. The MM4 ravaged AU infantry in Israel.

There was another useful weapon terrorizing the soldiers of the Annan's Army in Israel as well. The Raven PAH-6 Helicopter Gunship. The "Rav" was a sleek stealthily designed killing machine that was nearly impossible to take out by firing a shoulder missile because of its shape. Its weapons system had an amazing range of over 40 miles, and a radar dome mounted on the bottom could disperse an electromagnetic pulse rendering electronic missile systems useless for 8 minutes. It also carried a enormously large payload of Gatling guns, missiles, and cluster mines. They could spearhead an offensive with tanks out in front, or they could cover grounds and buy time for mass movements of soldiers to be completed.

In any case, Bakr had to breach Tel-Aviv, and try as he might, he could not. On August 4th he nudged Bramley back about 4 miles at a heavy cost of 13,000 dead. Type-3000 tanks from China fought Deterius tanks for the first time in open country for the first time. It was noticeable to even the most partisan person that the Deterius tanks were winning. In a desperate attempt to save his offensive against stiffening American resistance, Bakr paused on August 5th and demanded missile and air strikes. The AU jets came but few came back supplying the general with unsatisfactory results yet again. Bakr tried to finish the job with artillery. As soon as they began firing many of his mobile artillery guns were silenced because "Ravs" destroyed 4 of 10.

In the midst of dodging missiles Bramley used August 5th to reorganize his forces and began preparing a counterattack aimed at a point just south of Haifa, Israel. Moments before Bakr launched his own attack Bramley's 4th Corps hit Bakr with Ravs and armor yet again. Panic ensued throughout the entire AU ranks, which was steadied only by the careful observations and tacit moves of Bakr. AU soldiers fought with a vengeance, and for a few days it seemed that they would break up Bramley's offensive. Both sides pressed their men to "keep ever moving forward" but of course both could not. Bramley received support from both the air and sea, and eventually his stubbornness paid off on August 10th. Because of events in Turkey Bakr was forced to withdraw from both Israel and Turkey to protect the Arab Union proper.

Speedy 23rd Corps had made gnashing progress, and took Adana in southern Turkey on August 9th putting immense pressure on the thin and flimsy line of defense Bakr had installed. Incredibly 23 Corps had negotiated the rocky terrain of Turkey in about 2 weeks. Bakr quickly saw he was surrounded by two forces—one that was overpowering—if he stayed within the locality of Bramley. Bramley's 4th Corps had suffered 4,000 dead (a high number), but saved countless numbers of Jews from barbarous execution tactics used by Muslim strongmen. Former governor Sakr who perpetrated these acts was captured and killed in the aftermath. Bakr's losses in Turkey and Israel eclipsed the 30,000 dead marker at the very least. On the AU occupation of Israel, Bramley later reflected, "My men moved through the streets of Tel-Aviv with tear filled eyes. Dismembered bodies of small Jewish children were scattered through buildings like a painter creating abstract art. No hope, no care, just deliberate death with no regard for human life. Women were raped over and over some left to live, some shot, some cut to pieces in no particular manner after being used in a lecherous act. Men were tortured at every turn. Their genitals were removed with knives as some Arabs had the idea to end Jewish fatherhood forever. Most of the rest were killed in horrible ways and their was no way to tell whether the scattered body parts had once been corporeal. Everyman in 4th Corps knew they had to come here, and at that moment everyman in 4th Corps wanted every Arab dead." The intrigue surrounding the death of Sakr was covered up by Bramley. Sakr was reported dead on August 12th a casualty of the war, but he was actually shot after his capture on Bramley's orders. Bramley was not willing to waste time and he had a "gentleman's agreement" on how to handle Arab Union characters like Sakr.

With tear filled rage the small band of 4th Corps luridly continued across their now humanitarian effort in Israel. When Edward first heard of the atrocities being committed against Israel he began ordering all of Israel liberated by the military before pressing onward towards Syria, Jordan, and Iraq. Despite the fact that Edward wished to avoid clearing Israel, he really had no other alternative. It would have been a grand show of repugnance to continue with any other venture into the Arab Union while Jews were still suffering torture. If anything, Edward felt that the outrages in Israel bothered his allies much to little, he could not possibly—in his mind—be fastidious enough in saving Israelis.

Throughout August, Edward led 23rd Corps to elaborate victories, annihilating every enemy in his path until he reached Syria. Bakr now realized Edward's plan was to break into Israel with his army and link up with Bramley, which meant that Edward would travel southward in Syria. Bakr saw no reason to throw disorganized forces into the teeth of 23rd Corps so he merely let Edward traipse unabashed toward Israel. During the last half of August, Edward used his overpowering tank divisions to barrel straight through Syria capturing the cities of Aleppo and Homs on the rainier side of the country. Edward faced a showdown with a small—but tough—Chinese contingent, and nearly took all of them prisoner. The movement of 23rd Corps, which was now close to 4 million men was precise and quick. Edward's methodically quick nature resulted in not a single major battle fought in either Turkey or Syria, but every battle as an allied victory. The importunity filled drive had resulted in a fantastic string of blow out victories the likes never before seen for the allies in the war. While plunging through Syria towards Israel the only form of resistance became renegade soldiers or civilians who willingly blew themselves up according to their Islamic tenets.

These attackers had little effect on the morale of 23rd Corps who gallantly destroyed everything in their path. The men of 23rd Corps became the stars of freedom, and they represented a diverse background bringing comfort to a civilized world coming back into formation. The men came to embody the values and convictions their nations had held for centuries. The same nations they were now defending collectively. In less than one year, they and their leader Thomas Edward had become the finest fighting force ever. Even the Chinese elites who had opened the war could not help admiring these men who now moved with alacrity, audacity, and invincibility across the Middle East. This force would lead the allies to total victory like the famous divisions throughout history.

During 23rd Corps' remarkable movement Bramley had continued excavating Israel from any form of AU autonomy. By the end of August only traces of the prewar Israeli border were controlled by the AU. Bramley was spread dangerously thin throughout Israel, and needed support to firmament his entire army soon. But Bakr's men were to astonied to take any action, and spent their time lobbing artillery shells toward Israel and nervously guarding Damascus. The perfect chance for a fall offensive had been spoiled on the account of a temporarily broken force stuck in a state of atrophy. The first week of September spelled disaster again for Bakr as Edward's forces moved into Israel for good. Bramley moved his command north, and patiently waited for Edward to meet him.

By September 10th the link up was complete, and the allies had accomplished the first major step in the total defeat of the Arab Union. Operations Jupiter and Pluto had garnered immense success both numerically and logistically. The allies had liberated Turkey and Israel, and now could actually begin planning for a peaceful initiative after Annan was toppled from power in Baghdad. Over 300,000 AU soldiers were killed, captured, or wounded in Jupiter and Pluto. Conversely the death toll from the allies was a shade over 16,000, and amazingly almost a quarter of them were victims of partisan activities like snipers, or booby traps. The most lugubrious acts by the AU were dead or near dead G.I.'s strapped to claymores activated by Arabs in the area. Many medics and privates were killed upon checking these men.

Throughout September the largest military gathering in history took place along the sands, mountains, and hilltops of Israel. Over 30 countries were represented in some fashion, and the world could tell the AU's days were numbered just as much as Ali Annan. Interestingly enough the name of the gathering point of this host went nearly unnoticed by everyone except the worldwide newspapers. The world's newspapers soon realized they had a golden opportunity to take what was a story of biblical proportions and run. First, the place was referred to as its biblical name Megiddo in the world press. A few days' later media masses used the more popular, better known translation: Armageddon.

CHAPTER 14
EDWARD'S RETURN

While I have led you, not one of you has been killed from behind. Despite the wealthy feelings of pride that has already manifested itself in me; I have greater requests to ask of your courage. I shall not lie, this is either a judgment period, or it is not. If it is, then you have nothing to fear, as very quickly all of us will reach our end, at different places. If it is not, then we have the opportunity to create a new world, which maybe yourself, but certainly the majority of civilization will live in. Forever upheld during this war one symbol will forever stand out, and you may take it to your grave. That is the sight of the allied soldier appearing in cities, houses, and doorways always be synonymously linked with that of inspiration and hope, and you are that hope. If you take nothing else from your service take the feeling of immortal hope, which was brought by men before you, and now brought by yourselves to so many."

Thomas Edward delivered this succinct message to the enormous allied army gathered at Megiddo. He needed to make sure that at no time his troops would muddle into the "Valley of Tears." Whilst serving under Edward his soldiers had credited their general with knowing everything, from this they became supermen, fearlessly led by their commander. However, the next operation they would undertake was the most treacherous ever faced by any army.

The aptly named Operation Assassin got its name by what many top commanders believed the war in the Middle East would eventually resort too. Facing Edward was once again Bakr with 3 million AU soldiers backed up by 800,000 Chinese Elites, and the

Chinese brought their own equipment with enough for their friends. Zui had decided to send as many soldiers and supplies as necessary to keep the war out of the Chinese mainland. Both China and the AU due to allied aircraft attacks had now moved manufacturing, oil drilling, and training to protected underground centers.

The allied army once again was split into two factions with Edward in overall command. Romania's General Bogda—who was formerly deputy to Edward—was given the newly christened 1st Army, while Bramley who orchestrated a marvelous campaign in Israel was given nearly double his former forces for his performance and became 2nd Army. Together they had the best of everything produced by the allied nations, and faced the best that the Chinese could offer at a time when the Chinese were vacillating.

On September 25th Operation Assassin commenced when the two largest most advanced forces ever clashed over the most famous cities and landmarks in the Middle East. Assassin fell into two different priorities with one common goal—Baghdad. According to the plan 1st Army would take Damascus, Syria, and Mosul on the Tigris then move in on Baghdad. Bramley who constituted the south would take Amman, Jordan, before burrowing into southern Iraq with his multifaceted goals of Karbala, An Najf, and finally a meeting with 1st Army at Baghdad.

Bakr opposed both of them with his single force, and would not give into fettering away his men and material as he did in Syria. Instead he decided to count on one major advantage. He had unlimited soldiers all over the Arab Union in forms of civilians that hated the allies, and equally hated the thought of occupation. From these women, children, and even the elderly a national front could be established with almost no hitch in any other plan. By the end of the year the Middle East was completely uprooted by the devastation of the war, the death toll skyrocketed on all sides, and the sheer numbers of dead totaled millions because of this strategy.

Bogda's 1st Army arrived on the outskirts of Damascus on September 30th taking solace in the fact that all Israel had been cleansed of the AU presence. They were about to encounter their first difficult task; and were charged with investing a foreign city and keeping it from becoming a stultifying bloodbath. The fighting at Damascus was filled with slow progress and fury, but allied soldiers using all the tools in their arsenal inflicted an acrid defeat on Bakr's AU soldiers. Allied soldiers held superior numbers—for once—and won the street battle of Damascus based on proficiency in their training and technological expertise in their weapons, attributed directly to LWI systems. It was not until after the AU Army had been driven out that civilian trouble—egged on by television broadcasts from Annan—started. In another allied advantage Operation Shadow Agents had pinpointed massive amounts of explosives and mines in Damascus, which were confiscated and destroyed. Controlling individuals proved to be another problem all together.

One of the first landmarks in Damascus to be destroyed was the Great Mosque, which was obliterated by allied bombs from B-52's in early October. While some outraged citizens outside the AU looked on with scolding eyes the allies showed the aplomb to do what was necessary because enemy weapons and provisions were being centralized within the mosque. The outrage of this action by the citizens of Syria brought hate to a head, immediately revenge was on their mind. The citizens of Syria soon turned to suicide tactics to stop allied progress, as they tried to kill and destroy whatever allied target was available.

The war turned brutal after Damascus was taken by the allies because of the destruction of the Great Mosque. Hate filled Muslims attacked by the hundreds until the allies were forced to post sentries around the clock and shoot on sight. Edward saw Bogda making no progress, and also was observant that Bakr had begun to build immense fortifications around Baghdad. Losing time was not an option, and Damascus had to be settled as quickly as possible. The violence came to a head on October 2nd when 566 allied soldiers were killed in 10-hour battle with Arab civilians! As a result Edward made a controversial decision that showed massive amounts of barbarity, but also proved necesarry to bring a resolution to the madness. He ordered the top U.S. Air Force Commander, Blake

Wainwright, to carry out an air assault using 513 heavy bombers to fire bomb the city of Damascus. On October 5th following in the footsteps of Dresden in World War II, Damascus was devastated under allied bombs. The firebombing ordered by Edward killed 250,000 residents (the figure does not include thousands more who starved in the weeks after.) On October 8th the allied army marched back into the city proper. Not a single noise was detectable to human ears, and not a single obstruction from civilians again occurred in the city. Damascus was a dead city. Edward memoed the entire world, "A colonel who arrived with the first group into Damascus was peculiarly amazed at the exorbitant amount of destruction. It was as if the entire town had been exterminated, and in truth a large portion has been. However, once again, I am not on a mission of a pedagogical nature, and not one allied soldier has that responsibility either. This decision was heartbreaking, but even more heartbreaking would have been the lives lost on our side, and war lengthened indefinitely. There is already no way of detailing how much the longevity of the war has increased by pussyfooting in Damascus. Are we to sacrifice ourselves by our own virtues, or win a war? If the answer is yes, there might not be future for any of us."

Immediately, some international voices called for the removal of Edward from supreme command, some even recommending sentencing for war crimes. But President Powwer obtusely refused, he had developed an affinity with Edward, and Powwer understood his explanation—that was all that mattered. Powwer would not allow stabs like this to become perfunctory by nature against U.S. officers, only in dire circumstances would he actuate it by even listening. This did not qualify for even negligent attention in his mind.

When Annan first heard of the massacre at Damascus he responded to an aide, "I have nothing." On the contrary the destruction of Damascus had a two-pronged outcome that would affect the rest of the war. On one hand it stiffened the soldiers' resolve, and every siege the allies attempted became empirically tougher in some cases. On the other hand Annan knew power was what his people respected, and all over the Arab Union citizens began realizing that what happened to Damascus could ever presently happen to them as well. As a result civilians began to think twice before attacking allied soldiers the way the Syrians did. Most citizens just fled to Kazakhstan in order to avoid the allied army altogether. Squarely bequeathed to Edward was an improvement in his army's speed.

On October 10th after much pomp and circumstance, Bogda began rolling again in conjunction with Bramley who subdued Amman on October 6th. Lost in all the Damascus scandal was the fact that Bramley once again had purported himself masterfully against Bakr's southern force. This time however, the home of Annan became the objective Bramley was setting out for, or more specifically the city of Karbala. Bogda's destination was the familiar city of Kirkuk—taking both cities would put the allies in excellent position to surround Baghdad. Fighting was guaranteed to be bitter all the way, and as soon as Edward ordered both men moving Bakr's best forces confronted them.

It was on the borders of Iraq that Arab resolve solidified nearly ten-fold. Suddenly the allies were checked at all points they attempted to penetrate through. Millions of Arabs deemed unfit for combat had come to stop the allies from entering the greatest state in the Arab Union. By the end of October, after nearly four weeks the allies had barely nipped a miniscule salient into Iraq. While this was going on the allied nations began experiencing doubts about the outcome of the war. Many allied leaders were affrighted to the fact they may not be able to win the war in the Middle East.

But there was a plethora of key reasons the allies had become entranced in a quagmire. Bakr now was able to refit his troops back from Europe into their original divisions under their original commanders wherever possible. These men had won in India, Israel, and nearly all of Europe, they were his best, and they proved it; even against superior allied technology. Finally, they were reunited and Bakr with Chinese pilots in the latest Chinese jets, which at critical times kept Bakr's ground operations unhindered. Bakr also counted on veteran Chinese troops coming in fresh daily from

Donskoi's suspended Front. Support in Iraq from the highest class to the lowest mendicant prohibited a foreign invasion until a plan could be hatched to end it. The dramatic resistance allowed Annan to exclaim to the allied leaders, "In this case we are once again all united."

Not far from where life was first incubated 10 million soldiers took part in the great battles that came to define the second half of World War III. Bramley was pressing through desert lands in the south, while Bogda was dealing with formidable pressure and terrain in the north. Throughout October both sides had delivered and absorbed tremendous blows as witnessed by the fact that on October 25th over 17,000 Arabs died in 5 hours when two of Bakr's reserve infantry divisions were committed to stopping 4 Allied Armored Divisions. It looked as though the tank brigades Edward trained would lead the way to Baghdad, but just two weeks later Edward took the fall for the worst American defeat in Iraq when AU divisions acting independently attacked massing allied convoys along the banks of the Euphrates. When it was all said and done the outnumbered allies had taken 8,500 deaths, and sadly enough three of every four deaths were Americans.

By early November Edward had seen enough viscid allied blood that it was about time to make an audacious move. Originally, Edward planned to drive straight for Baghdad, but he decided he needed to revert back to a step-by-step approach. After all, Edward had the most mobile force ever assembled, but what good was it if he could never really do some open running? Now he decided to jump Bogda's force in a three-pronged assault at Mosul, Irbil, and Kirkuk, while Bramley would still drive for the southern objectives of Karbala and An Najf. Edward added Mosul and Irbil as tangent assaults that would give the allies control of the entire western part of Iraq. These battles became known as The Early Crusader Battles. They would put the allies in a strategically brilliant position in Iraq.

The battles commenced on November 1st as the allies had regrouped and were ready to drive to their initial objectives in the land of two rivers. Another concerted effort was made by the U.S.A.F., but this time they dropped hundreds of thousands of pounds of bombs in Saudi Arabia securing Bramley's right flank—something Bramley had been clamoring about since Jupiter and Pluto. Then a tactful cruise missile assault on communications stations, followed by artillery fire on AU forward positions characterized the opening phases of The Early Crusader Battle. Artillery was nearly lined up across the country, and protected by gun ships, SAM's, and aircraft, reigning death all over Bakr's lines. When the armored vehicles began moving droves of AU soldiers surrendered wounded or near starvation. The traumatized Middle Eastern faces that emerged from the front lines were not particularly Bakr's best. Once again, during a brief lull from the last few days of October to November Bakr had once again shifted his best troops across the Euphrates to prepare for defense of the capital. This move by Bakr allowed the success of the Early Crusader assaults.

Nevertheless, after weeks of stalemates the allies had finally broken out of the Western Desert, and were finally in the open ground. Bakr's forward lines had broken, and the top AU general had lost 11,000 men to prison camps before retreating. Cogitating his new situation Bakr decided to withdraw from his current position to places where the allies could be drawn into traps; the river crossings.

Three days later the Battle of Mosul took place to thundering noises of descending and then exploding artillery shells. It was at Mosul where Edward ordered the utilization of artillery as the primary weapon of siege. Without fighting inside the city, or leveling it with the air force his only recourse was to starve it. U.S. Self-propelled artillery really won the Battle of Mosul. It constantly abnegated any hope for Bakr to relieve the city, while reducing the city to a heap of rubble. Artillery was now dropping laser-guided shells in key military areas of the city. Precise shells guided by aircraft and satellite technology tore holes in infantry foolish enough to wander around within certain parts of the city. Then during the cover of night Edward sent Rav choppers to destroy any remaining military vehicles in Mosul. They polished off the remaining amount of tanks and artillery left behind, and assured the soldiers of the burned out city could launch no large offensive. In addition, radio and television stations were also destroyed and Mosul became a city without contact to the outside world. Regretfully, Bakr abandoned it to its fate when he announced on November 13th no further relief attempts would be made for the citizens of Mosul. Though no one will ever know for sure, it is estimated that during the siege of Mosul 95,000 civilians died of hunger, disease, and lack of water.

Alackaday, too late, Bakr's position in the north was untenable, and Mosul ended in a complete allied victory. Now Irbil and Kirkuk were also forsaken to the allies since the Chinese 10th Army had arrived late with their 1st Air Corps. Bakr now had to wait in order to launch his final offensive before defending Baghdad. Which was saved for the moment from U.S. bombers that were needed more urgently in the south to expedite Bramley's campaign.

Bramley, for his part, was performing trencherman like duty moving with celerity in the south. Bramley was facing the AU coupled with Chinese arrivals, and because of that his road was a much tougher one than Bogda's. With great certitude in the early part of November he simultaneously attacked Karbala and An Najf. Almost no one believed he could accomplish a victory, but Edward gave him the OK to strike. After three days of sadistic fighting Bramley was repulsed by expert Chinese divisions. At this point Bramley halted his offensive and waited for more armor, artillery, and Ravs. While Bramley took a week hiatus to visit Edward headquartered in Turkey his men lobbed rockets, artillery, missiles, and virtually anything else they had to weaken the defenders. At the same time the U.S.A.F. combined with the newly formed Allied Air Force picked up the slack by commencing Plan Blue—the operation to destroy all tactical units outside Baghdad—opening up large cavities on the Bakr's circumscribed lines around Najf and Karbala to devastating effect. Acting desperately the Chinese had introduced their own hypersonic jet known as the A1-YT a sloppy copy of the F-44. It was hardly an answer to the U.S. F-44, and not enough were yet produced, and low production numbers of aircraft never allowed the AU/Chinese forces to get control of the air. And as long as they were denied control of the air any offensive they could possibly scrape together stood no chance of success.

But that axiom meant nothing to General Bakr who cast military logic aside, and prodigiously launched a new southern offensive to clear his holy cities. Bakr named his new offensive Plan Alcazar after great structures the Arabs once built. He planned to build a new defense line after the success of this offensive. Brand new columns of newly conscripted troops were floating across the Euphrates, and they were numbered in millions. After taking countless shells of U.S. artillery they reformed and deployed in a manner retrospect to a new offensive. Immediately many on Bramley's staff urged for an all out withdrawal, but that would leave the northern force in a very dangerous position. Bramley proclaimed his feelings at a crucial meeting between his staff and Edward, "I will not surrender a position won by expertise, skill, and lives to reports. As it stands now there is no definitive answer on this 'battle of annihilation.' If it comes, let it, for we will not be uprooted. In any event there will be a tremendous battle for Najf and Karbala—did you think they will just give it to us?"

Bramley received full support from his Deputy German Commander Otto Kohl who had 4 divisions of the Wehrmacht under his command, and anchoring the left flank meant he would assuredly be the first to make contact with the AU. He echoed Bramley by saying, "There is another round, a tough job lay ahead, but it will be done."

December 2nd became a critical day for the allies as Bogda completed his navigation past the Euphrates and was closing in on Baghdad itself. It was also the day where the largest battle in the history of Iraq took place, and it was the German soldier more so than any other that outshined all. The German soldiers had always maintained an excellent unmatched skill in battle whatever the reason. Now on December 2nd two divisions under Kohl felt the brunt of over 14 AU/Chinese divisions in a head on clash.

The Wehrmacht formed the left most flank of Bramley's line in the south. German panzers put up a stiff resistance, and gave ground grudgingly and at high cost to the Chinese in particular. Their Leopard tanks were the best manufactured machines in the entire world, and ingenious features like a hybrid fuel system of gas, solar, and electric power added speed and proved German ingenuity was capable of making high grades. So was their ability. Bakr who had taken command of the offensive permanently wanted to turn Bramley to Saudi Arabia, and allow himself the chance to move north and face Bogda with superior forces and destroy northern force. But he had to break the stubborn Germans to do it who dug in with fiery resolve. During the first week of the Battle of the Euphrates German panzers inflicted irreplaceable losses on Chinese armor and armed vehicles. But after six days of brutal fighting Bakr began pushing Kohl and the rest of Germans backward.

They had accomplished one amazing feat because Bakr's new precious force was going to keep moving and the initial losses made it very likely the offensive would peter out sooner rather than later. Bakr was blinded by the opportunity to fully break the German lines, and chop up the rest of the allied divisions. He attacked automatically, and never thought of stopping despite faulty intelligence reports. By December 13th after nearly 4,000 Germans had died, Bakr summoned them to a final decisive battle known by history as the Second Battle of Karbala, which fully showcased the mastery of Bramley in lucubrated tone.

AU intelligence on the allies was very poor, and unbeknownst to Bakr, Bramley had reinforced the Germans with French and Greek divisions, while pivoting small but effective American forces outside the original German lines. With no satellite photography and unreliable air reconnaissance Bakr committed the balance of his force into a cauldron. On December 14th the allies were ready, and ensconced in well made fortifications. Bakr made his final push to eradicate the allies from the south of Iraq. Now it was a different story though. Bakr ran into the Germans plus 5 French divisions, 2 Greek divisions, and 3 U.S. battalions who counterattacked a day later. The opposing forces clashed for two days in the scorching sun of winter in southern Iraq. Bakr turned part of his forces to puncture the American attack, but in another of many ironic twists the 16th Greek Infantry Division arrived just in time to firmament the tiny American squad in a time of crises.

In the south of Iraq the Greeks had come to save a small American force from near destruction. It showed yet again how full circle and united allied cooperation had become. The final battle of southern Iraq ended inconclusively, but for all intensive purposes the allies had stopped Bakr's brand new force. During the course of fighting the allies lost 13,000 dead, while the AU suffered another Earth shattering loss of 88,000 dead, and 200,000 taken prisoner. The number of casualties gives one an idea of the scope of the fighting reinforced by the fact that only a few miles exchanged hands. Bramley's stubbornness had won!

Bakr began relegating his lower units to duties such as holding actions and sloppy, unorganized offensives. He took his elite troops and moved them back to cover Baghdad, as the next fight would involve his capital. Although it would take the allies into January of the next year to regroup and recover their losses, by mid-January 2020, Bramley and Bogda led over 8 million allied soldiers to the toughest defenses they would ever face. Once again the allies had achieved just enough to win, and they won through superior handling of forces; not numbers.

Over the last week of December, Bakr reconvened with his Emperor in the now tattering capital of Baghdad. Bakr apologized for the loss of men and material that now left the city on the verge of decay. "You do not need to apologize to me Auda, the citizens of the Arab Union—some already conquered—can already feel your mistakes resoundingly. But the Arab soldier is not dead yet, he can still win this war. I myself have now calculated that we have 5 million troops who serve as our main army. Forty-percent of them can be classified as elite. I will rally them and every citizen in the AU to do their duty for the land. If the allies do indeed conquer us, let them not have a single man to pit against the Chinese. We will kill as many as possible. I have no aspirations to be sitting here when the war is over, and the last period of this war will be fought with a desperate hate. Hate of the allies, hate of occupation, and hate of man, woman, and child who support them! You can count on uprisings all over the world in the name of Allah, and the allies will suffer as much as we do now. So fear not Auda, your business is to do your duty, and defend the capital of the Arab Union, which will live on." Annan's words foreshadowed the next step in the war, and throughout the world the allies would pay a terrible price in blood for their visions of the capital. In truth though, this moment had to come. It signified the end of the Arab Union and to perceive that would come without cost would be categorically foolish. The noose was tightening, and Annan as well as the entire AU felt it.

CHAPTER 15
THE END OF THE ARAB UNION

While August 2019 was quickly approaching its end the situation in the Middle East was still very much up in the air for one part of the allied side. For the Northern Front Operation Assassin was still weeks away, but the allies had already carved out a hard fought foothold in one section of the Middle East. It was largely due to the posthumous success of Deathgleaner, which reached the decadent city of Ashgabat—at a heavy price in lives. General Donskoi was in no mood for ebullience when he saw the casualty lists from the start of the campaign to the brief pause he now took to refit his army. Donskoi openly labeled Deathgleaner, "A success over terrain only." Donskoi was beginning to lose confidence in himself and his ability to lead this final and critical phase of the war effort. The increasing death toll escalated on his mind evermore, and became worse as bad news traveled back to him from the front. Donskoi began questioning and second-guessing himself at nearly every turn during the early part of September 2019. His subordinates saw him as a man whose skill was deteriorating. He was rapidly nearing a nervous breakdown.

Nevertheless, Donskoi did not have time (in his mind) to wait in Ashgabat; he had to keep moving and tying up many AU and Chinese divisions from fighting in the west. During the summer of 2019 he had finalized his next mission that would circumambient Annan in Iraq. Donskoi had garnered a plan that would capture Iran and block any possible escape of AU forces into India, Pakistan, or China. With the advent of Bogda's and Bramley's successful invasion into Turkey and Israel, Donskoi set out to control all territory from

Tehran to Bushehr, or more explicitly to build a line from the Caspian to the Persian Gulf where no enemy could travel east.

Donskoi could claim a few advantages that Edward did not have available on the Western Front. When Chinese soldiers first crossed into Russia in January of 2019 the United States and UK sent not only soldiers but also scientists. Together the men from those nations pooled their technology, and came up with startling new weapons that in peacetime would not have been shared and certainly never created together. CANU or (Combined Arms Network Utility) focused on the creation of dominating ground weapons molded with the best technology the three nations had to offer at the time. Their first production was just hitting the war effort, and it was a magnificent weapon codenamed the Fortitude. The Fortitude was a tank that contained the newest radar systems of allied jets, but more importantly it was made with a new type of alloy known to everyone else as "memory metal." Simply "memory metal" could take a hit then immediately begin molding itself back to its original shape. Together with the latest weapons features including missiles, UAV's, and a 178mm cannon this tank became a formidable animal. The only way to stop them was to destroy the well-protected engine, steal it, or blow out a tread. They could even evade enemy radar due to their stealthy shape. Donskoi mitigated these tanks throughout his force to try and conceal reports of their existence to the media. Eventually the media found out and claimed the material from these tanks was that of UFO spaceships that had crashed throughout North America and Russia. No one ever commented on the design, material, or idea to create the Fortitude. Donskoi received 10 of them in total, and when he reached Tehran not a single one had been lost.

The other "weapon" was not in the sense a weapon. However, it was a crucial device in securing bases, supply lines, and preventing sabotage. It could also stop residents in cities and towns from attacking prone fixed allied positions. Hypersonic sound had been in incubation for three decades before it appeared in Iran under the guise of Instrument-PN. Sound was maintained through sonogram directing lasers and could be diverted to a single spot or single person rendering movement impossible due the strength of decibel frequency. The crippling result would cause a person to become instantly paralyzed. Named after two men who pioneered research on the topic Instrument-PN became a great advantage. Ironically, it had been used in the Iraqi war in the early 2000's, but was kept clandestine to news media and foreign governments. It also came with a psychological advantage because Annan's guerillas lost the motivation to attack allied bases in the Middle East when they saw the incapacitating affects it had on their countrymen. It gave Iranians first the chance to see what life was like without war, and they adapted to this new life very quickly and very happily.

With these new perfections in hand Donskoi hurriedly began preparations to pave an allied path and victory to Tehran. The fact that Donskoi began his final campaign facing a flurry of numbers bothered him greatly. Donskoi's personal inhibitions were deteriorating him from the inside. Rarely he slept more than two hours a night after Operation Eagle began.

Operation Eagle kept Odets, Tukachev, and Whitney in a tightly coordinated formation. Their front had been drastically shortened from its original form in Russia so long ago. Luckily for Donskoi he had three great generals in his force capable of executing difficult commands and producing initiative entirely on their own. As the forces turned to drive towards Tehran, they once again reshuffled themselves with Odets' becoming Northern Force, Tukachev as Central Force, and Whitney as Southern Force. Odets was strictly a support unit after his disaster against the Caspian sent him reeling. Tukachev was charged with taking Tehran, while Whitney received the most difficult challenge controlling everything from Tehran to the Persian Gulf.

Operation Eagle began September 15th with massive air strikes aimed at decimating all critical parts of Rahim's frontline on the border of Iran and Turkmenistan. The Allied Air Force, which was still the premier weapon of the day was utilized to a maximum extent. Allied jets like the F-44 and Bloodhound B's were superior to everything the Arabs could now operate, and their presence prevented Rahim from launching a counterattack—the only action that could have saved his force throughout the winter months. The precise tactical strikes left Rahim with gaping holes all over his lines. Unfortunately, the allies did not exploit them to their greatest extent because of Donskoi's caution and inability to judge AU reserves. The air force had done a magnificent job, and Tehran could have been taken in a matter of days, but languid opening movements stung the allies.

By the time Donskoi was determined to destroy the AU, Rahim had dramatically saved his position and bogged the allies down by Gorgan near the Atrak River. But Whitney controlled the flank and decided to extend the battlefront by attacking Sabzevar not initially an allied goal. Whitney used his tanks in the open terrain to stunning results at the expense of Rahim's infantry. Rahim offered little resistance and the city crumbled by the end of September. Sabzevar allowed the allies to break out completely and forced Rahim to fight on a wider front opening up necessary ground to finally begin exploiting the debilitating strikes the airmen had inflicted. In response though, Rahim tapped reserves from India in the hope of surrounding the allies in Iran. These forces were weak, but were not afraid and were ready to fight.

The AU Western Army (around 18 divisions) commanded by Yasir al-Karawei was a force largely comprised of irregulars and men not fit for service with the AU regulars. Karawei spared 13 of these divisions in defense for the assault Whitney scheduled in early October. The Arabs arrived October 3rd, and departed in shambles on October 6th. Whitney turned his artillery, tanks, and infantry loose and they were protected from the flank by Tukachev's army who kept Rahim at bay. What looked like a dangerous allied position became a reverberating defeat for the AU. Karawei's forces suffered a 57% casualty rate—terribly high and sapping all morale from his soldiers who surrendered quickly. Donskoi criticized Whitney for careless use of his tanks—of which he lost 35—but the chance of any large-scale attack, or continued build-up of defense from India was nil. Whitney returned to Sabzevar for brief respite before moving again.

Tukachev asserted himself into taking greater control of the campaign, and assured his friends he would kick down the door to Tehran. Tukachev turned his attention to the city of Babol and adopted the age-old Russian vices of a methodical drumming. He committed huge resources especially air support and artillery to reduce Babol to shambles. It's important to remember that Babol had come to resemble modern cities with skyscrapers and industry, but after Tukachev was through it looked more like a primitive disaster area. Tukachev conducted a thorough examination of the residents, and then began setting up Hypersonic Sound Stations— HSS to assure nothing would happen to cause delay or unnecessary casualties. Tukachev was painstakingly accurate, but never cruel. When his work was done on October 25th he took four days to reorganize before spearheading to Tehran.

Whitney on the other hand was confronted with constant violent counterattacks from Rahim and even Tran's army. But Whitney consistently bested his counterparts in every aspect of war, and began pushing their combined forces southward. Whitney won every single decisive battle until the end of hostilities. The more men attacked him the stronger his army became and from October 20th to December 16th, Whitney rolled through the Iranian cities of Qom, Esfahan, Yazd, Shiraz, and finally Bushehr. The movement to Bushehr completed Whitney's drive effectively breaking the resistance and the backs of the AU and Chinese army in Iran for good. By making such epic advances Whitney had solidified the allied position, and by himself had brought the southern army to the point of surrender.

When Whitney reached Bushehr he had little to do except consolidate his gains. Rahim's southern army surrendered in Iran under Mohammed al-Terpa on December 16th receiving a backlash from Annan. Tran escaped back to China by submarine along with thousands of his soldiers who were evacuated as Zui saw the writing on the wall in Iran. Tran reported on allied strength and began drafting the first plan to protect China from allied invasion. Two million Arabs and Chinese died defending the south, while another two million were taken prisoner. HSS were set up to control prisoners as well and Kazakhstan was soon overrunning with POW's. Whitney had finished his job, he finished consolidating his position and protecting Tukachev who refused his direct help. Tukachev wanted Whitney's men to refit and prepare for a possible Chinese attack to save Iran, and to stop any AU leaders from escaping to China. Whitney's mostly American force had sealed off any escape route, but suffered a much-lamented 25,000 casualties doing it.

Meanwhile, Tukachev headed for Tehran on October 31. The Elburz Mountains covered him from the north, and Rahim had almost nothing to pit against him until Tehran itself. Tukachev then incorporated Odets' force to bulk up his own powerful army pitted against a rag-tag force of Arabs. Tukachev arrived at Tehran on November 5th obliterating every thing in his way without remorse. Tukachev struck with virtual impunity flashing through Iran suffering less than 400 deaths. Rahim was in disarray receiving no help from Annan or Bakr who had stopped communicating with him due to their situation in Baghdad. Rahim's countenance would not let him surrender, but he was in a hopeless position against a superior force. Beaten at every turn Rahim doggedly dug into Tehran.

Tukachev first needed to control the skies above Tehran and accomplished this on November 15th for good. All AU fighters had been grounded permanently in Iran. Next Tukachev surrounded the city with artillery and posted sentries outside his bombardment line to protect against guerillas. Tukachev opened the wrath of death on Tehran. For ten days Tehran was subject to constant air attack and artillery fire. Citizens fled in droves and Tukachev humanely let them go. When asked why he let them flee Tukachev responded in his classic curtness, "They are no threat, they are as broken as anyone I have seen in this war. They will try to live." But AU soldiers were embedded in the shambles, and continued trying to dig into the rubble. When the hellish fire stopped Rahim mounted one last offensive to drive Tukachev back, but Rahim's last stand was repulsed for good on December 1st, and it was only a matter of time before surrender became necessary. Rahim had lost 200,000 men only in Tehran so far, and asked Tukachev for a three-day cease-fire on December 3rd to plan his options. Rahim gathered with his staff who determined there was no possible way out but surrender, and desperately tried to contact Annan for permission. Annan was reduced to living underground but sent a message to Rahim that any surrender would be paid for by his blood. The cease-fire had expired by December 6th when Tukachev sent his Land Warrior Infantry into Tehran to flush out the rest of the Arabs. The emaciated defenders put up little fight as they were clearly bludgeoned for the final time. Again on December 8th Rahim requested a cease-fire and a meeting with Tukachev. Tukachev granted both, and formally accepted the surrender of all Arab units in Iran on December 9th.

Rahim then asked if he could address his troops before being retained for questions by allied intelligence agents. He succinctly told them, "Men, the war is over for us now. It is with a heavy heart I surrender us, but it would be with an even heavier heart if one more of you had fallen. The time is right to go back to our families, and pursue our most noble ventures for the glory of all Arab people. Put down your weapons, forget, and live. We do not need to take revenge and this talk about infidels must end before the world ends." New Persia was broken for good.

Two events were immediately triggered by Rahim's surrender. First, on December 10th General Donskoi who had become less and less of a leader during Operation Eagle checked himself into a mental institution. It was well known to virtually everyone except the enemy that Donskoi was a shell of the man he was, and Tukachev had really controlled the allied drive to Tehran. He died 3 years later in Siberia at the age of 59 almost unknown except for a small portion in the newspaper. Statues and monuments have since been erected of Donskoi during Tukachev's presidency, but Donskoi is a man history should never forget. Peril befall them if they do forget.

Second, the Arab Union as well as peace was dealt a crumbling blow on December 16th when General Rahim was killed while being shuttled out of Iran. A group of AU loyalists murdered Rahim and the 12 Russian soldiers guarding him from the detention to the train station. Annan's sympathizers made sure Rahim paid for his surrender with his death. Tukachev was affronted; he felt Rahim would have made a great postwar leader for the entirety of the Arab people. The crushing news of Rahim's death made all the Arab nations mourn. Tukachev issued only one statement, "Let Rahim's blood sow the seeds of peace."

In the following days Tukachev was inundated with AU/Chinese intelligence documents that were carelessly not destroyed before occupying Tehran. Tukachev quickly realized he was in possession of papers that in all probability even Rahim had never seen. As Tukachev plowed through papers in his freshly built office, he spent days alone with no contact from anyone except Salaval and Powwer. Tukachev had discovered documents that told a dangerous story that could still transpire before the end of the war. Most were blueprints for the end of war, and steps to be carried out following the implied surrender of Russia, Europe, and the United States. One concerned Zui's okay for the extinction of all Israelis in the world, and a complete Arab state that would ultimately exist in Europe. The allied nations would be forced to live in subsistence by their superiors who would confiscate food, resources, and money to raise their lifestyle. China planned to destroy the U.S. economy and to exploit America for food to feed its starving millions. Some were even more frightening like the documents that confirmed Chinese scientists were experimenting with a device capable of controlling weather. With this type of technology Zui could control the spreading of diseases from one end of the world to the other. It would then be possible to exterminate the entire U.S. population and make it seem like an accident before anyone knew what was going on. The possibilities for terror were limitless, but there is no idea how far the Chinese got, or even if they started on this machine. Tukachev did not have that ability, he took everything he read at fact value for he had no other choice. However, nothing was more frightening to Tukachev than **Directive 14**, which was a blueprint on the final days of the war if the Armies of East were defeated.

Directive No. 14

In the event that mutual cooperation between the forces of the Arab Union and those of the People's Republic of China become impossible the following document will illustrate what steps are to be taken. The leaders of China will gather for a final meeting to decide to what extent weapons of mass destruction will be used in order to inflict the highest possible degree of damage to allied lands. AU agents acting in place of the Arab Union government will destroy all oil producing establishments located in the Arab Union; this will proceed all other courses of action. The People's Republic of China rather than concede defeat through its current administration will attempt a final extermination of its opposing nations. Nuclear strikes will occur in Russia, Europe, United States, United Kingdom, and Israel through ballistic missiles or other means. If this is not possible biological weapons will be released by China near the end of the war. It is hoped that the scale of the death will be so high that the Chinese administration—which will hide in a clandestine location until danger has passed—will return to take power. Foreign currency will also be stored in select locations throughout China and the Arab Union to propagate any return to power. Though biological weapons are preferable nuclear weapon use will not be restrained in the event that there is no hope for a reinstatement. The people's Republic of China will not suffer a defeat like anyone before in history. The Arab Union will also employ small nuclear weapons to exterminate as many parts of the allied military as possible. These weapons will be delivered by ship to predetermined agents in the Arab Union.

Refer to Directives 23 and 25 for specific details on dates, placements, and other valuable information. This document is to be destroyed before capture and only viewed by those who Ali Annan deems noteworthy.

When Tukachev read the full directive (8 pages long) he was confused about the fact that there were no signatures and all information was in general terms. But the document spurned more questions than it answered and Tukachev wandered about the viability of the document. No signatures, nothing formally addressed. It did connect with the Chinese art of subtlety that their military thrived on. Tukachev had recently replaced Donskoi as the Supreme Commander of the Iran Occupational Force, and now had access to nearly everything he wanted intelligence wise. He quickly organized a meeting in Moscow between his president, President Powwer, and Prime Minister Bollingworth complete with the entire staff of generals from the Western Force.

Near the end of January the hopes of the Arab Union disintegrated in the streets of Baghdad, while a meeting in Moscow determined what would guide policy. For one week in January nine members of the allied war effort ironed out war and post-war policy barely ever reaching consensus. General Tukachev was in favor of attacking China with nuclear weapons immediately; no matter what anyone else thought. Edward favored Tukachev, but Salaval, Powwer, and Bollingworth were skeptical to the truth of the document. The leaders came to no definite decision, but their response would be incriminating and terrible when it came.

Before Edward could completely turn his attention to Directive 14, he first had to crush the remnants of the Arab Union once and for all. Bakr was inheriting plenty of material caught in flux from the Rahim surrender when Annan attempted to rally his entire nation to defend Baghdad. The Iraqi citizens were too broken to endure any more signs of war. Bramley and Bogda reformed one more time and by the beginning of the year mounted the final offensive—Operation Fox on January 3rd 2020. The allied divisions swept right through all obstacles including the Tigris, Kirkuk, and Karbala leaving masses of dead AU soldiers in the way.

Annan's vaunted 5 million plus never heeded his last call mostly because Annan had lost all ways to communicate with the outside world and his citizens had lost all stomach to fight. All television and radio stations had been destroyed by allied cruise missiles specifically to stop Annan from rallying the nation. Bakr was woefully running short of airfields, tanks, and artillery the only weapons that could slow the allied onslaught. Since the Rahim surrender and subsequent death morale steadily declined within every AU military member. Only inspired Arab soldiers in isolated pockets still fanatically resisted in an effort to cost the allies as many lives as possible. Because these few obsessive soldiers the war dragged on until the end of January, but the most shocking events occurred when the first allied troops entered the city of Baghdad.

Finally through the skill and perseverance of Bramley and Bogda there troops reached the city of Baghdad on January 10th and prepared to end the hold of Annan over the Arab Union. Tukachev and Whitney had sealed off any corridor, eliminating any possibility of escape. The idea was simple but the siege of Baghdad was another story altogether. Annan sat in solitude in his underground shelter below his palace; he had lost nearly all communication from his troops. Bakr was determined to coordinate the final operations from within the parameters of the city, and there were only a few radical legions that would fight indefinitely.

The allied position by January 10th was easily recognizable as triumphant—even to the Chinese government who abandoned all hope in the theatre after Rahim surrendered. Annan could no longer impassion any more people while huge conflagrations rose above Baghdad from all lines of sight. Food was becoming harder and harder to find—at least for the civilians—who begged for food from allied soldiers. Immediately, Edward requisitioned supplies and distributed them to the Iraqis to build the goodwill he had to obtain immediately after the surrender. But at the same time Bakr threw in his last few divisions to protect the city and buy time to find an escape route for his leader. However, these Arabs and even some Chinese remnants were massacred by superior allied weaponry and organization unparalleled in the pursuit of war. The last real divisions of the Arab Union Army were extinct; of the Army that once nearly conquered Europe it was gone, entirely gone.

Since the landing in Turkey 8.4 million Arab soldiers had perished defending their homeland, but an even more alarming number stood out. That was 42 million. Just fewer than 42 million AU civilians lost their lives in various forms of firebombing, hunger, and suicide attack. Edward responded by saying, "We carried out all the necessary events to end the war in the quickest amount of time without destroying the world. It was not a butchery, I can live with myself and actions." Though no one admitted it, most of world believed these terrible facts that emerged did more to guarantee postwar peace than anything else. The sheer brutality of the situation made lasting peace in the Middle East possible.

The seizure of the Imperial Palace was the only thing on the mind of the allied soldiers methodically plowing through Baghdad. Brutality was not something they were concerned about in the least with the end of the war in the Middle East in sight. On January 20th for the first time in a long time, and the last time ever, Annan addressed his staff in the surface-level parlor of the palace. Annan disregarded any more strikes because he felt only his people would continue to suffer for his mistakes not the ones who caused them. The broken leader who accepted all responsibility began speaking in that famous rough toned voice, though franetically. "This war has marked the greatest successes of the Middle Eastern peoples. It proved we could bind together for the greatest the good, and in time they will undoubtedly do it again in a more fruitful venture. Those of us who live must subject ourselves to the allies' mercy. But those of us who started this war have a duty to remain accountable to the end. I ask you now to stand and fight with me until the bitter end." Annan grabbed a rifle and continued. "You have served me so faithfully, please allow me to return the favor before I die."

Annan was in danger anywhere on the surface level. U.S. intelligence had placed Ravs to virtually stake out the palace, and thanks to amazing intelligence and UAV's fired munitions into the palace. The entire lobby was turned into a complete fireball, and Annan along with his staff began their journey to perdition. The bodies were obliterated and there was no sign of any living human being inside. Annan left nothing behind of his corporeal body. Auda Bakr heard that the palace had been hit and quickly raced through the flaming pestilent streets to reach the palace. When he arrived he found soldiers trying to extinguish flames from the parlor. Bakr was shocked that Annan was no longer alive. He had no desire to outlive his Emperor. Bakr hurried to find his Deputy General Walid

Rushad, and gave him final orders on how to handle Annan's death. Then Bakr took gasoline, lighters, and an American made 9mm pistol, and ran into a bombed out building next door. He poured gasoline around him, lit separate fires, and in the midst of the flames raised the pistol to the side of his head and squeezed the trigger. His body soon burned.

Rushad was put in an impossible situation and on January 23rd agreed to a cease-fire. Edward waited two days while Rushad tried to get his hands around the situation, and never attempted contact with the Chinese something the allies were anxious to find out. Rushad was practical and only tried to prepare for the succession of order in the Arab Union. He stopped all activities involving the AU army, launched no attacks, and therefore helped the allies hunt down guerillas. On January 25th Rushad met with Edward and unconditionally surrendered the entire Arab Union from Iraq to Pakistan to the allies. By submitting to the allies Rushad set himself up to become a profitable member in the postwar Middle East. He carried little hostilities to his new role. Edward felt Rushad was prudent, and ideally favored him over anyone else to head the Arab Union. Rushad was also clearly in the dark to any continuing partnership to the Chinese, which eased their worries about a triggering nuclear escalation of the war.

Nevertheless, the war in the Middle East was over and China's ally was no more. There was some insurgent activity, but the allies quickly put it to rest. Most of the fanatics had already been killed in the previous weeks, and postwar trouble was classified as "extremely light." The allies also had sustained heavy losses throughout the entire campaign. In just the Iraqi theatre alone the allies suffered 78,000 casualties. An unheard of number due to their advantages, but realistic in terms of the fanatical resistance they encountered. Edward responded by saying that a specter of evil was removed from mankind, and finally defeated forever. Therefore, a steep price must be paid to ensure this—that price was delivered in blood. On January 27th the first allied soldiers arrived in Baghdad from Bramley's division and began setting up camp. In four days Camp

Powwer was constructed, and the world now looked China squarely in the eye. Edward now turned his attention to the Chinese problem that came festering after Tukachev had discovered Directive 14. Firmly rooted in Edward's mind was the fact that a nuclear outbreak in Powwer's words was "very likely" between now and the end of the war.

CHAPTER 16
10,000 HELIOS

The meetings revolving around Directive 14 swirled into February with a resounding question circling the heads of the allied command: What is the best course of action? No one needed reminding of the Chinese ability to continue to fight a war. China had taken control of India per Zui's orders in the wake of the AU collapse, and some loose remnants of the Arab Union had even moved to support the desperate Chinese on their own accord. The Chinese also had the advantage of fighting only a defensive war, and despite fighting in their territory the Chinese were capable of turning India into a meat grinder if they gave it the proper commitment. Finally, the Chinese also scrambled to produce new jets, tanks, and scramjet missiles to deliver a crushing opening blow if and when the allies attacked. In response the allies shuffled their forces placing Edward at the top, Tukachev as deputy, and the four generals kept their armies. Unfortunately, the earliest the four armies could be organized was April. By that time China would have more than enough firepower and equipment to bitterly resist any allied attack. China had moved 95% of their production facilities underground safe from allied bombs—even the allied bombs meant to destroy underground facilities. The most allied bombers could do was reduce the standard of life for the Chinese civilians, which they were already doing daily.

Numerous allied think tanks were formed to gauge Chinese strategy, while more and more documents became available to the allied leaders. China was working on stealth nuclear warheads to evade American missile defense systems, an answer to the Fortitude tanks, and eventually an aerospace fleet to bomb anywhere in the world in minutes. They also had spent billions developing neutron missile warheads aimed directly at the major cities of allied nations.

The allied leaders met for three weeks in March in the historical city of London where Prime Minister Bollingworth opened the meetings by saying, "We have the power to set the course for the rest of world history. God help us that we make the right decisions. If we men are capable of guaranteeing anything; let it be our survival and let everything else assume a backseat."

For the first two weeks the allies accomplished very little, but decided on a policy in the Arab Union. The Arab Union would be retained if desired by the people, and the Middle East would be rebuilt. Israel was reinstated and given generous borders, and while a few Arabs protested the Middle East had been cleansed of those who would still have war. The most positive fact was the death of nearly all of the fundamentalists who had stopped peace in the past, but much innocent Arab blood was also shed for this reality in the process—a deplorable, but necessary byproduct. There were some other bright spots because Annan's administration had already brought all the Muslim peoples together. This made it easy for the allies to bluntly say, "Your all in it together. So now for the first time in history you must cooperate with your neighbors and the world." General Rushad was the main cog in the new AU governmental wheel. Through Rushad—a peaceful man—a peaceful transition occurred. The Middle East was full of peace worshippers because the fanatics were now filling the graves.

The second series of allied meetings focused on the ability of the Chinese to still fight a full-scale war in defense of their homeland. To the Chinese the war was still far from over. Zui still had a large army, air force, and excellent field equipment that equaled what they were up against. The Chinese also had more weapons on the way. They had developed their own aerospace force and were within months of launching it against the United States. They were quickly producing an opponent to the Fortitude known as the Dynasty Tank, and had more soldiers than anyone could still predict. In addition, brand new stealth nuclear weapons would be available for use soon, and they could easily evade any existing missile defense system deployed—except the hereto-undiscovered U.S. ESP Satellites.

A frightening prospect still stood before the allies if they chose to invade China, but an even more frightening nuclear scenario took precedence over the conventional invasion. The third series of allied meetings took place late March 26th-28th where allied policy was decided by consensus, and the final plans agreed upon. China's only remaining allies were North Korea and Vietnam; the latter was ready to quit the war entirely, while the former was virtually decaying rapidly. The Chinese also had allies in smaller satellite nations like Laos and Cambodia, but all these nations were looked at as minor in importance. When the beast fell, they would soon topple so a plan was never hatched to attack them.

Zui was prepared to use nuclear weapons in order to avoid his toppling, and ordered his intelligence ring to acquire pertinent information. The Chinese intelligence ring was the best in the world, and confirmed that hasty installation of missile defense systems was underway in Russia and Europe. Zui waited to see when an invasion would come if at all, and stepped up production on nuclear stealth missiles, while his civilians were pounded and his air force in constant disarray.

In early April General George Odets led a small offensive into India against General Tran's 3 million strong 2nd Corps. The superiority of the Allied Air Force and the full-scale production of the Fortitude proved to be a crushing combination to the Chinese. Invading from Pakistan Odets reached New Delhi by April 12th despite a few outbreaks of tough fighting. The Chinese resistance was bloodthirsty and hellish; Odets continually noted this in his reports that were sent back to Tukachev and Edward. Odets conveyed a strong tone of the considerable fight left in the Chinese soldier, then continued to drive the Chinese out of India permanently. By the end of April Odets reached and stormed Calcutta—Tran's last major defense—and liberated India for good. The Indians were rightly joyful, and many Indians were ready to march into China. In a quirky move India demanded the freedom of Tibet, or they would attack China.

Zhen Zui had begun to feel what Annan had gone through months earlier. He felt the allied noose tightening, and the continued news of his once proud cities leveled to rubble did not inspire confidence in his mind. Zui needed a quick resolution because he was also beginning to feel trouble stemming from a much closer source. There was daily grumbling of a possible uprising against Zui led by some of his generals—most notably the former Chinese Supreme Commander Hung Nguyen. All this combined to lead Zui to one of the most destructive acts ever carried out on humanity, which happened on the night of May 5, 2020.

On that night Zui unloaded the majority of the 155 aging CSS-5 nuclear missiles in the Chinese arsenal aimed everywhere from the United States, Japan, Russia, and Europe. All but two of the warheads were destroyed, but both landed in the Russian cities of Tula and Krasnodar on the Black Sea. The destruction was absolute and the death toll was terrifying awful, easily surpassing one million combined. Russia had two sores on her that would not be healed in the lifetime of anyone currently living in the country. All told both cities were devoid of life for what seemed like eternity. When the first pictures came out of the cities they reminded the world of Hiroshima, but an even greater sense of disaster had overtaken the world. The fact that there was no suffering, no one to help, only the dead, bothered everyone on a subconscious level. There was no equivalency between the allied bombing raids and the Chinese use of nuclear weapons. The Chinese attack was dastardly and meant to harm civilians. The allied bombing raids operated on the idea that cities must be destroyed to stop resistance. The Chinese attacks were strictly supposed to exterminate life on Earth. No equivalency could possibly be drawn among those two ideas.

A moment after the first impact at Tula the allies responded without hesitation and their reaction was even more ferocious. Russia and the United States both launched nuclear missiles at nearly every major Chinese city, the list was long and strewn with casualties: Yumen, Lanzhou, Changsha, Chengdu, Chongqing, Kunming, Jinan, Fushun, Hong Kong, and the capital Beijing. The death toll was estimated at over 110 million. The wholesale suffering of the entire Chinese nation was witnessed firsthand by many who quickly saw photos out of the area, and could only describe it as "10,000 Suns." Civilians would not eat for days, do without clean water for months, and would never have the same lives again. Even the allied bombing raids, which had been particularly destructive did not compare in the least to the nuclear ordnance and the wrecked Chinese homeland.

The Chinese government knew the game was up when they heard reports of what had happened. Zui released even more nuclear missiles, but U.S. satellites that were now entirely online disposed them of easily. On May 6th the Chinese leaders emerged from their bunker at Da Qaidam, but to a massive shock. General Nguyen had pulled together what Chinese forces he could, appealed to them as countrymen, and ordered Zui and his followers killed. Nguyen ordered the deaths of over 600 Chinese officials, but remanded custody over the entire nation. On May 7th Nguyen contacted Edward and sued for peace. World War III was over.

CHAPTER 17
THE LEGACY

The legacy of World War III is one that must never die. It taught and showed the world the worst it had ever seen and been, and demonstrated what could be done again. The memory of it became a blessing of magnificent proportions. Hundreds of years from the now the world could look back on how it almost destroyed all its races. Former Chinese General Hung Nguyen echoed these sentiments when he signed the unconditional surrender of China to the allies on May 9th. The aging general signed the peace accords in London (one of the few major cities untouched by the war).

On May 10th the world started to rebuild itself, and the victorious countries began lending hands to the vanquished. There were obvious tensions and war crimes trials were months away, but the everyday citizens banded together to survive until help came. They survived and help did arrive. The World Health Organization estimated that 16 million Chinese were saved from death due to starvation, dehydration, and disease that could have gripped the country after the nuclear retaliation. In time China was rebuilt into a modern country, and new cities began to appear. Fuzhou became the new capital where China's government was recreated. China went through a Renaissance and the best minds of China started producing ingenious new ideas dealing with environmental cleanup. In five years China had rebuilt its expansive network of buildings, roads, and communications. Though many of their cities were still uninhabitable China was just as productive as they were before the war. The Chinese also adapted a new understanding of human rights, and though the government became socialist it was a humanitarian socialist. The nation was forever altered, but with Nguyen to bring them together and the new leader Ilgyan Qinhai China became the nation it wanted without the violence. Today, as they once were, China is the top exporting nation in the world.

Russia rebuilt itself as well with help from their greatest soldier. General Tukachev took control for Salaval in 2024. Tukachev restored Russia to world prominence by 2030. Russia became a technological state built upon pioneering discoveries in the field of medical technology. In 2032 Tukachev's last year in office of Russian presidency his country launched the world's first military aerospace fleet. Tukachev garnered the best economists, and rebuilt all the cities of Russia to a new splendor—save for Tula and Krasnodar. He encouraged Russians to expand business all over the globe, especially in China and the Middle East. It was said that Tukachev rebuilt Russia with the Chinese Huan—post World War III made strange bedfellows. Russia became the leading military exporter, and capitalism completely took hold of the country. Russia profited so well they never looked back. Today the Russian people live in peace with every nation on Earth.

The world did not put down their weapons; on the contrary technology soon raced to find itself with space planes and unmanned weapons that were the next wave of war. There was much more responsibility, however, in using weapons and determining policies. Everyone kept an eye on each other, and the reluctance to go to war remained high. Many nations had become friendly with each other on a level never seen before in history. Israelis could dine openly in a new Palestine, travel to Egypt, while Americans could frolic anywhere, and Middle Easterners soon became masterful learned citizens all over the world. All of this was thanks to Benjamin Wolfshiem who became the Israeli leader after the war, and the architect of the Middle East. Wolfshiem kept Israel's 1949 borders, and returned the all Muslim countries to their original borders. Wolfshiem counseled all the leaders of the various AU nations, and became friends with all. Soon Israelis and Muslims lived in peace, and mutually benefited each other. Post World War III allowed dreams that had never before been possible. Coupled with these factors were the feelings of harmony each citizen of the world felt with each other.

Freedom had become the benchmark in nearly every country on Earth. However, there was no one freedom. Freedom is what each nation made, and now finally at long last each nation could shape the freedom they wanted. Some like China held on to high government control, while there were those like Russia who sprinted ahead unabashedly. Even in Africa new agricultural technologies soon produced food for the Middle East and Russia. After World War III communist states and dictatorships were reduced to single digits worldwide. As President Powwer said in his first speech after the war, " Individual freedom will be the greatest factor in determining that another World War will never occur again." He was right. The citizens of the world realized they did not need a governing body of the world to look our for them. The world realized they needed personal responsibility in constructing policies to look out for themselves, and if they did this the best interest of every nation would be served.

There was a new postwar United Nations as well. This U.N. was now one that forced communication and cooperation. No more money came flowing in to the institution, just communicators. The world would stand for no more tainted dealings of corruption. Problem solving was the name of the day, and representatives came here to resolve world hunger, education, and morality.

Thomas Powwer remained in office until January 2025. He had the major hand in rebuilding the world, and the new United Nations was his brainchild. Powwer is now remembered as the greatest president ever, and this man single-handedly made each American proud to be one again. Tukachev once said, "The greatest thing America could now export was Thomas Powwer. It will take Thomas Powwer's everywhere to ensure a peaceful world." Powwer accomplished the unthinkable. He saved a country on the verge of extinction after he had saved it economically. Powwer deserved the name of "miracle worker."

But there was one other man whose iron resolve and pragmatic planning saved Powwer's administration. After World War III the two Thomas's became the story in the United States. But while Powwer continued to live in the open giving speeches, and helping other nations organize their policies, Edward became a recluse. Edward who was born June 13th, 1981 retired from the military one year after the war. Intense studies of Edward suggest he was disturbed by the amount of death he caused in his campaigns across the Middle East. He rarely spoke, wrote, or made public appearances, and when he did he was brief and unyielding. Edward died of a stroke June 16th, 2034 only 53 years old. In one last move from Thomas Powwer he lobbied to dedicate the largest gravesite in Arlington National Cemetery to belong to Edward. Powwer also paid for an inscription so the vast amount of visitors who would come throughout the world could read a brief but brilliant description of the life of Edward found in a Chinese proverb. It read:

> Tzu-fan (who was sent by his commander to the besieged city's commander) said, "How are things with your state?"
> Hua Yuan said, "We are exhausted! We exchange our children and eat them, splitting and cooking the bones."
> Tzu-fan said, "Alas! Extreme straits indeed! However, I have heard that in besieged states they gag their horses when they give them grain and send out the fat ones to meet the enemy. Now, how is it that you, sir, are so frank?"
> Hua Yuan said, "I have heard that the superior man, seeing another's distress, has compassion on him; while the mean man, seeing another's distress, rejoices in it. I saw that you seemed to be a superior man, and that is why I was so frank."
> Tzu-fan said, "It is so. May you exert yourself. Our army has only seven days' rations." (And returned to camp).

Tzu-fan reported to King Chuang. King Chuang said, "How are they?"

Tzu-fan said, "They are exhausted. They exchange children and eat them, splitting and cooking the bones"

King Chuang said, "Alas! Extreme straits indeed. Now all we have to do is conquer them and return."

Tzu-fan said, "We cannot do it. I have already told them that our army for its part has only seven days' rations."

King Chuang was angry and said, "I sent you to observe them. Why did you tell them?"

Tzu-fan said, "If a state as small as Sung still has a subject who does not practice deceit, how can Ch'u lack them? This is why I told him."

King Chuang said, "Nevertheless we shall presently just take them and return."

Tzu-fan said, "Let your Highness stay here; I will just go home if I may."

The King said, "If you return, leaving me, with whom shall I stay here? I shall return as you wish." Whereupon he went back with his army.

The superior man approves their making peace themselves. Hua Yuan told Tzu-fan the truth and succeeded thereby in raising the siege and keeping intact the fortune of the two states.

And no one ever wrote the book World War IV. The End.

The Author's email is corpks@aol.com to discuss and thank, the Library of the University of Texas Online for all maps, Sun Tzu's—*The Art of War* for the Chinese story, and of course you.